MW01119871

I am deeply grateful to...

Joel DelValle and Thalia DelValle, my children, for your patience when I immersed myself in a world where both of you couldn't go. With your support, I achieved an exciting goal: I accomplished my biggest passion—this book.

Don Gervich, my wonderful editor, for critiquing and polishing my writing in its early stages.

Marcellus Parker, my friend, my ace. Thank you for being with me through all my difficult times—never wavering. Without your wisdom and constant motivation, little of this would be possible.

Francisco Clark, my cousin, for the encouragement. Thank you for having faith in me and always helping me look at the bigger picture. Although we didn't come together until our adult years, we have the rest of our lives to make up for it.

1

"I am broken. Like porcelain that has been shattered into many pieces, I am not fixable. You can save pieces with a few breaks, but it will never again be the same doll."

BROKEN

The medical response team arrived quickly at the accident scene on the Storrow Drive expressway, near the Charles River at 1:39 am. I was lying on the concrete in glass wondering what just happened. Last I remember I screamed and then my body took flight through the windshield with quite a force.

Everything was moving in fast motion. I was placed on a stretcher and pushed into the back of the ambulance. They checked my pulse and blood pressure. Because I suffered massive blood loss, an intravenous line was inserted into my vein to help prevent me from going into shock. I was in and out of consciousness, but I remember the paramedics working hard to save me. At that moment, I didn't want to be saved.

I arrived at the hospital. The ceiling lights were bright against my squinting eyes. My body jerked from side to side as the paramedics rushed me in to the trauma center at the Boston Medical Center. Every part of my body was in excruciating pain. It felt like my body was being pressed against needle pins and broken glass. I could hear the faint sound of voices at a distance because the blow to my head blurred my senses. At the hospital, physicians and surgeons took over...I fell back into a faint.

Later that night, as I lay on the hospital bed, my eyes began to open. I was still fading in and out of consciousness but slowly coming around. Seeing all the tubes and bandages triggered my nerves with frustration. An eerie feeling consumed that deserted room. All I could hear was the hum of the air conditioner blowing and the heart monitor machine. My body remained still on the bed, shivering. I moaned in anguish as I hurled up images of my past mistakes, the issues I dealt with in childhood, and now the life I

4

trumped up for myself left me here broken with regrets. A stream of tears trickled down my face while the edges of my vision turned black. It was all coming to an end.

18 YEARS EARLIER

The judge ordered me to enroll in anger management in lieu of probation. Therefore, I had to attend ten sessions of therapy and bring a letter of completion from the facility back to the judge at my next court date. When I arrived home, I picked up the yellow pages and searched for my new therapist. I chose a clinic in Cambridge, near the Galleria Mall to make my commute to Northeastern University a lot easier. And if I had time to spare in between the two, I would be able to sneak in a little shopping.

On the day of my first appointment, I wore a pair of gray slacks, dress shoes and a white blouse. I wanted to be taken seriously and win legitimacy from the therapist. As I waited for the elevator to descend, an older gentleman wearing sunglasses and carrying a cup of tea walked in.

"Good afternoon." He greeted me with a smile.

"Hi, do you know what floor the mental health department is on?" I asked.

"Yes, it's on the 9th floor."

"Thanks."

The man had a deep, rich, and curiously fluid voice. When he turned away to sip his tea I sized him up. He was tall and dark, with shoulder length dreads that were pulled back in a pony tail. He wore a long sleeve shirt, faded blue jeans, sneakers, and a pair of Oakley shades. The elevator finally arrived. We were both heading to the 9th floor. Midway, the elevator jolted and then stopped. Afraid to say anything, I held on to the wall and looked at the gentleman. He seemed to be calm as if it was normal for this machine to jam. He pressed the emergency button and informed a woman named Jane that we were stuck in there.

6

"Don't worry, either it will start back up or the fire department will be here shortly." He assured me we were safe and it was a minor issue we were experiencing. However, I was scared. Despite the confident exterior I was adept at showing, a part of me wanted to press that emergency button again and yell out to Jane to put a rush on the fire department.

"So who are you here to see?" he asked as he looked at his watch.

"A head shrink by the name of Roman Wesley. I can only imagine him being a geek with tape between his glasses and wearing a corny looking neck tie. The classic tale of the geek who never got laid in High School." I continued to crack jokes to help alleviate the fear of being trapped in that elevator.

"They probably said the same thing about Bill Gates. He was called a geek, but now they call him boss." The man was clever and witty.

I couldn't help but laugh at his remark. "Oh man. So I am right, he is a geek!"

The man also laughed as he sipped his tea. The elevator gave another jolt and ascended to the 9th floor. We both got off the elevator. I looked around for the doctor's office. The gentleman pointed to a red door on my right.

"Wesley's office is right here," he said. Meanwhile he walked in the other direction towards a conference room.

"Thanks." I mumbled before walking through the red door. I checked in at the front desk and waited about five minutes for this shrink to call me in.

A lovely young lady came out and said to me; "Doctor Wesley is ready to see you, Ms. Pino." I opened the door and snuck my head in before entering. The office was astonishing. One wall was red brick. Across from the brick wall was a waterfall wall made of Japanese stacked stone. The rest of the walls were a shade of light gray with impressionist paintings of Parisian cafes, bars and theatres from the 19th century. The windows stretched from the floor to the ceiling and it overlooked the Charles River. The whole environment was conducive to having patients feel comfortable enough to open up. The doctor walked in and greeted me, "Hello again."

I swung around and was face to face with the gentleman from the elevator. The look on my face must have been priceless because he said the one thing he knew would embarrass me, "Well it's a good thing I got laid in High School." He threw jabs at me. "Why do you think you need your head shrunk Ms. Pino?"

I just stood there in disbelief and didn't want to embarrass myself more than what I already had. He sat down on his lazy boy and asked me to take a seat also.

Despite how deep and comfortable the couch was, I wasn't able to mask my own discomfort. "Are we going to talk here or should we go back to the elevator?" He kept jabbing me. Had I kept my mouth shut, I wouldn't have been this uneasy. Just as I was ready to excuse myself from his office, he put an end to his teasing.

"It's all in good jest and will go no further than this." He grabbed a notepad and pen and proceeded, "Now let's get started, because your time is valuable."

"How are you a doctor?" I couldn't help but ask. He dressed casual, he was witty, and had a tattoo of a quote by Buddha on his forearm: Even death is not to be feared by one who has lived wisely. He was clearly not the geek doctor I had imagined him to be.

"It was by chance. I seemed to have a knack for people to talk to me. Probably from all the reefer I used to smoke. Growing up, everyone always felt comfortable divulging their secrets." He definitely had a knack for saying the right thing.

"You just seem different."

"We're all pretty much the same, except some of us have a hard time expressing our feelings. I entered this field to help people with behavior and social adjustments. My job is to help you explore yourself as you are today, as you were in the past, and as you see yourself in the future."

"Where's your shirt and tie? You don't look like a doctor is supposed to."

He finished his tea. "Too corporate. I feel constricted in a shirt and tie. I like to keep myself informal. If you look around, my space is neutral and I want my patients to feel relaxed and free of judgment."

Resistance to opening up was always my way of protecting me. I worried about sharing my feelings and thoughts to anyone, especially because they were wild and unconventional. A part of me was upset that bitch judge ordered me to anger management but another part of me thought maybe this man had the solution to rid my night terrors. I pulled an envelope out my purse and handed it to him.

"What's this?" he asked.

"I've been ordered by the court to seek anger management. You have to sign it after I complete ten sessions." He looked at the page and inserted it between the sheets of his notepad.

"I'm going to briefly interview you to get a sense of who you are Ms. Pino." He crossed his legs.

"Please call me Sky. Everyone calls me Sky."

"All right then, Sky, where do you live?"

"Boston."

"Are you married?"

"No."

"Are you currently employed?"

"Yes."

He wrote my answers in his notepad. After a few seconds of silence, he looked up at me and asked, "Where do you work?"

"For the City Police."

9

"What do you do there?"

"I'm a 911 operator," I muttered.

Usually when I told people what I did for work, I always got the stupid question: what's the craziest 911 call you've ever heard? There's no such thing. Every call has some level of insanity. So I waited for Doctor Wesley to ask it.

Instead he asked, "How do you feel about your job?"

I was in no mood to explain how significant my job was. "Schizophrenic."

He wrote that down. "You want to talk about that?"

"No."

"All right we'll move on. Tell me a little about your background."

LIFE MUCH MORE THAN DEATH

I am a Cuban American born in Miami, Florida. My mother, Lucia Velez, was in the Cuban exodus. She secretly exited Cuba to the United States via a boat back in the late 1970s, along with her older sister, Isabella Velez, Isabella's husband, and their two sons. They were searching for a way to improve their lives, at least economically. My mother was only fifteen at the time and Isabella was nine years her senior.

When the group arrived to the United States, my mother cared for her two nephews while Isabella and her husband were out working. One summer afternoon, my mother took a nap with the boys. The oldest, Enrique, who was five years old, woke up from his nap first. His younger brother Elias who was three, woke up afterwards. Enrique and Elias were playing around the house, when they found a box of matches. Enrique lit the match in the living room and set the couch on fire.

At the sight of the blazing fire they both ran off in different directions of the house. Enrique went back into the bedroom where my mother was resting. He sat on the edge of the bed swinging his legs nervously against the box spring, crying. His whimpering woke my mother up from her sleep as she tried to figure out what was wrong with him. The fire alarm went off. When she opened the bedroom door, heavy black smoke emerged. She picked up Enrique and pressed his face against her chest, making sure he didn't inhale the smoke. She called out for Elias and tried to look for a way through the smoke. She screamed for help as she struggled to find her way out the house.

The neighbors were standing around watching the fire rip through. In a panic, she sat Enrique on the sidewalk and rushed back

11

towards the burning house. A young man grabbed her and stopped her from going back inside. She fought with him to release her. He then had the neighbors restrain her while he tried to go in to save Elias. Unfortunately, he couldn't make it through the front door because the fire was too fierce.

A few men ran around the house breaking all the windows. One of the men lifted the young man as he climbed through on of them. The firefighters arrived and were then looking for the gentleman and Elias. The firefighters rescued the gentleman but there was still no sign of Elias. A few women were outside trying to calm my mother down as her panic increased.

The fire was quickly put out. The firemen all came out one after the other. One of them carried Elias' lifeless body out the house. The firefighter found Elias hiding in a closet. He placed the boy on the ground and performed mouth to mouth resuscitation, but failed to save him. Elias died from smoke inhalation. The young man escaped from the fire with only a few scuffs and bruises.

The death of Elias disturbed everyone, including the young brave gentleman who tried to rescue the boy. Isabella blamed my mother for her son's death which caused tension between them. This made it more difficult for my mother to adjust to the United States.

Over the ensuing months, my mother and the young man from the fire began dating. His name was Ivan Pino. Ivan was an 18 year old Cuban but he was Americanized. His parents settled in Miami and opened a cigar shop before the Cuban revolution in the 1960s. This made Ivan well above average in business skills. My mother not only leaned on him for emotional support but she saw the means of a comfortable economic base for herself. It wasn't long before he asked her to move in with him, and she did.

Ivan was noted for his courageous and fiery nature! Considering that he was combative and willful, he was surprisingly gentle and nurturing towards my mother. My mother loved Ivan for his energy and initiative. He helped her enlist in a federally funded Cuban refugee program, which provided free medical care. He also helped her get a job at a garment district and taught her how to drive a car. Their ability to work together as a single unit blended well. After six months of living together, my mother became pregnant with me. She was only sixteen and half years old.

On the day I was born, my mother recalls the moon having the shape of a Cheshire cat's grin and the delivery ward being quiet. She named me Cecilia after my grandmother. Yet my mother and her never bonded well. I never knew why. But despite their differences, my mother always tried to please my grandmother, and naming me Cecilia was one of those ways.

Three weeks after my birth, my mother experienced severe post partum depression. It started with an overwhelming feeling of anxiety. Then it turned into paranoia. She would lock herself in the apartment because she believed someone was trying to kill me. She became exhausted and cried all the time. Through this horrible ordeal, no one was there to help her. My father worked two jobs and found little time for his home and family. This triggered constant arguments between them.

By the end of 1978, the Cuban government agreed to promote reunification of Cuban families. This allowed my mother, who was still living in Miami, to visit my grandmother and the rest of her siblings back in Cuba. Once I turned a year old, my mother packed a suitcase and left.

MY GRANDMOTHER - THE SANTERA
(VOODOOIST)

Cuba, which is known as a Catholic country, is also known for its practice of another religious tradition we recognize as Santeria or Voodoo. Although Santeria is often blended with Catholicism, it must be mentioned that we maintain a strict secrecy about our involvement with it because of the negative image that it portrays to the non-believers. With it comes: fortune telling, reading dreams, animal sacrificing, summoning spirits, and casting spell work upon adversaries. This is a blind force which can be used for good or evil.

My grandmother was a well-known Santera in Havana, Cuba. She specialized in all types of spell work. She mainly practiced Santeria to help heal the sick. Many sought this remedy due to their inability to afford medical insurance. Others were just believers and put their faith into her talent. No matter their reasons for seeking her, she was effective with her practice.

As the most emotionally intense woman I've ever known, little escaped my grandmother. She could walk into a room filled with strangers and she immediately swallowed up a flow of intuitive information about those around her. This gave her migraines and at times her body would become weak from the stress of communing with spirits even when she tried to reject them. But she told me, this was her calling and she must accept everything that came with it.

For some reason, she enjoyed reading me. There was something about me she found special. She called me Cielo, which means sky in Spanish. She told me the thoughts that crossed my mind were like passing clouds. She tried to keep me centered but I was a child who loved to wander. Instead of playing with other children my age, I spent a lot of time watching the boats sail by and gazing out at the endless sky. I was a daydreamer. Most of my thoughts were hidden and scattered just like an iceberg. I only shared what I wanted you to know. So much went on inside my head as I tried to figure out where I belonged in the scheme of things, I didn't know how to simplify any of it.

When I wasn't at the dock watching the boats, I followed my grandmother's every move around the house. I watched her slaughter goats and chickens in our back yard. She told me that they were for stews. It's no wonder I had a hard time expressing myself. It traumatized me to watch these animals take their last breaths. Half the time we weren't actually eating these animals for dinner. She sacrificed them for her ritual activities. She would use their blood and different parts of their bodies as offerings. I learned later, that the blood of these animals had a special life force to it. One time she stuffed a dead rooster with a special cloth that she prepared to free a man from prison. She placed the cloth in its mouth, prayed over it and then buried it in our town's cemetery. A week later, the spell freed the man. He visited my grandmother with yellow flowers, as an offering of gratitude.

From my childhood days, I would encounter some unknown being. Many times I saw a big black figure walking down the hall of our house. Other times an oppressive presence filled my room. I didn't understand what was happening but it frightened me. One morning, I told my grandmother about the black figure in the hall but she told me that the discerning of spirits was a gift. She advised me to embrace it, but I never got used to it.

My grandmother held her card readings Monday through Thursdays in her house. She had me write down people's name on a sheet of paper in the order they came in. It was my duty to watch them and make sure no one got out of line. At times, my grandmother was so busy she asked me to help her in the kitchen between her appointments with clients. It was awkward watching her

15

cook chicken after seeing it butchered. I'm surprised I didn't turn into a vegetarian.

My grandmother always kept me busy by helping her around the house. I never complained. I did anything to keep away from my mother. I was terrified of her. Whether it was wetting the bed or failing to do as I was told, she would always spank me. I could not reason with my mother when it came down to disciplining me. No one seemed to understand that everything I was exposed to brought terror to my sleep, causing me to wet the bed. Therefore I followed my grandmother's every move to avoid my mother and her spankings.

Every Tuesday and Friday night my grandmother locked herself in her room to pray and practice her rituals. The night I received my first spiritual consultation, I was 10 years old. My mother was brushing my hair before going to bed but couldn't get me to stay still. I was fidgeting so much; she hit me across the head with the hairbrush. I cried out loud and my grandmother came out and pulled me inside her room. Once I walked in, I was spooked and intrigued all at once. Different candles were lit around statues and artifacts. I sat quietly on the edge of her bed and observed her as she prayed to the spirits. First she mixed hibiscus flowers, honey, oils and different types of liquid to concoct a love potion. Then she folded a picture into a cloth and tied it up with a red string. I was amazed at how fast she worked.

As I watched her spell preparations, my eyes opened wide from the fear when she stopped and turned her attention to me. She stood in front of me and ordered me not to be afraid. Her voice changed to a strange, deep, and raspy tone. She began to speak words that remained with me into adulthood.

"You are a dreamer. Pay attention to your dreams because they will guide you. Learn to trust yourself. Trust your inner voice, rather than the voices around you. Honor it! Allow yourself freedom to take off at any moment's notice. Your impulsivity will help manifest what your intuition is trying to tell you. Envy will be your biggest enemy in life. Many men and women will envy you. You will always do well with money and you will possess lots of it, however, your love life will suffer because of it." I never told anyone about what took place in that room that night. I was astonished at how the spirit that entered my grandmother spoke to me. Even at such a young age, I knew, people would find that crazy. Besides, I didn't want the life everyone else would envy. I wanted the life everyone would be proud of me having.

MOTHER AND FATHER

Growing up, I remember secretly traveling back and forth between Cuba and Florida. My mother befriended a smuggler who took us in his speed boat for a small fee. Whenever she fought with my father in Florida, we moved in with my grandmother in Cuba. This went on until my parents reconciled their differences. When we weren't living in Cuba, we were back in Florida with my father.

I was happiest in my father's presence. We watched movies together every night. I would sit under his arm as he enjoyed his beers. He always explained everything on TV, including commercials. We talked for hours at a time about anything and everything. He walked me to school and picked me up every day. I loved him more than anyone else in the world. Unfortunately, my mother felt differently. They were always arguing.

"One day, sweetie, I'm going to own a Jaguar like this one." He showed me a picture of the car.

My mother butted in, "Sometimes you need to be smacked to get off that cloud."

When I was 12 years old, things became hectic between my parents. I never witnessed my father physically abuse my mother but she wore a small bruise underneath her eye the last time we moved out his house. He pulled me aside, gave me his phone number, and told me that I could call him at any time for anything.

My aunt Isabella, who still lived in Miami, allowed us to stay with her until my mother found a place of her own. The three-bedroom apartment my aunt lived in with her four children was too small and uncomfortable. I shared a room with my younger cousin Raquel. Raquel always complained that I wet the bed. So I was given a sleeping bag to sleep on the floor.

One morning at 5:30am, I heard a loud breathing close to me. I knew only Raquel and I were in that room. I shut my eyes tight and covered my ears hoping it would stop. After a few minutes I uncovered my ears. Suddenly I was held down. The breathing noise was now a demonic screech. I couldn't move and I didn't dare open my eyes. This force of energy abruptly let me go. I sat up and checked my sleeping bag for a sign of urine. No, I didn't piss on myself. I leaned on the side of Raquel's bed and placed my hands over my face. As I sobbed, I heard someone speaking in the next room. I stood up and tip toed out the room to see who it was. My older cousin Enrique was in his room praying.

I listened to him closely. "With the blood of Jesus, I rebuke all demonic forces out my room. Father, please forgive me for any sins that I've committed. I take my stand with you, God, against Satan and all his demons. Send an angel to fight for me. Please come into my heart and cleanse me with your blood. I cast out all evil spirits by the power of the Holy Spirit."

I stood behind the wall listening to him ask God to help him cast out the spirits with authority and no fear. I felt safe that he was throwing them out. He ended his prayer by saying, "Praise you, Lord. Your power surpasses all others. Fill me with your Spirit so the enemy is not able to return, in Jesus' name, Amen." I tip toed back to Raquel's room.

Our living situation frustrated my mother. The strain of having seven people under one small roof was affecting my mother's mood. Her spankings turned to beatings. Everything I did or said was wrong. If I sat still to stay out of everyone's way, she hit me for being lazy. If I washed the dishes or swept the floor poorly, I was guaranteed a beating. No one ever stopped her like my father and grandmother used to. Everyone just looked in the other direction.

Depression set in. I didn't enjoy being around my cousins anymore. Life didn't seem worth living at the age of twelve. I missed my father deeply but it was almost impossible to call him because I feared my mother would beat me to death! I hadn't seen or talk to him in three months. His absence burdened me. He wasn't allowed to pick me up from school or have any contact with me. This made me shut everyone out, including my mother. I stayed to myself all the time. My cousins found this to be annoying. They would speak to me and tried to get my attention, but I purposely ignored them. Pulling away and shutting out that household sent all of them in a tizzy, especially my mother. I must admit, I got a little kick from it.

CHURCH

One Saturday afternoon, my cousins and I were left home alone while our mothers went out shopping. We were left in the care of our oldest cousin Enrique. Enrique was 19 years old and a devout Christian. He was a youth leader at a nearby Pentecostal Church and taught Sunday school. He was short and scrawny. He gave the impression that he was timid, but when he spoke with a sharp tone, I was a bit intimidated by him. He also kept to himself most of the time because his siblings made fun of him and my aunt Isabella didn't care for his religious beliefs. To her, he was just a Jesus freak. She made sure he kept his preachy ways outside her home.

On this particular day, while our mothers shopped, Enrique studied the Bible in the kitchen. He ordered us to play outside and not disturb him. I didn't want to play with the others. I thought this was the perfect opportunity to sneak a call to my father. While the others played outside and Enrique studied in the kitchen, I snuck in Isabella's bedroom to dial my father's number. My hands trembled. When he picked up the phone, I hung up. I was scared of getting caught by Enrique. I thought if I did, he would rat me out to my mother. But then I thought if I was going to get a beating, this was certainly worth taking one for.

I called him again. "Hi dad."

He was surprised to hear my voice. We cried on the phone together. I missed him so much. Enrique walked in and I dropped the phone.

"It's alright, Sky. I'm just here to get a pen." He picked up a pen, showed it to me, and then he shut the door behind him. It was commendable of him in allowing me to speak with my father. We

21

spoke briefly. He promised me that he was doing everything he could to get visitation rights from the court.

After speaking to my father I wiped my tears and went to sit on the couch. Enrique called me over. "Come here and sit down." He pulled out the chair for me. He opened his Bible and began explaining to me what it was.

"This is a Bible. It is God's word and it's an essential part of Christian living."

I interrupted him and asked, "Is that why you asked God to help you get rid of the evil spirit that was here the other morning?"

"Yes. I'm committed to Him and I apply myself to the principles of the scripture, that's why when I tell those evil forces to go away, they must obey, because it's not me, it's God in me. This," he lifted the Bible mid-air, "isn't just to inform, but to transform."

He smiled and continued. "The devil isn't going to want you to hear this message, but he is completely off base, because the Lord has a word for you. And it will be delivered."

He bowed his head and prayed. "Lord, allow me to deliver your word, with no interruptions, in the name of Jesus, Amen."

I was amazed at the power of Enrique's words. "What are you studying?" I asked him.

"I'm preparing my sermon about Peter. He was one of the twelve disciples. He was impulsive and outspoken. When Jesus walked on water, Peter was the only bold one to join Jesus. Peter walked on water for a second but then became afraid when he saw the boisterous wind and the waves lift up. His courage was mixed with fear, causing him to sink. He cried out, Lord, save me. It's the shortest but most effective prayer in the Bible."

I sat at the table with both hands under my chin listening to him. "Did Jesus save him?"

"Of course he did, he stretched out his hand and caught him. The Lord will deliver you from all your fears."

When our mothers returned from shopping, Enrique asked my mother if he could bring me to church on Sunday. She turned to look at me, confused, thinking I was up to something. My aunt Isabella said, "Oh let her go with him, it's just church. What's the worst that can happen? She'll turn out into a little church fanatic like him."

My mother and Isabella both laughed. Enrique looked at me and winked. It was the first time in a long time I looked forward to something.

The following morning, I woke up early and got dressed for Sunday school. A white van came to pick us up. My cousins were ridiculing me and mumbling, "There goes the next freak in the house." I paid them no mind. Nothing was going to discourage me from visiting the place that taught Enrique his God-given basis for faith and spiritual power.

The van brought us to a pale green church with a cross above the wooden double doors. We heard the people praising and singing from outside the temple. I sat down on the bench and watched how some were clapping their hands to the music and others were shaking and striking tambourines. I looked up at the pulpit and read: Make a joyful noise unto the Lord, all ye lands. Psalm 100:1

After the singing and praising, I was sent with the rest of the children to a separate room for Bible study. The incessant heat in that small room made it difficult for me to sit still and pay attention. About fifteen minutes into the class, I excused myself and went back downstairs to join the adults. I sat behind a heavy set woman, to avoid being noticed. I listened to the preacher.

"I've been in my highest and lowest and God hasn't forsaken me. God never creates something without purpose. Amen?"

The congregation all shouted, "Amen!"

The preacher continued, "Lucifer had a purpose. He was created for praise."

I thought to myself, *who was Lucifer?*

The preacher must have read my mind. "Lucifer was an angel, the anointed cherub. He was created with wisdom and beauty. His vestment was full of precious stones. He was the angel of light."

Another question crossed my mind; *what happened to Lucifer?* It was bizarre how the preacher was answering the questions in my head.

"He wanted God's position, so he went up to the holy mountain of God and was cast down from heaven. He corrupted his wisdom by wanting to exalt himself above God. He saw how God created the world without much work, just with his words. In the book of Genesis, where God created man, he created man in His likeness. The power of likeness allowed Adam to rule over everything on Earth. Lucifer figured that if he was cast down, he wanted man to be so too. The reason Satan hates you so much is because you have the greatest thing God gave you; His image, His likeness. His likeness is what gives you power. Angels will move at your command because you have the likeness of God. You can speak to the darkness with authority to leave, and it will obey."

The congregation clapped their hands and shouted praises to God. Everyone was tuned in with what the preacher was saying. I understood at that moment why Enrique had the authority to cast out that evil force that was in the house. Hopefully it would work for me if I had to cast out that shadowy figure if it ever returned.

Bible study came to an end and we headed back home.

"How was church?" My mother asked me.

I replied with a shrug.

My cousins all teased me. "Did you jump around and speak in tongues like the rest of them?" They started moving their bodies like they were having a seizure.

24

Even Raquel laughed at their idiocy. I didn't know what they were referring to but I didn't find it amusing. I left and sought solitude in Raquel's room where no one would bother me.

ANDRE MEDEIROS

It wasn't long before my mother started dating a Portuguese police officer, Andre Medeiros. Andre was from Massachusetts, but traveled frequently to Florida to visit her. He had short, black, wavy hair; dark brown eyes, and wore a thin clean-cut goatee. He was tall, masculine and attractive to women. I'm not sure how they met because they both told their side of the story differently. I rarely saw Andre the first year he and my mother were together. Nevertheless, when I did, he exhibited an aura of kindness and patience. He showered my mother with expensive gifts and even put us into a two-bedroom condominium.

Whenever Andre came to Miami to visit my mother, I would spend the weekend at my aunt Isabella house. Those weekends were unpleasant for me because I couldn't stomach my cousins and their shenanigans. One day my cousins were feeling mischievous and started telling Bloody Mary stories. Bloody Mary was a ghostly English folklore about a witch who appeared when you called her name in a dark room. They sensed the fear this myth had on me; therefore they decided to prank me. They locked me in the bathroom, with no light, and called for Bloody Mary. I screamed and banged on the door. As they chanted for Bloody Mary, a cold hand grabbed my leg. I swung my arms and kicked my legs. The door opened and the light came on. Isabella was standing at the door. I pushed her out the way as I ran to the kitchen. I grabbed the phone and called my father. I was trembling uncontrollably and crying hard. My aunt snatched me by my arm, hung up the phone, and tossed me on the couch. She yelled at me for pushing her out the way and giving my cousin a bloody nose. Apparently, he was hiding behind the bath curtains when I lost control in the bathroom. I was put in the corner on timeout.

I stood in the corner with angry tears running down my face. A few times I would look back and lock eyes with my cousin who wiped the dripping blood from his nose. My aunt yelled, "Turn around! Wait until your mother hears about this." I didn't care anymore. My mother's beatings didn't faze me like they used to.

There was a loud knock at the door. My father stormed in the apartment looking for me. I ran to his arms crying. He told me to get my things and I left with him. On the ride to his house, I mentioned how my mother was dating Andre. Even though I was young, I noticed the pain in his eyes from hearing me talk about it. I regretted telling him about my mother's affair with Andre, but no one ever warned me not to. He sat there listening to me, but never said a word.

The following morning my mother showed up at my father's door with the Miami Police. He tried to speak to her but my mother didn't want to hear him out. He pleaded with her to let me stay. We both knew I was going to receive a merciless beating. My father explained to the police officers that I was unsafe with her but they sided with my mother after she told them he was a jealous ex-boyfriend. The police officer advised my father to go to court and speak to a judge.

Once I arrived at our condo apartment, my mother sent me to my room. Andre was sitting on our sofa waiting for us. I sat on my bed thinking how fortunate I was to have dodged a beating. I overheard my mother talking to Andre and learned that he had advised my mother to show up with the local authorities at my father's house. Instantly, I felt hatred towards Andre for interfering in my father's business. Then my mother walked in and told me to take off my clothes except for my underwear. She left and came back with a belt and whipped me with it. Andre barged in and yanked her off of me. I squatted, covering my half naked body, and looking down to the floor in shame. He began yelling at her in the hallway. They argued for a while and he started walking out the front door. My mother came back in the room and ordered me to take a bath. I watched her run behind Andre.

The bath water stung the welts on my back and legs. I cringed from the pain. For the first time, I thought of running away. Even though I wasn't sure of how and when, I entertained the thought of it while I sat in the tub. My mother walked in the bathroom sobbing. She looked at me with remorse and apologized. She had never done that before. So I turned my face away from her. Her apology meant shit to me.

A few weeks later I was sent to stay with my grandmother in Cuba. But something was strange and different about this visit. My grandmother was acting secretive and even stopped interacting with me as much. She would send me outside to play every day. I guessed she was working on something she didn't want me to know about. I would just go sit by the dock to try and fight against the great tide of sorrow that consumed me.

This went on for several months until my grandmother sat me down and gave me a spiritual reading. She told me many changes were soon to enter my life.

"Allow yourself to open up to the changes that are coming. Although the change will be uncomfortable for you, always remember that a diamond cannot be polished without friction. Andre is a good man and he will do everything he can to see your mother and you happy. It won't always be clear what's right or what's wrong, but the intensity of everything you see will be more emotional than it is visual. There will be several Santeras like me to cross your path, but not all will have your best interest. Don't allow every one of them to give you a reading, for they may curse you. Be patient for the time being. Your relationship with your father will come into a spotlight again. I also see many people of all walks of life who will befriend you. Many will admire you, but some will be against you, so be certain in whom you place your trust in. Most importantly, always remain humble, Sky. Don't let power and money get to your head."

ZIP CODE: 02130

My mother continued her relationship with Andre. Eventually he proposed to her and they married. We moved up North. It was a cold and snowy evening when we arrived in Boston. What a difference! I had never been anywhere else besides Cuba and Florida. I spent my life in a tropical setting, where it was hot all year long, with beaches and palm trees that never lost their beauty. Boston had no palm trees; only leafless branches on hideous barks of trees. It was a small city with winter snow that covered just about everything in sight. It was so cuttingly cold; it sent chills through my thin jacket. Andre seemed oblivious to this frosty temperature so I walked behind him to the car, using him as a shield against the frigid wind.

The city appeared lifeless, which coincided with how I felt inside—cold and empty. But there was something dramatic about the scenery I couldn't explain. The naked trees moved fiercely back and forth without breaking down, and the snowflakes gently descended on the bare branches, lacing the limbs with its white patches. I thought where were these roots getting all their strength from since the violent gust of wind couldn't knock them down? I began to notice the rage in these leafless trees with all their imperfections and their true self uncovered. I came to realize that I was going to find it in my heart to love this city and its unique charm.

Andre noticed I was less than thrilled about this move. I resented being thousands of miles away from my father. I was extremely uncomfortable with the changes Andre brought on me. My mother on the other hand was excited and looking forward to the great opportunities Boston offered. Andre attempted to cheer me up.

"Look for the gray house with the burgundy shutters and a wooden swing set on the side of it."

I was thirteen years old. How stupid of him to not know that my days of playing on a swing set were over. I never even liked playing on a swing set. I admit though, I was mesmerized after getting a good look at this place. We moved to a two-family vintage Victorian home on Jamaica Street. The outside looked Victorian, but the inside had modern kitchens and bathrooms. The front porch extended along the side of the house. Our driveway was long and wide, leading to a two-car garage in the rear. The driveway had enough space to accommodate ten parked cars. The house was built on the top of the hill. It was the most extravagant house on this street. Although all the other homes on Jamaica Street were decent, the surroundings at the bottom of the hill were not. There, a set of brick stairs lead to a rundown basketball court. Right across the basketball court was a housing complex full of cruddy old brick buildings. Andre warned me to stay out of the complex. There were only two possible routes to our house and cutting through the complex was strictly forbidden.

Sleep didn't come easy for me my first week in our new home. My bedroom had a creeping sensation where a chill always seemed to be in the air. I could feel the presence of someone or something every time I closed my eyes. Covering my head with a pillow and curling up like a fetus didn't help one bit. I even tried placing a Bible on my night stand. After a week, I slept with the lights and television on. My mother would come in to shut everything off, but I, after a few minutes, turned everything back on.

Despite the fact I had so much animosity towards my mother and her new found love, her marriage to Andre did change some things for the better. He didn't accept her way of discipline. In fact, he made her stop beating me. It was a shame that this help was too late; I was already damaged from years of abuse. But on the bright side, the best change was reuniting with my father. I was allowed to spend my summer vacations in Florida with him.

FRESHMAN

In late summer of 1992, I received a confirmation letter in the mail assigning me to Boston High School for my freshman year. Boston High had a work-study program I wanted to join. Their program assigned us to a job for half of the school day. I was thrilled about entering a new school, especially one that offered a paid internship at a bank or medical facility.

The first day of school was chaotic. My name didn't appear in the school's computer system and I didn't think to bring my confirmation letter with me. I had to go back home and return the next day with it. When I arrived home I noticed Andre's car was parked in the driveway, so I decided to enter through the back door, which lead straight to my bedroom. I walked in quietly to avoid running into him. Once inside, I heard strange noises coming from the kitchen. I made my way in and caught Andre in a vulgar display of passion with our upstairs tenant, Sharon Miller. He was sitting at the kitchen table with his uniform pants down and Ms. Miller was on her knees running her tongue down his crotch. They were mortified when they heard me come in and catch them in the act.

I turned away and locked myself in my bedroom, disgusted and shocked. Andre banged on my door, begging to explain his actions to me. I didn't want to look at him, let alone listen to his reason.

"Open the door! It's not what you think, Sky." He continued to bang on my door.

From the hall he said if I told my mother about his cheating act, she would leave him and move back to Florida. "You know this would really upset your mother if she found out about it. You would leave me no choice but to deny it and accuse you of wanting to break us up. We both know how monstrous she can be when she gets mad at you."

I couldn't believe this! He made me think that if I told my mother what I saw, she would become violent and even turn on me. I couldn't shake the thought of him getting a blow job from that trifling tenant of ours who smiled in my mother's face. But the thought of my mother beating me was far more disturbing. I never opened my bedroom door. He just got tired of knocking and left the house.

It was a quarter to six that evening when my mother arrived home from work. She was overpowered by the smell of bleach I was using to disinfect the kitchen. "Why on Earth are you using so much bleach?" She mumbled as she covered her face with her hand.

"I found two roaches in here today," I said with sarcasm; except she didn't get it.

Andre came home with an arrangement of flowers and guilt written all over his face. My mother placed the flowers inside a vase in the center of the table. I told her how the school didn't have me registered as a new student and I needed to bring the confirmation letter in the next day. Andre had been listening to our entire conversation from his office, just so, he walked in the kitchen and handed me the school letter. Then he sat at the kitchen table to clean his gun. He ejected the clip, checked that it was empty or full, slid it back into place, and wiped it all around. Unlike me, he looked comfortable with that gun in his hand. It was his way of intimidating me, keeping me quiet. From that moment, I became a rebellious teenager. I despised them both but for the first time in my life, I pitied my mother for marrying this man.

"Could I please be excused from dinner tonight?"

"Why so?"

"I feel sick." I touched my stomach in an effort to convince her.

34

"You may be excused. You're probably sick from all that bleach you whiffed today."

She turned to Andre and said, "I was dumbfounded when Sky told me she saw two roaches in here today."

Andre locked eyes with mine. He didn't know what to do or say. I felt this was the perfect opportunity to ask for anything I wanted.

"I want an allowance." I blurted out.

My mother was alarmed. "Oh, the bleach got to your head too, Sky. You receive money from your father's social security pension; why else would you need more?"

I should have thought of a reason before I blurted that out, but if I had thought of it, I probably wouldn't have had the courage to ask. Now I had no legitimate reason to give her, so I turned my attention back to Andre. He eyed me for a moment, and then wiped his mouth with a napkin.

Andre glared at me. "Okay, how much do you want?"

"Forty dollars...a week."

Although money wasn't going to wipe out the image of Ms. Miller sucking Andre off in my mind, forty dollars a week was enough to keep me quiet. For this, I thanked my father in taking the time to explain what extortion was from a movie we watched together when I was younger.

"For forty dollars a week, you're responsible in keeping your bedroom and bathroom clean," Andre ordered. He wasn't going to make this easy on me, but I agreed to the deal.

Besides the incident with Andre and Ms. Miller, freshman year was starting off smooth. I was partnered up with a twin named Jade for an American History project. Jade was exceptionally smart but painfully introverted. Her twin sister Sasha was the complete opposite. They were both attractive girls. They had almond shaped eyes, round faces, olive skin, and bodacious figures. Sasha was

35

slimmer than Jade. She dressed radical while Jade's style was more conservative. Although I got along well with both of them, I felt drawn to Jade. She came over the house twice a week to work on our history project. We built a solid friendship during the time we studied together.

Another interesting thing about the school was that our advisor handed us a list of electives available to all freshmen. I chose wood working class and Jade chose culinary. She weighed about 20 lbs more than her sister so it didn't come as a surprise to me when she elected a cooking class. I wanted to do something different, to build something with my own hands. There were mostly boys in my class building miniature bookshelves but I chose to build a basic box. It didn't make sense for me to build a bookshelf when I didn't have any books to store in it.

Designing my basic box was difficult. I couldn't come up with any creative ideas for it. I painted it all black, to keep it simple, but my teacher said it was unacceptable. He wanted a more artful look. I argued that it was my box and I should design it the way I desired. He argued back that if I wanted a desirable grade, I'd better vivify my box.

In the class was a crafty Asian boy named Li. His English was poor, so I was almost afraid to ask for his help but his artistic skill was out of this world. I walked over to his work station and whispered, "Could you help me design a skull and cross bone for my box with big letters that read: BLACKMAIL BOX."

He nodded yes. A week went by, yet Li never once came to my workstation to help me. Did he understand what I asked him? I printed out pictures of white skulls and crossbones trying to figure out how to design this box and earn a passing grade. With thirty minutes left for class to end, Li secretly came over to my work station with the wooden skull and cross bone. The words-BLACK-MAIL-BOX were also carved in wood; designed with dripping blood underneath the letters.

"All you have to do is paint it," he said.

Overwhelmed with joy, I hugged him. Everyone stopped to stare at us. The teacher cleared his throat and told us to get back to work. My work was simple in design, yet beautifully carved. I painted the skull with letters, and nailed the pieces to my box. I earned a B. That grade worked for me. I brought my project home in a large sneaker bag. It was created to store my new "allowance" money. Before hiding it in my closet, I pondered the box, studying it at leisure. I knew Andre's little secret with Ms. Miller would eventually unravel one day. Until then, his secret would be safe in my blackmail box.

THE MIDNIGHT INTRUDER

I was falling asleep in my bed one night, when I felt someone was watching me. Gasping for breath, I shot up in bed. My night light had burned out. Stumbling through the dark looking for the light switch, a shadowed figure intruded my closet, and my flesh crept. Never mind the light switch at that point! I ran to the bathroom instead to wash my face. I shivered from the coldness of the water. I couldn't explain why these midnight visitants terrorized me. From that moment, I decided to sleep with the lights on again.

I called my grandmother the next day and asked her to help me rid the omen once and for all. She sent me a package with hyssop soap, a white candle, and incense. She instructed me to bath with the hyssop soap for three days.

In those three days, I had to step out the shower completely wet, let my body dry naturally, and light the white candle which was anointed with special oil. Then I had to read the prayer she wrote for me. I felt awkward at first but anything was better than the fear this omen imposed on me.

I recited. "Whatever evil comes to me, I demand that it disappear. I'm protected, I've been cleansed and I am no longer in fear. With the speed of the wind, and the darkness of the night, I order your presence to take flight."

While the candle burned, I had to light the incense. Then while standing in front of the candle and the incense, my grandmother instructed me to close my eyes and visualize a white ray of light entering my body from the crown of my head. This was the light of protection to end my night terrors.

This ritual brought a new peaceful energy into my bedroom. I slept well for a while without the night light, though I kept it in my drawer just in case. I didn't know how long this pleasant ambiance was going to last. I had my doubts, but I tried to push them out my head. At times I was annoyed by my own paranoia. So I would light a white candle and say the prayer to feel secure again.

SOPHOMORE

Over the course of my sophomore year in high school, I walked home after school along the side of the housing complex like I always did. I never thought of disobeying Andre by cutting through the complex, but one day the weather was warm and breezy, with the advent of spring, and my feelings, like the season, was changing. I was more observant of the neighborhood kids who gathered by the basketball court.

Taking the chance, I walked through the complex that Thursday afternoon. Everything seemed safe until a girl with hazel eyes, a pound of lip-gloss, and a bad attitude became problematic.

She pushed her face up to mine. "What the fuck are you looking at?"

I hesitated.

"Yes, I'm talking to you bitch! Do you have a problem?"

"I don't, but clearly you do." I didn't back down even though I was scared inside.

She was with two other girls who began instigating. Then she threatened me, "Stay off this block unless you want me to wipe your face on it."

I climbed the brick stairs and made it home safely. In the house, I found Andre and my mother dancing Salsa in the kitchen. I leaned in the doorway to watch them. It was as if I wasn't even there. While I forged ahead to the refrigerator, my presence didn't stop them from unhooking themselves. They were hypnotized in each other's arms. I grabbed a juice box and headed to my room. I locked the door behind me and dropped my schoolbag on the bed. The thought of that girl threatening me didn't settle right with me. I imagined ways to kick her ass if she ever confronted me again. I threw punches in the air and shook my pillow, pretending it was her neck. After my shadow fighting, I picked up my homework and went upstairs to visit my upstairs neighbor, Shelley, to get my mind off the incident.

Shelley was Sharon Miller's daughter. She was short and heavy set, with dark brown hair and eyes. She wore glasses and was friendly. Shelley was a year older than me; we were both an only child and liked Heavy Metal music. I told her about what happened near the basketball court earlier that day with the hazel-eyed girl. She was baffled that I even considered walking through the complex. She wasn't allowed to affiliate with people of such a distinct class.

"Do you think it was a good idea to cut through the complex?" Shelley sounded disappointed, "Those girls could have beaten you up."

"I wasn't scared." I lied; trying to appear tough.

"You shouldn't walk through there again. Your step-father already warned you."

"He's my mother's husband Shelley, stop calling him my step-father. Augh!"

I could see this was a one-way conversation so I just pulled out my homework to change the subject. Shelley was intellectually gifted. I usually paid her a few dollars to do my homework. Her facility with language and ideas were a major plus when it came to writing. Even though I was intelligent, I didn't apply myself to school. I was too lazy to put my energy in schoolbooks. As a result, when Shelley handed back my homework assignments, I studied her answers closely because my teachers were always impressed with it. I had to be careful not to get caught up if I wasn't prepared when they questioned me.

SERIOUS ABOUT SECURITY

Andre worked in the Canine Unit and his partner was a German Sheppard named Syrus. For a while, the dog and I didn't mesh. Syrus knew I wasn't fond of him or Andre, so he stayed out of my way. It seemed I was outnumbered now with that damn dog living with us. I often would walk by Syrus and whisper "stupid mutt," and he would growl back. The urge of slapping him for no reason was always on my mind, but I was scared he would bite me.

One evening before Andre left to work, he and my mother were in the kitchen fondling each other. I caught his hand under her blouse and her hand over the crotch of his pants. My presence startled them. I pretended to have not seen what was going on as I almost regurgitated some of my food I had for lunch. Andre asked me to walk Syrus. I stood there in disbelief. Why did I have to walk that dog? He knew I didn't like the stupid dog. He ordered me again to go and not come back until Syrus finished his business. I sucked my teeth and snatched the leash as I walked out. No sooner than stepping outside I realized this was my chance to walk by the basketball court again. There was something about that neighborhood that was intriguing to me.

"Syrus!" The four-legged creature looked confused that I was calling him. "Come on, boy."

He stepped up slowly but led the way. We walked down the hill and all I could think of were these people as beggarly or dangerous as Shelley described them to be.

As I approached the stairs, a sudden, uneasy feeling surfaced inside me. A group of kids were all watching Syrus. We continued to walk along the side of the stairs where a group of boys were sitting. A tall, pale skinned boy, wearing a blue New York Yankees hat and a short sleeved black t-shirt, asked me, "Hey, you live around here?"

"Yeah." I answered him.

"What's your name?"

I didn't respond immediately. I tried pulling Syrus who decided to poop at that moment. I was flushed with embarrassment that he was on full display.

"Sky."

The boy didn't bother looking at the dog. He persisted in speaking with me. "Does that dog bite?"

"Yeah," I kept my answers short.

"Well I better stay away from you," he said, smiling.

Then from somewhere behind me came a girl's voice, "No, *she* needs to stay away! Didn't I check you already about coming through here? I thought you had an eye problem but I see you're hard of hearing too."

It was the girl with the hazel eyes. I thought of pounding this gremlin on the concrete. She wasn't going to get away with embarrassing me again. I left Syrus behind on the sidewalk and charged towards her. She wouldn't shut up! I bashed her in her face. We pulled on each other's hairs and fell sideways on the ground. I punched her repeatedly on the side of her face while she yanked my hair harder. A bunch of kids gathered around us and this girl wouldn't shut up while we fought.

She kept shouting. "You stupid bitch!"

During the rumble, I felt someone hit me several times on my back. That's when I became infuriated and clawed my nails in the first girl's face. My clawing made her shut up. Eventually, we were pulled apart. When I looked up, I was surprised to see the mob of people that stood around us.

While being held back, I looked around for Syrus in the crowd. Why I worried about this dog and not my own safety was

43

beyond me. I probably trembled over what Andre would do if anything happened to his partner. Out of nowhere, Syrus came up and lunged at me, knocking both me and the unknown person who had separated me from the fight. Syrus attacked the stranger, who happened to be a young guy, by biting him on the leg. He yelled and kicked Syrus in the attempt to get him off his leg. I tried grabbing Syrus but I was powerless against him.

During the struggle, the boy pulled out a nickel plated gun but it fell from his hand, to the ground! The dog released him but was barking uncontrollably. I prayed for someone to get me out of there. I held on to Syrus while the crowd scattered. That's when I realized Andre was standing in front of me in full uniform. I couldn't have felt safer or happier to have seen him.

Within minutes the police and ambulance arrived. Andre approached me with two other officers and the youngster whose leg had Syrus' teeth mark. One officer asked, "Did you see this boy with a gun?"

I took a good look at the boy. He appeared daunted and his eyes begged me to deny seeing the gun. Andre also asked me, "Did this punk have a gun on him, Sky?"

I snapped out of my fog and lied, "No, I didn't see a gun."

"A witness stated she saw a gun fall beside you two during the struggle. Syrus must have attacked him if he had drugs or a gun on him." Andre was suspicious.

"Andre," I grumbled, just wanting to end this interrogation, "My head hurts."

Andre told the paramedics to take good care of me and the doors to the ambulance were shut. The gun was never found and we were all transported to Beth Israel Hospital.

My mother arrived at the emergency room before I did. She was an employee there as well, working her way to become a Registered Nurse. Everyone at the hospital loved my mother. As a professional courtesy, they treated my head without delay. I sat in the hospital room, throbbing with pain, ignoring the lecture my mother was giving me. She almost convinced me that she was actually concerned about my well being. I walked out and left her with her words in her mouth.

She went over to the nurse's station to pick up my discharge papers. While I roamed in the hallway, I heard a voice come from one of the rooms, "Psst, hey!"

I peeked inside and found the boy Syrus bit in a hospital gown. "Thank you for saving my ass, that was pretty brave of you."

I removed the clipboard from the wall and responded as I read his name off the medical chart, "No problem, Calvin D. Matthews."

"Now that you know my name, what's yours?"

"Sky." I didn't take my eyes off his medical chart.

He kind of snickered when I told him my name.

"What's funny about my name?" I snapped at him.

"Nothing. Nothing at all," he softened the response with a smile.

I walked away and met my mother in the waiting area. I thought I was going to be grounded after that ordeal, but she didn't say a word during the ride home. I closed my eyes and sat quietly, replaying the fight in my head.

A few days went by and I witnessed my mother taking medication. I asked her what the pills were for. She said they were to help her sleep.

"There's a letter from your grandmother on your dresser," she said as she put her empty glass in the sink.

I ran to my room to read my letter and watch TV. My grandmother stated she always prayed for me and always had candles lit for my protection. The letter comforted me. I flipped through the channels but nothing piqued my interest. I looked outside my window and saw Syrus outside. I found it strange of Andre to be at work without his canine partner, but it wasn't important for me to know. I hadn't seen Syrus since the incident so I went out to the backyard to give him a drink of water. I sat on the swing set beside the house. He just stared at me. I called him over. He stood in front of me with his tongue hanging out. I couldn't help but pet the dog. Then I tapped him gently on the jaw and whispered, "You're not a stupid mutt anymore."

My mother was in her deepest sleep when I walked back in the house and Andre was off working for the rest of the night. I snuck out to the basketball court, hoping to run into Calvin or the handsome boy with the New York Yankees cap—nervous—not knowing what to expect. God forbid I get into some type of trouble again. I reached the end of Jamaica Street and saw smoke coming from the stairs. I headed towards the court to get a closer look. Five male teenagers were sitting there. They all stopped talking and smoking to turn their attention to me.

I lifted my hand up as I greeted them. "Hey."

"What's up, Sky?" Calvin greeted back.

"Just came to see how your leg was holding up."

"Come look at it."

He pulled up his pant leg to show me thirteen stitches from the dog bite. The boy with the NY Yankees cap interrupted, "Your dad's a cop?"

"No. I mean yes, but he's not my father."

I noticed how gorgeous he was: tall, slender but muscular, pale-skinned, black hair and chestnut colored eyes. He was down to Earth but had a hint of toughness about him. He introduced himself along with the others; "I'm Xavier, everyone calls me X. You met Calvin. This is Adrian, Sean, and Rodney."

Xavier Cruz was half Puerto Rican and half Dominican. He was 16 years old, like me, but appeared mature for his age. He was

46

about 5'10" and walked with a sure, masculine stride. He lived in the complex buildings with his father and older brother Miguel.

Calvin Matthews was mulatto. His father was African American and his mother was Irish. He was three years older than I was. He had brown complexion, a bit stocky at an average height. He dressed well and was clean shaved. He didn't live in the complex like the others. He just visited his relatives who lived there.

Adrian Merced was an 18-year-old Dominican high school dropout, who also lived in the complex. He was well known in the neighborhood for his car thieving skills. He looked like a guy who had lived through hard times. Adrian was short, heavy set, and had a long ponytail that ran down his back. When he turned to Xavier, to pass a joint, I noticed a four-inch surgical scar near his hairline.

Sean and Rodney Owens were brothers from Kingston, Jamaica. They were both tall, slim, and dark skinned. They fled to the United States after their father went to prison for killing a man on their island. Rodney was 19 years old and Sean was two years younger. Sean had a down to Earth personality but he was stealthy. He and Adrian were partners in crime when it came to hot-wiring cars. Sean had a tendency of sneaking behind Adrian's back in negotiating other deals with these cars to make an extra profit on the side. Adrian always fought with him about it, but always forgave him because Sean was a better car thief than he was.

Rodney was reserved and wore a mean mug. Quietly, he stood with his back against a tree to blow on the joint. He had an uninviting presence. But I learned later on he was all heart when you got to know him. He held up a tough wall in order to screen people before letting them in to his personal space. The downfall of crossing him was quite dangerous. He had a bad temper and wore a gold chain with a machete pendant.

"Wa gwan! Wha pawt yuh from?" Rodney asked me.

I didn't understand a word he said. I looked over at the rest of the guys and Calvin translated, "He said what's up. Where are you from?"

"Oh...I'm Cuban but I moved here three years ago from Florida."

As I was making my assessment on all of them, I studied Xavier. I recognized him. He went to my school.

"Hey, don't you go to Boston High?"

"I do." He answered with a hard smile.

"You must be a freshman."

"No, I'm a sophomore," he lied.

"No you're not. I'm a sophomore and you're not in any of my classes."

The rest of the guys all laughed and started giving Xavier a hard time. He looked down and shook his head. Apparently, he had misrepresented his grade to the others. Although he was smart, he was held back a grade when his mother passed away.

"Sorry." I apologized for putting that out in the open.

He leaned over on the stair railing and his eyes traveled up and down my body and said, "Don't worry, you can make it up to me by taking me to the movies."

"I don't think so." I rolled my eyes. The rest of the group burst into a cackle.

He ignored them. "How do you get to school? I never see you at Forest Hills."

"My mother drops me off in the mornings. I only ride the train back home."

I thought getting a ride to school by my mother was about to change. Xavier pointed at Calvin and says, "He picks me up after school. That explains why we haven't bumped into each other."

Calvin's pager started beeping. He looked at it and said, "Money. Hey, Rodney let's take care of that tomorrow." He placed the pager back in his pocket.

"Naa worry bout it, C," Rodney responded as he took a drag from the joint.

I leaned towards Xavier and whispered, "What did he say?"

"He said don't worry about it."

The guys all understood him. I found his dialect quite interesting but hard to grasp. Calvin dismissed himself from us and took off in a nice silver Volkswagen Passat with chrome rims. After he left, the rest of the guys took off one by one and Xavier offered to walk me home.

We headed up Jamaica Street and stood in front of my house, talking for an hour. He asked a lot of questions. It made me feel uncomfortable because I didn't know him. I decided to change the subject.

"Who was that girl I fought? Why'd she pick a fight with me?"

"That was Calvin's cousin, Charlene. She's a trouble maker. Trust me, she will never mess with you again."

"Who jumped in? That was fucking dirty."

"Kyla, she's Charlene's best friend. I pulled her off of you and Calvin pulled you off Charlene. That was one hell of a fight! Did you get in trouble with your step-father?"

"He's not my step-father! Let's get that straight."

He threw his hands up. "I'm sorry. I'm sorry. I meant did you get in trouble?"

"No. Thanks for walking me home. Maybe I'll see you around school or something."

"Sure."

NEW COMMUTE

My mother was running around the house, stressed about everything that morning. Andre was scheduled to attend a hearing regarding Syrus biting Calvin. Consequently, the police department sent the dog to Texas, while Andre was issued a transfer notice to the Motorcycle Unit. More importantly, Andre was devastated that after two years of loyal partnership with Syrus, he didn't get a chance to say goodbye to the dog. My mother not only had to console Andre that morning before he headed out, but she had to mentally prepare herself for a promotion interview. That meant there was not enough time in the morning for her to fix us breakfast and take me to school like she usually did.

"I can take the train to school today."

Relieved that it was one less task my mother had to complete that morning, she finished her hair and makeup on time. I stepped out the house hoping to come across Xavier. Sure enough I did. I took a short cut through the complex and ran into him on the corner of Hall Street. He was pleased to see me. Eventually, this turned out to be a daily commute between us. I would meet him every morning at 6:45 outside his building to ride the train together.

Xavier spoke about becoming a professional boxer every morning during our walk to Forest Hills train station. Sometimes I just wanted him to shut up. He had taken Martial Arts for many years as a child, but Boxing was his passion. He told me he had all types of fighting equipment at his house that he wanted to show me, but I never took him up on the offer. After weeks of listening to his boxing dream, my mind would wander off and his voice became a distant echo.

50

CALVIN MATTHEWS

It was a warm spring day in June, with the school year close to ending. Xavier was absent but Calvin showed up after school. Only this time, he parked his car on the side street I normally crossed.

I approached his window. "X didn't come to school today."

"I know. I came for you." He was a bit shy about it.

"Why me?"

He grinned. "Just wanted to see you."

Saying nothing, I opened the passenger side door to his car. Once I sat down he asked, "Can I make a stop before I drop you off?"

I shrugged. On that beautiful spring day, how could I resist a joyride with him? Besides, he had a super nice car: chrome rims, a fresh new silver paint job, black and gray leather seats, and it even had a cool 8-ball stick shift knob.

A moment later, he turned on Green Street. He opened the front cover of his air vent, reached inside of it, and pulled out a sandwich bag full of marijuana. He placed the bag on his lap and pushed the vent back into place. Then he drove back around. We parked in front of Brigham's Ice Cream Shop on Centre Street.

"Come inside with me."

We entered the ice cream shop and he shook the manager's hand. Calvin turned to me and said, "Order whatever you want. I'll be back."

The manager escorted him to the back of the store, where they met for several minutes. Meanwhile, I ordered a mint chocolate chip ice cream in a waffle cone and waited for Calvin. When they finished their transaction in the back room, Calvin placed money on the counter as we exited.

Just after we sat back in the car, I became curious. "How come I never see you smoke with the rest of the guys?"

"It's not my thing. I prefer to make money."

"I want to try it."

He was nonchalant. "Ok...what are you doing later?"

"I'll be smoking with you."

Giggling nervously, I caught a piece of my waffle cone falling from the side of my mouth as I said that. He laughed at my mishap. Then he gave me his pager number. My numeric code was eleven. He pulled up in front of my house and we made plans to meet up. I thanked him for the ride.

Later that night he picked me up. I made sure my mother was comatose and Andre was out working overtime before sneaking out. Calvin met me at the bottom of the hill. We drove to Jamaica Pond and he parked on the side of it. He rolled the weed in a cigar's outer leaf. I watched him smoke. He then taught me how to inhale before passing it to me. I hit the joint, bringing down the smoke to my lungs. I started coughing and choking on the spot.

Calvin laughed at me. "Don't fill your lungs completely with smoke, sweetie. Leave a little room to breathe in through your mouth. Let me show you again."

I watched him carefully the second time. As he smoked, his pager went off. All at once, he choked and I made fun of him.

"Now you got me coughing." He glanced at his pager, and then put it away.

"Me?"

"Here, try it again."

This time, I inhaled the smoke gently into my lungs. "Hold it there," he said. I held it and exhaled.

"You got it, sweetheart."

We smoked, we coughed, and we laughed about it. After a few drags, I gave up. He took his last one too, held my chin and blew the smoke in my face. I closed my eyes and breathed in the contact smoke.

His pager went off again and he mumbled, "Money."

I knew he had to leave. He put out the joint and handed it to me. "You can have the rest of this."

He started the engine but sat there thinking for a minute. He turned to me and asked, "Do you mind coming with me to make this delivery?"

I didn't mind. He opened the vent again, except this time he pulled out a bag of fine white powder.

"Hold this in your bra." He handed it over to me.

"I feel weird," I said, "I can see that you...why you, um...never mind." I couldn't formulate my words properly so I just burst into laughter.

"You're definitely high, because you can't even speak."

"I know, thanks."

He turned up the car stereo and played the Ready To Die album by The Notorious B.I.G (God rest his soul). I was attentive to the sound and lyrics. It felt like I was in an unfamiliar place—a different world. Surrounded by danger—just waiting for something to happen. The suspense was amazing.

Calvin interrupted my trance. "What do you listen to?"

"Metallica, Guns and Roses, I'm into that metal sound."

"You listen to heavy metal?" He seemed disturbed.

"Yeah and I like it," I said shrugging my shoulders, "Is that a problem?"

"That explains why you're always dressed in black."

"Whatever."

Calvin drove for a while. I noticed we were no longer in Boston. We entered a beautiful suburban area. Then, looking out my side mirror, I saw a car was speeding towards us. Blue lights were flashing! My stomach knotted up. I thought: *shit*! Calvin pulled over to the side of the road and the police cruiser bolted by us. I was no longer blunted after that brief panic. We both looked at each other and laughed.

He was so composed. "Don't worry. I'm careful with how I do things."

SUMMER HEATS UP

My mother came in my room early morning. "Are you ready to visit your father?"

"Can I just stay for a month?"

"Why only a month?"

"I haven't spent a summer here in Boston."

My mother purchased a two-way flight to Florida. I was excited to be leaving but sad of the fun and trouble I was going to miss out with my friends.

The day before I was leaving, I called Jade and asked her if she could blow dry my hair. The hair bun I always sported was boring me. I wanted to let my long hair down for a change. Instead of packing my clothes; I took off. As I walked through the complex to see if Xavier was around, I saw Charlene. I hadn't seen her since our fight and it made me nervous.

Xavier was right. Charlene didn't bother me. So I continued towards his building and rang the door bell. He stuck his head out the window and told me to come upstairs. He buzzed me in and I made my way to the second floor. I stood by the door. His father was lounging on the couch with a large shot glass of Spanish rum. I caught the heavy scent of alcohol from the entrance. He was watching television in his boxer shorts with no shirt on. When he saw me come in, he left the living room.

"What's up Sky?" Xavier said, putting on his sneakers.

"Nothing, I'm going to Jade's, can you walk me to Forest Hills?"

"Yeah, give me two minutes." He went into his room.

At that moment, his father came back out into the living room wearing a white t-shirt. He shook my hand and introduced himself as Xavier's father.

"Have a seat, child." He was polite.

I sat down and noticed how poorly they lived. The sofa was torn and the 25 inch television was on a wooden stand that was scraped and missing a drawer. Hidden in the corner next to the television stand was a small shelf with a statue I didn't recognize, a ceramic bowl in front of it filled with coins and dollars, and burned out candles. They were believers too. I studied the altar for a few minutes. Usually, the immaterial power of a Saint conveys to something material for the believer when given offerings. In this case, Xavier's father was a miser who sat on whatever money he had.

Once Xavier was done, we left. I said, "Let's take the bike route to the Hills."

Xavier gave me a strange look. "That's the long way."

"I know." I pulled out the joint Calvin gave me the night at Jamaica Pond. "I wanted to finish smoking this."

Xavier's face was lined with confusion. "Since when do you smoke?" He pulled out his lighter and snatched the joint from my hand.

"I tried it the other day with Calvin and he let me keep the rest of it."

"Calvin?" Xavier seemed upset. "How did you get him to smoke with you?"

"By asking."

Xavier scoffed, "Why didn't you ask me?"

"I don't know, but who cares, I'm smoking with you now."

I took a drag of the joint and choked. Xavier shook his head. "You smoked with an amateur, that's why you're choking. Watch me."

We sat on a humongous rock next to a tree by the park. He took a hit of the joint but didn't inhale it. He opened his mouth, letting the smoke float out for a moment before inhaling it back in. It was pot etiquette 101 with Xavier.

"You got it?"

I grabbed the joint and mimicked his style. He grinned when he saw I picked up on it. It was cool smoking with him.

"Now I have to warn you about a few things." He ran down the rules. "One, never smoke with anyone who has a joint already rolled up. You don't want some scumbag lacing the weed with crack or anything else for that matter. Two, don't put your lips on it when you're smoking with more than one person. Back your lips in your mouth." He almost dropped it showing me, but he caught it fast. "Three is for three puffs and pass!" He pulled on the joint. "I bet Calvin, didn't tell you that."

After we finished the smoking session, he escorted me to Forest Hills Station. I took the 32 bus to Jade's house in Hyde Park. Dazing out the bus window, I thought about the most random things, like what I needed to pack for my trip, chocolate éclairs, and getting my driver's permit when I returned from Florida. But what I kept repeating in between thoughts were: *damn I'm dumb high.*

I got to Jade's house and knocked on her door. Her little brother answered and said she was up in her bedroom. I tripped on the third step going up the stairs. Her brother got a good laugh in. I entered the room where Jade had a mini beauty parlor set up for me.

"Are you ready to let that bun go?"

"Yeah." I pulled out my rubber band and let my hair fall. After the wash and blow, Jade asked me if she could iron my hair.

"What?" I thought the idea was crazy but she was serious.

"That's how I straighten Sasha's hair."

Either I was high or I really trusted Jade. Nonetheless, she ironed it and I was more than pleased with the results.

I left Jade's house feeling and looking good. On my way back home, I cut through the complex. The smoke in the air that came from the basketball court was a sign that the guys were on the stairs. When I approached them they were all stunned at my new look. Judging by Calvin's face, I could tell he found me attractive. Xavier, who was more openly flirtatious with me, kept running his hand through my hair. It didn't matter how many times I slapped his hand off, he continued to touch it.

Naturally, I stayed with the fabulous five: Xavier, Calvin, Rodney, Sean, and Adrian, longer than I should have. Adrian and Sean had a stolen Mustang convertible they needed to stash somewhere for the night. I told them to leave it in front of my house. They were all puzzled at my suggestion. I assured them Andre wouldn't think anything of it, since our neighbor across the street always had company. Always.

Morning came and my alarm woke me up at 4:30. My mother was already awake cooking breakfast. I could hear her and Andre arguing about him never being home. I tried to block them out but their voices were loud and irritating. Somehow I caught the wrath of their argument when I stepped into the kitchen. I didn't clean the bathroom like I was supposed to and it caused an uproar. I kept my mouth shut. It was too early in the morning to be scolded over an unclean bathroom. As if listening to my mother rant about it wasn't enough, Andre felt the need to tell me off too.

I mumbled as low as I could, "Why are you even speaking?"

"Because this is my God damn house!" He threw his cup of coffee in the sink, splashing a speck of it on my mother's uniform. Now that coffee spill was another argument on top of their underlying issues. They were both in rare bitter form. I rushed in my bedroom to bring out my suitcases. When I got to the hallway, I slammed the door behind me.

Andre came out fuming. "Adjust your attitude and let it be the last time you slam my door."

58

"Don't tell me what to do, you're not my father," I snapped back. Never once, in the years that Andre was a part of my life, had I ever said that out loud.

He got closer to me. "You ungrateful, spoiled, little bitch! I should have listened to your mother when she wanted to leave you with your father."

The world for me paused at that moment. All my mother's beatings didn't compare to the pain of finding out that my mother wanted to leave me in Florida with my father, and that rat bastard Andre stopped her. My stomach turned upside down. Those words became a seed of grudge planted in my heart.

It was a bumpy airplane ride and I was restless. After landing in Miami Airport, I dragged myself to baggage claim. The place swarmed with so many people. On top of that, my father wasn't even at the airport when I arrived, making me more aggravated.

After waiting outside for twenty minutes, my father pulled up in an old beat up gold Cadillac with no air conditioner. It didn't matter to me what he drove because being with him meant more than anything else.

Things never changed between us since I was a kid. We still sat on the couch to discuss what was on television. He held a beer in one hand and the remote in the other. He spoke to me as a person; not like a child, but as an equal. It's exactly how I wanted to be treated.

He had an opinion about everything. "I don't know why they put golf on TV, it's just ridiculous! It's boring."

"Well dad, it's interesting to some people."

"It's a conspiracy. The Jews run Hollywood. That's a racist statement but I know it's true."

"What are you talking about?"

He was clearly drunk. "It's all propaganda. I sound like I'm a Nazi, even though I don't want to see them dead like they do, but it's true. Just look at all the content that comes out of television. We're at the mercy of what they want us to watch. I think the whole Neilsen Group shit is farce."

"The what group?"

"The Nielsen Group. They're a group of people that determine what gets played on television. They're a bunch of consumers that sit around and focus group a show. Let's say one will represent about 100,000 people and if they say okay I like this, then it gets airtime."

I laughed. "Where do you come up with this stuff?"

"I'm not making it up! I was just looking at golf and it made me think how I don't understand the point of it."

My father was an equal opportunity fuck up. It's one of the things that I found interesting about him. He didn't care what color, race, or religion a person was. When he drank, he'd let his tongue take flight. And although I loved my time spent with him, I was anxious to return to Boston.

As soon as I arrived home, I called Xavier and Calvin to let them know I was back. Calvin invited me to Canobie Lake Amusement Park in New Hampshire that weekend. His father planned a family trip and Xavier was also going.

"You should come with us and invite one of your friends."

"Will your father mind?" I asked.

"You're riding with me. He'll love to meet the girl whose vicious dog bit me."

"Oh great!" I said sarcastically.

I invited Jade. She really wanted to go but her mother didn't have any money to spare. "I have enough for the both of us, just get her permission."

It was 98 degrees on Saturday, the day of the trip. Xavier and I waited for Calvin to pick us up under a shaded tree near the stairs.

"Damn, it's hot out here." I fanned myself with my hand and complained, "Calvin needs to hurry up."

"You think Jade will like Calvin? They would make a good couple, right?" Xavier asked.

He had in mind to play matchmaker between Calvin and Jade. He suspected Calvin liked me but felt he, himself, was better for me. I tried not to listen to him but it was impossible since we were the only two standing underneath that tree.

"I don't know, X. I've never had a boyfriend and if I wanted one, if surely wouldn't be with any one of you all. You guys are just my friends."

He frowned. "You don't think we'd be good together?"

"You're a player. I've seen more pussy play in your corner than HBO."

"I would change for you."

Now I was the one laughing. I wasn't convinced. He was cute but his looks alone weren't going to get me involved with him.

Calvin pulled up. Xavier sat in the passenger seat and I jumped in the back. Calvin asked Xavier, "Why don't you let Sky sit in the front?"

"Nah, let her stay there. She was talking shit to me this morning." He adjusted the seat to lay back.

He didn't even bother asking me if I had enough leg room. Calvin looked at me and I smiled at him. I didn't care. I was just excited to be going to an amusement park. The only time I had ever been to one was with my father when I was a child.

We picked up Jade at her house. When she came out, Xavier opened the car door and offered her the passenger seat. She didn't want to sit in the front but he insisted by acting like he was trying to be a gentleman. When he sat beside me in the back, he gave me a sly grin and stuck his middle finger out.

During the ride to the park, I could see that there was no chemistry between Calvin and Jade. He tried making small talk with her but she barely said anything back to him. He jokingly said he was going to leave her on the side of the highway if she didn't speak up. They seemed to be bored with one another. I almost thought Calvin was really going to leave her on the breakdown lane when he pulled over to check for a noise he thought he heard coming from underneath the car.

After we met up with Calvin's family at Canobie Lake, the four of us took off to enjoy the rides. While in the park, Xavier started flirting with Jade, in an effort to get her to lighten up. Since Jade told us she wasn't going to ride the roller coaster, I figured I'd stay with her while the guys got on. After they got off the Yankee Cannonball, Calvin grabbed me by my hand, and pulled me into the roller coaster line.

"Don't think you weren't going to get on because Jade isn't." I thought it was cool he brought me with him.

"I didn't want to leave her alone."

"Well, now she's with X, so you can have your turn."

We sat in the front row. I didn't want to admit I was scared. Anticipating the stomach drop was the best and worst feeling I experienced. I closed my eyes and held on tight as the clattering sound of the ride sped down the track. It was mind blowing.

Down from the ride, Calvin and I noticed Jade laughing with Xavier when we approached them. However, I wasn't surprised because Xavier had a charming way with the ladies. Calvin and I walked behind them to get something to eat. We were secretly creating and improvising what we thought they were saying to one another. Calvin was pretending to be Jade and I was acting like Xavier. They had no clue that we were making fun of them from the sidelines. I'll never forget the way Calvin laughed with me that day.

Our stomachs were hurting from it. The entire day was a good time. I didn't want it to end.

When we returned home from the park, Calvin dropped Jade off at her house and took off to catch up on the money he missed out on that day. Xavier and I hung out by the basketball court, talking about our day together and his connection with Jade. He claimed he wasn't interested in her; he wanted to make me his girl. I kept reminding him that I didn't want a boyfriend. Besides, no matter how much I liked him, Xavier had a bad reputation of being a panty chaser. He wasn't the type of guy to wait for any female, so he agreed to stop pursuing me and give Jade a chance. By the end of the summer, Jade and Xavier became a couple.

RUTH JANKOWSKI (THE NOSEY NEIGHBOR)

Ruth Jankowski was a lonely and imprudent neighbor who lived in the ginger bread look-a-like house next to ours. After her husband Charles passed away, she would sweep our street every day with her flying broom and became too involved with the neighbors. If you asked me, she was 120 years old and a poor neighborhood crime watch. She lived with a raccoon for a cat that was fat and dirty. Sadly, she spoke to it like a baby and kissed it all the time. It was disgusting.

She always spoke negatively about me to Shelley's mom. She would say I shouldn't be allowed to hang with Shelley, I was a bad influence, and I had no values. Well, I knew why she felt that way. A couple years back, she brought a crate of ancient books over to Shelley because she knew Shelley loved to read. I picked up a dusty book, made a nauseating gesture, and threw the book back in the crate. Ever since then, she despised me. But what she didn't know was I found an interesting dream book Shelley let me have. It helped me interpret my dreams.

The afternoon was hot and muggy. Andre and my mother were off working and I strolled down to the complex. Xavier was coming out his building with a trash bag and waved at me. We stood around—talking. Bored with nothing to do, we walked back to my house, to eat left over rice and beans with steak. Xavier ate like a prisoner, guarding his food with a fork and knife, and his face close to the plate. I could tell he hadn't eaten a good home cooked meal in a long time. After we ate, we went in my room to roll up some weed in a cigar leaf and go back outside to smoke it.

Mrs. Jankowski spotted us arriving and leaving from behind her shabby curtains. I pretended not to notice her, but I did. She was known for snooping. Xavier and I walked back to the complex and sat on the roof of his building to smoke. We felt like spies looking at everyone from up there. The fiends, drug dealers, maintenance employees, and families were all outside. The fire hydrant was turned on for the children to stay cool in that humid weather. The maintenance staff didn't seem to mind. According to Xavier, they were more afraid of what the neighborhood thugs would do to them if they made the children turn the hydrant off. As we smoked on the roof top, I observed how everyone behaved down at the complex. Some sat around chatting, some looked suspicious doing transactions in plain sight, and the rest played in the water among the children.

"Do you know how fortunate you are?" asked Xavier.

"Excuse me?"

"You come from a good home. Why do you come down here with us poor folks?"

"Things aren't always what they seem, X. I come from a humble background. My mother married into this lifestyle and landed a good paying position at the hospital. Lucky me, huh?"

"I can't seem to understand you. Can you break it down for me?" It was hard to take Xavier seriously whenever he was this sarcastic.

"Have you always been this damn nosey?"

"Have you always been this difficult?"

We sat there quietly for a minute or two smoking the joint. I could feel Xavier staring at me. "Do you know I can kill you right now and no one will ever know I did it? I can toss you off this roof and be done with you."

What?! I thought how Mrs. Jankowski was the last to see me with Xavier. He continued with his horrific plot. "Or it might turn to a murder suicide because I wouldn't be able to live with myself. I'd

65

jump after you. It would be a tale of Romeo and Juliet in the ghetto." Xavier let out a chuckle.

"What is in that weed?" I became paranoid. "I don't want anymore."

He laughed too long and urged me to continue smoking. "I'm joking. I just wanted to get a reaction out of you."

"You're insane. That's not funny." When I stood up and left the rooftop, he came after me and grabbed my arm.

"Here." He pushed the joint in my face.

"Don't touch me! You fucked up my high." I pulled away from his grip.

"Come on Sky, I was kidding." Xavier couldn't stop laughing as he followed me down the stairs, out the building. "O Romeo, o Romeo. Wherefore art thou Romeo?"

"Shut up, asshole!"

"She speaks, yet she says nothing. I take thee at thy word."

I shoved him and crossed the basketball court to go back home. He just watched me leave.

My mother walked in hours later from work. She was in good spirits. "Andre and I are going to New York this weekend to a Salsa Concert. I don't want anyone here while we're gone." She ran down the rules as she prepared dinner. "Ms. Miller will be keeping an eye on you while we're out and there's plenty of food and snacks for you."

I wondered how the mistress felt about that.

My mother left to New York on a Friday night. I went upstairs to hang out with Shelley. Ms. Miller was extremely nice to me since I caught her in my kitchen blowing Andre. Although I couldn't blackmail her like I was doing Andre, she let me do what I wanted while under her supervision. She grabbed her keys and purse and headed out to a bar. Shelley and I were left in the house by ourselves.

66

I invited her to walk with me to the complex but she was reluctant to leave.

I didn't want to brush Shelley off but I wanted to hang out with the guys. So while her mother was gone, I invited Adrian, Sean, Xavier, and Calvin over. It never mattered to me how different they were. They brought out the best in me and time with them was always a diversion.

We hung out in the basement. Xavier brought boxing gloves to put together some hard hitting action. The guys each paired up for a match while Shelley and I kept busy playing judges. We shouted, laughed, and argued over whom out boxed who. We enjoyed every moment of that night; especially how welcoming the crew was to Shelley. I was certain her perception of them had changed.

"Where's your bathroom?" Calvin asked.

"Follow me." I led him upstairs.

Calvin moved all through my house, poking his head in all the rooms. I stood outside my bathroom waiting for him to finish his self given tour. He came up to me and complimented my house.

"Can I ask you something?" He was now standing inches away from my face.

"Go ahead."

"Why don't you have a boyfriend?"

I didn't know how to answer him. My back was against the wall and I felt like he was leaning in for a kiss. And I was right. He pressed his lips onto mine. Then he gently parted my mouth with his moist tongue. It darted in and out my mouth. It was my first kiss and it was gratifying.

"When are you going to be my girl?" He placed his hands around my waist, positioning himself to kiss me again.

I became nervous. He leaned in, but I placed my hand on his chest and stopped him.

"What about X?"

67

Calvin was not concerned. "What about him?"

I anticipated another embrace, but I felt guilty for rejecting Xavier many times before. "He likes me too, Calvin."

"He likes all the girls. I'll talk to him about it, don't worry." We kissed again and just like that, I became his girlfriend.

We walked back down stairs to the basement. The boys wanted to leave. I escorted them out and watched them all get in Calvin's car.

When Andre and my mother returned from their trip the next day, Mrs. Jankowski greeted them outside. That old hag told them I snuck a bunch of hoodlums in the house. She gave them every detail of what went on while they were gone.

My mother was livid. She stormed in the living room while I was watching television, reached over and pulled me by my hair. She punched me on my back repeatedly as she yelled at me for disobeying her. That's how I found out that Mrs. Jankowski snitched on me.

Andre intervened. I ran off and locked myself in my bedroom. Enraged, I pushed my television off the dresser, watching it crash. I smashed my stereo against the mirror. I pulled my hair and even clawed my own face in fury. Andre attempted to come in. I picked up my radio from the floor and threw it at the door.

Later on, when I calmed down, Andre told me I was grounded for two weeks with no phone, no television, and no freedom. These orders came from my mother and he agreed that it was reasonable because I disobeyed her.

Two weeks passed, I came home with my face half asleep from a dental appointment. The Animal Rescue League and a police officer were at Mrs. Jankowski's home. She was devastated when she found her cat stiff—dead. She screamed at me, from in front of her house.

"You killed my cat, you little shit! Your mother should have aborted you."

I stood there and watched this insane woman. I wanted her to understand how much I didn't care what she was yelling. I even caught myself giving her a devilish grin. The police officer managed to settle her down and then make his way to me.

"Try not to antagonize her. She's distraught over this."

"Poor pussy." I responded with a fake frown.

"Yeah, I'm a cat lover myself."

"I wasn't referring to the cat, officer. And tell the rescue team to disinfect themselves thoroughly after they get rid of that raccoon." I turned away and left the scene. I never saw Mrs. Jankowski again. Rumor had it she was placed in a nursing home.

I walked in the house and forgot about the dead feline when I found a letter on the kitchen table from my grandmother. I hadn't heard from her in a while. She told me she had a vision and she was concerned. In her vision, she saw me broken hearted and crying. She told me whatever was coming my way was going to knock me into a heavy depression. She lit candles every night and prayed for no harm to come to me. I became a little worried but soon forgot about it. I believed in my grandmother's work. I watched her breathe fire into her rituals as a child.

JUNIOR YEAR

Someone was calling me in my dream, "Sky!" It sounded like my mother from afar. I opened my eyes and rose from my sleep.

"Sky!" my mother called again.

I woke up feeling groggy, sluggish, and wet. My mother was standing over me yelling something, but all I could do was see her mouth moving.

"You've been in bed all day; it's time for you to get up! I'm going to class now. I left some lasagna for you on top of the stove." She turned around and shut the door.

I don't know how my mother missed the strong odor of urine coming from my bed. All I could think was this can't be happening to me. The bed was soaked and I was mortified. It was strange that after so many years of staying dry at night, it came back at sixteen and a half. As a child bed wetter, she rarely showed me compassion and would strike her belt squarely on my ass. I needed sympathy, not blame. But that time was different. I suspected she just didn't care anymore. So I undressed the bed and me, placing the wet garments in a trash bag, and then hid the bag under my bed until I figured out where to dispose it.

After I showered and wolfed down my lasagna, I decided to go down to the housing complex to find the crew. As I made my way down the hill with my trash bag, I discreetly left it next to a neighbor's trash barrel at the bottom of the hill and continued walking.

Everyone from the neighborhood was outside enjoying the cool and comfortable weather. I searched for the guys and found them behind Calvin's aunt's apartment building, hunched over an Acura Integra. Adrian and Sean were stripping the car of its entire interior. Calvin's aunt wanted to collect money from the insurance company for it, so they set up the car to look like it was stolen. Calvin smiled hard when he saw me approaching. He walked half way to hug and kiss me. Xavier, as usual, was smoking grass. When he caught sight of Calvin kissing me, his eyes turned red from the fury. He didn't know Calvin had made me his girlfriend. It wasn't my fault.

Xavier stopped speaking to me until school. Like always, I waited for him in front of his building to ride the train together every morning. Even then he wouldn't speak much during our commute to school. It bothered me that he was upset with the choice I made but I didn't know how to talk about it. What I did know, was that I didn't want to lose him as a friend.

During late fall, I caught driving fever, from being around so many stolen cars. Calvin gave me lessons in a blue Mercedes C Class he claimed belonged to a friend. After I mastered automatic transmission, he taught me to drive manual in his Passat. Whenever Andre worked overnight on the weekends, I'd take his Volvo out for a spin. Xavier and I would go to Jamaica Pond to smoke reefer. Things were starting to get back to wonderful between Xavier and me.

I persuaded Jade to sneak out her house one day because she wanted to see Xavier. After she got a taste of that sweet escape, she came out a few more times until her mother caught her and she was punished. What started off as a little mischievous act ended with a heavy consequence for her, because Jade's punishment meant she had to stay away from Xavier and me.

Junior year wasn't going too well after Jade was forbidden to hang with us. She blamed me for not being able to see Xavier anymore. Jade avoided me. I tried speaking to her about a homework assignment one day, but she brushed me off. I was so angry at her, that I actually pictured slamming her face on the desk. Worse, our teachers chose Jade and I to work a paid internship at the Federal

71

Reserve Bank. Not only did she ask to work in another bank, but also tried to change some of her classes.

Many times, in school, I sat in the cafeteria alone. Xavier had a different lunch hour than I did and Jade avoided lunch so she wouldn't see me. One day, as I was leaving the cafeteria, a girl who was twice my size blocked me at the doorway. "Are you Cecilia?"

"Yeah." I knew this wasn't a friendly meet and greet. I didn't know her but she wanted me to.

"I heard you've been running around with my boyfriend."

I paused, "Who's your boyfriend?"

"Xavier!"

I explained to lady bigfoot that I didn't know who she was and Xavier and I were just friends, but she closed her mind to what I said and lifted her finger, poking it in my face. She warned me to stay away from Xavier or else. I knew what she meant and I wanted no part of it. She staged this unpleasant scene in the cafeteria for all to see. It was something I hated the most: being humiliated. Although I didn't want to fight her, I would have liked to knock the teeth out her mouth.

I skipped my next class to look for Xavier. I needed to find out who this girl was and what gave her the right to threaten me. He was in the gym playing basketball. I walked up to the hoop and stood there with both hands around my waist, waiting to be noticed. He had a goofy grin when he saw me standing there. I curled my pointer finger for him to come over.

He ran up to me. "What's up?"

I told him what happened down at the cafeteria and asked, "Who's lady big foot?"

"That's Felicia, she's nobody. She's just jealous because she likes me. I'll speak to her."

Irritated at his response, I barked, "Speak? The bitch threatened me!"

He playfully slapped me on the side of my head and ran back in the game. "Don't worry about it. I'll tell her to step back or you'll pounce on her."

"I don't think that's a good idea, X!"

THE OTHER GIRLFRIEND

At the dinner table Andre and my mother avoided eye contact and conversation. I joined them in silence for a bit, lazily eating my pork chops, rice, and fried plantains. Felicia's threat was assaulting my mind.

"Why are you eating so slow?" asked my mother.

I glared at her. "Because I'm not an animal!"

My mother dropped her fork and knife on her plate. She was about to tell me off but Andre cut in.

"What's bothering you, Sky?"

I took another bite of my pork chop and chewed it. Finally, I looked up at Andre and asked, "Have you ever been afraid of anyone?"

He picked up his napkin and wiped his mouth. "Yes."

"What did you do about it?"

"I married her," his face contorted into laughter. My mother stood up from the dinner table and stormed off.

"Is someone bothering you at school, Sky?"

"Yeah," I couldn't believe I was telling Andre this.

"What's her name? I'll speak to the school police to keep an eye out for you."

I got up from the table to throw out the rest of my food. "Never mind, I'll be fine."

I didn't want to add more humiliation to myself. As weeks went by, Felicia taunted me whenever we passed each other in the halls. I ignored her menacing ways. A few times, she tried bumping into me but I moved to the side. Until one day, I was fed up with her bullying, I didn't move when she tried bumping me.

She opened her big mouth, "Bitch!"

My stomach was churning when I threw the first punch at her mouth. She grabbed my hair and swung me from side to side. I held on to her hair while students shouted, "Fight! Fight!"

My body hit the lockers hard. When her hand reached for my face, I bit her until she screamed. School police arrived and broke us up. By the end of that fight we both looked like a couple of trolls with our hairs sticking out in the air. School police escorted me to the principal's office, while Felicia was brought to the nurse's office because her mouth was saturated in blood.

Andre was called and asked to pick me up. I received a three day suspension and a huge bruise on my hip from being slammed against the locker. Andre spoke with the school police as I waited for him out in the hallway. Xavier heard about the brawl and ran to me with a foolish smirk. "Damn Tyson!" He said as he positioned himself in a boxer's stance.

"That's real funny, X! What's the deal with Felicia?"

"She thinks you're my girlfriend."

"What? Aren't you and Jade still together?"

He looked down at his feet. "Yeah, but Jade can't come out her house so I don't get to spend much time with her. Felicia heard I had a girl with long black hair and assumed it was you."

Apparently he was playing the both of them and I caught the girl's wrath over mistaken identity. Xavier and I were close friends, but people at school always thought we were more than that. Jade was so reserved that no one knew she was the actual girlfriend.

When Andre finished speaking with school police, he came through the hallway where Xavier and I were chatting. "Let's go, you two."

Xavier caught a ride home with us. During the ride, Xavier and Andre spoke about sports. I stared out the window and thought of Jade. Our friendship was already precarious; and this fight over Xavier was making it all worse.

As we approached the complex, Xavier ducked his head in the back seat. "I can't be seen getting out of this cop car!"

I laughed. "All right, punk, you can get out with me in front of my house."

Andre dropped us off in front of the house. Before leaving us, he rolled down the window and said, "Don't borrow trouble, Sky."

Xavier waved his fists in the air saying, "I'm going to teach you how to fight."

I shoved his hands out my face. "Does it look like I need to learn?"

He held my face up. "Let me see the damage...um...yes you do."

I pulled up my sweatshirt and showed him my hip. He didn't say anything but I could tell he felt bad about the whole stupid thing.

He turned serious. "Can I ask you something?"

"Here we go with the questions."

"Why did you choose Calvin over me?"

I just shrugged. I couldn't bring myself to tell him that I thought Calvin was more mature, dressed nice, and the fact that he had a car was a bonus. How could I say that without offending him? Saying I don't know, was much easier. I walked in my house and said goodbye.

JADE'S SECRET

Two seconds after the bell rung for the first period of the day, Jade rushed out of homeroom. I, for some odd reason, felt sluggish, so I left last. I arrived late to math class. My teacher made me turn back to get a late pass from the office. I growled. As I headed down the stairs, I saw Jade sneaking out the side door and I ran after her. "Jade, where are you going?" It was unlike her to skip class.

"I have to pay my godmother a visit."

"Can I go with you?" I wanted to get out too.

"Whatever, but this stays between us."

To my surprise, Jade brought me to a botanica near Dudley Station in Roxbury, which is a shop that specializes in readings, spiritual candles, and spiritual icons. It was located on the second floor above a Spanish grocery store called El Platanero. A heavyset woman, Iris, came out and kissed Jade on the cheek. She had dark complexion, a lazy eye, and wore long blonde braids. Her presence and her shop gave me an ominous feeling. They spoke quickly and left towards the back of the shop.

"Sky, wait here." Jade pointed at a chair.

Jade's consultation took about twenty minutes. She came out the room looking jaded. I wondered what her reading was, because she was so private. Iris went to bag up a large red candle for Jade.

I blurted, "Hell, you look like you saw her conjure up the devil." Iris handed her the bag and told her to watch the company she kept.

Iris asked if I wanted to receive a consultation also. No. I wasn't interested. My grandmother taught me to trust my instincts. And my spine-chilling senses were on high gear with that woman.

While we left the botanica, and took the bus back home, Jade's silence made me uncomfortable. "What did she say to you?"

"Xavier is in love with you."

I pretended to be surprised. "What?"

"What's going on between you and him?"

"Nothing! I swear Jade, I don't have those types of feelings for Xavier. He's...he's like a brother to me."

She didn't say anything after that. I knew she was jealous of my friendship with Xavier and now that Iris confirmed his feelings for me, Jade was heartbroken.

THE FIRST TIME

Andre and my mother were both working overtime on the overnight shift. Ms. Miller agreed to keep an eye on me since I didn't want to have a sleepover with Shelley. It was my chance to let Calvin stay with me for the night. Shelley came up with the plan to place a white t-shirt out her window when her mother wasn't on guard. I ran around the house making sure everything was ready.

The phone rang and the voice on the other end said, "I'm on my way."

"Ok, hurry."

Calvin stepped in my house with a strong, yet alluring scent of cologne. He pulled out a bottle of Hennessey and a cigar, placed them on the kitchen table. This was a good start to an unforgettable night. I grabbed a couple of glasses and we went to my room. Calvin sat on the edge of my bed and began to take off his sneakers and clothes. He left nothing on but his socks and boxer briefs. I wore a white tank top and black Nike basketball shorts. Then we took a few shots of the cognac as he rolled up some reefer in the cigar leaf. Once the joint was rolled up, he dipped it into the cognac, and placed it on my nightstand to dry. I caught him a few times watching my body. I sat next to him on the bed. He rubbed my thigh as he listened to me speak about my day. I was rambling. He just laid there sideways laughing at me and rubbing my thigh. He knew I was nervous so he didn't rush me.

After an awkward silence, he leaned forward. "Come here."

"Calvin...I've never done this."

He seemed to know already and kissed me gently. "I will only go as far as you let me."

I was ready to let him have me. He began to move his kisses down my neck and place my hand on his cock. It got hard as I rubbed it. He made his way to my breasts and I removed my hand. He grabbed me tight and whispered, "Don't take your hands off me."

My body tensed up. He told me to relax so I gradually slid my hands up and down his back. Then he caressed my breasts and sucked on my nipples. He left a heavy residue of saliva on one of them to rub it with his fingers while he sucked on the other one. It felt like two mouths were on my breasts. His tongue bath rushed chills through my body. He continued to move downwards and sucked on my stomach, leaving a hickey on it. Then he parted my legs and worked his way to my clitoris. I remember letting out light moans. I couldn't shake how uncomfortable yet aroused I was, naked and exposed. He stopped to put on a condom. He slowly began to penetrate. I screeched! I pushed him off me. He stopped for a few seconds but went inside me again.

His strokes were slow and gentle. Our eyes met as he moved back and forth. He had a disappointing look in his eyes; as if he was ashamed of what he was doing. Maybe I misread his expression since it was my first time.

After he buckled to an orgasm, he jumped off me and ran to the bathroom. I was motionless on the bed. He came back in the room and told me to wash myself. I took a quick shower and when I came back in the room he was in deep thought. Maybe my performance was not up to his expectation.

He snatched the joint from my nightstand and lit it up. We smoked without uttering a word. He fell asleep as I spent an hour eliminating the smell of marijuana from my bedroom. It was now 5:00am and either Andre or my mother could have walked in at any minute. I woke him up and he kissed me goodbye.

The following evening, I sat at the table with a bag of sunflower seeds, looking over my report card, while my mother mopped the kitchen floor. She stopped mopping midway, gave me a stern look and asked, "What is your fascination with that black kid?"

Shocked, I just sat there staring at her. She walked up to me and slammed her hand on the table and asked again, "Tell me now or I'll ask him myself!"

Some sunflower seeds fell on the floor. She was on the verge of striking me. She brought her tone to a normal level but her wrath stung me. "What is going on between you and him?"

I stuttered as I picked up the seeds from the kitchen floor, "We, uh, uh, we...nothing, he kind of likes me."

"Well I don't like it!" She swiped the mop across the tiled floor. "Are you having sex with him?"

I made a choking sound and hurried to pick up the rest of the seeds off the floor. "No."

She knew I was lying. I stormed out the kitchen to avoid being struck by her. Andre came in the house a little while after that, but she continued mopping. I overheard her tell him she found a condom wrapper in my bedroom and she suspected that I was having sex with the black kid, as she called him.

I paged Calvin, emergency. I needed to get out the house and away from mommy dearest. He showed up in the blue Mercedes Benz—both extremely attractive.

He held my hand and asked, "You hungry?"

I nodded yes. After he made his last drug run, he brought me to Moon Villa Restaurant in Chinatown.

"How do you feel about last night?"

I was afraid to tell him how uncomfortable I was about losing my virginity. "I'm glad it was with you."

"When can I have you again?"

I held his hand and didn't answer him; instead I deflected the conversation. "My mother found the condom wrapper in my room. You almost got me killed."

"My fault." He looked down, not at me. "Did you get in trouble?"

"Not exactly." I said with my mouth full of fried rice.

"Then I have the green light to go back."

"It won't be through the front door, that's for sure." I chuckled. "My mother hates you."

"Really?" He motioned the waiter over to our table. "Is it because I'm black and handsome?"

After we left Moon Villa, Calvin drove me home. We sat in the car for a few minutes in my driveway. "I have to make a few more runs and then I'm coming in like Spiderman."

"Alright...but please don't get caught."

TOO HOT IN THE KITCHEN

It was bright and early, Andre and I walked out the house together. He offered to take me to school. Even though I hated riding with him in his cherry top, I accepted the ride because I was too sore and tired from Calvin keeping me up all night. Before pulling out, Ms. Miller came running out the house to the cruiser. Andre rolled down his window.

"Hi Andre, oh and hi, Sky." After several seconds of staring at her, Andre cleared his throat, and I realized I hadn't acknowledged her greeting.

"Hi, Ms. Miller," I mumbled back.

"I appreciate you getting me a new Hotpoint stove, but one of the burners won't turn on. You think you can come by sometime when you're not busy and take a look at it?" She flicked her long hair seductively at him and judging by her eyes, they were saying come turn on the hot point—in my bed.

"Of course. I'll come up later today when I get off." He responded like a complete sap. Andre gravitated to Ms. Miller's amorous advances. They didn't even try to hide it from me. I was sick to my stomach just listening to them go back and forth about a stove, when they were clearly sending innuendos.

I dozed a little on the ride to school.

"You would sleep better if you turned off the lights and television at night."

I ignored him. I'd sleep better if I lived elsewhere without him.

Calvin picked me up after school. He made a few drug runs then took me home. On arrival, Ms. Miller was outside talking to my mother. Judging by the look on their faces, my mother caught Andre cheating with Ms. Miller that same day. We sat in the car and rolled down the window to listen in on the argument. My mother slapped Ms. Miller across the face with an open hand. I gasped for air. I couldn't believe it. They grabbed each other by the hair and my mother swung her down to the ground. Andre rushed out from the porch and pulled my mother off Ms. Miller.

"Now get the fuck out of my house, you whore!" My mother shouted. "And you," she turned to Andre, "I'll handle you inside."

Sharon Miller and her daughter Shelley moved out the second floor apartment within two days. From behind the curtains of my living room I watched them leave with a strange man. Just as they were ready to leave, Ms. Miller tossed the house keys on our front lawn and then spit on them.

Gloomy thoughts filled my mind. I lost my friend Shelley. I thought my mother would divorce Andre and move us back to Florida. I pictured having to say good bye to Calvin and my friends. My worst feeling was that I knew about Andre's infidelity all along and never told her.

A week later, Andre asked me if Xavier would come over and help him throw out some things and paint the apartment. Andre and my mother weren't fond of Calvin like they were of Xavier. They knew Calvin sold drugs and even though they disapproved of our relationship, they allowed me to keep seeing him. On the other hand, they loved Xavier. He was polite and won my mother over with his manners. Whenever my mother carried groceries, he helped with the bags. When he ate at our house, he washed the dishes. If Andre was outside washing the cars, Xavier helped wash the cars also. The only thing they didn't know about Xavier was that he smoked pot. Luckily they didn't know or they probably would have disapproved of our friendship also.

Andre wanted to rent out the apartment as soon as possible. The two painted it and threw away whatever junk was left behind. My mother had me bring them lunch upstairs. Andre was painting the living room and Xavier was in the kitchen sweeping when I walked in. Ms. Miller had left behind the furniture, so I placed the sandwiches on the dining table.

Xavier wiped the sweat from his forehead with his forearm and whispered, "I found something you should read."

I moved back a little. "Read what?"

"Your home girl Shelley left a crate of old dusty books in the attic. I looked through it just to see what kind of nerd she was and I stumbled across her diary. She had nothing nice to say about us."

"Where is it?" I asked.

He pointed at the trash that was piled up in the hallway. "Look inside the crate. It's a pink notebook with a key lock."

I rummaged inside the crate and found the diary. I pulled up my t-shirt and placed it underneath my sweatpants.

"Do that again!" Xavier said with a sly face.

I flipped my middle finger at him and went back downstairs. The diary shocked me. Shelley wrote that she hated me. Our friendship was never real. The only reason she did my homework was because I paid her. She said I lacked intellectual acuity and I would never amount to anything. She resented me for hanging out with what she called a bunch of low-lives and guttersnipes. She wrote how dirty I was for losing my virginity to a nigger. I was appalled that she used such a disparaging term to describe Calvin. To her I was a slut hiding behind baggy clothing. She expressed how much she hated that Andre wouldn't leave my mother for hers. Damn. She knew about the affair too. She ended the diary by writing: If you get to read this one day Sky, may this house burn down with all of you in it!

My heart sunk with sorrow. The affair between Andre and Ms. Miller was no fault of mine. It saddened me to know Shelley hated me. I read the diary over and over again. I felt nausea and hot inside every time I read it. I finally closed the diary and threw it across my bedroom, hitting my door.

TO BOSTON FROM MIAMI

My mother rented out the second floor apartment to a cousin of hers who flew in from Florida. Her name was Sonia. She was my mother's cousin from my grandmother's side. This meant she was also born into the generation of Santeria. Although one is not automatically born into voodoo, most of my family, with a few exceptions, chose to follow tradition. I knew from the aroma of Sonia's apartment—which always had that medicinal and herbs' scent—she practiced it faithfully.

Sonia kept a clear cup of water with a white boxy thing called camphor outside her doorway beside a statue of Santa Anaisa (Saint Anne). This Saint is the special guardian of money, love, and general happiness. Ironically, she didn't look happy and love didn't appear to be there also.

She was a heavy set, single older woman with long thin black hair that passed her waist. She had pale skin, wore a massive amount of makeup, and tight fitting clothes that marked every lump on her body.

Sonia looked older than her age. She had crow's feet and a partially wrinkled neck. This was probably from too many cigarettes. Every time I saw her she was smoking. Whenever my mother sent me upstairs for anything, Sonia would be sitting at the kitchen table smoking a cigarette. It was mind boggling how she always looked at me with dead eyes. It was eerie and mysterious.

Sonia moved in with her 22 year old son Rafael who we affectionately called Felo. He was tall and slim; with dark complexion, a small afro and slanted eyes. It was hard to believe that he was her son. Nothing about him physically resembled her, besides the dead eyes.

Felo had the gift for readings. At the age of fifteen, he was initiated into Santeria, to perform rituals and readings. He was given the attic as a bedroom, where he was able to freely practice his voodoo. Besides a twin bed and his dresser, the entire attic was set up as his own private altar. This was three levels of shelves with candles, statues of Indians, black faced women in long skirts, a horse, flowers, various saints, and skulls with snakes. Each shelf was covered in aluminum foil underneath every candle, and artifacts. He had clear cups of holy water with camphor inside, sacred beads, and other knickknacks that held money. It was a creepy attic with a stink of cigar smoke and dirty feet.

After I left the attic, Sonia stopped me to share an interesting story about my grandmother. According to her, Sonia had been having trouble getting pregnant. My grandmother prepared a remedy and prayed to Caridad del Cobre (Lady of Charity) to help in the fertility process. Soon after, Sonia became pregnant with her son, Felo. She was forever grateful to the powers of this Saint and my grandmother for the miracle that transpired.

Felo joined the conversation and ended up inviting me back to his sanctuary for a reading. I stood in the kitchen and paused. Even though his room was musty and creepy, I was curious about his reading skills.

"How many people have you read their cards to, Felo?"

"I've only practiced readings on other people. You would be the first out the family besides my mom." He had a low and effeminate voice.

We walked back upstairs to his room. He sat Indian style on his bed and I sat across from him. He pulled out a piece of flat wood from under his bed and placed it between us. He had me shuffle the cards and break them into three stacks. He touched each stack and mumbled something I couldn't understand. He took the cards in his hands and put them together in one pile. One by one he placed the cards side by side neatly in five rows.

"You're a dreamer." He studied the cards. "Your dreams speak to you but you don't know how to interpret them. I'm going to give you something to help your dreams become more vivid. The cards reveal to me that this house will no longer exist for you. I can't explain why or what's going on, but I see a crowd of people surrounding it and you will be forced to move out. You will be in a state of confusion, anger, and frustration. During this time a tall, fair skinned man with light eyes, will be by your side. I see him crazy about you and you will feel the same about him, but it will be no trail for true love. He will be your reason to escape whatever troubles you face. I see you attending a friend's wedding. Enjoy this time, for it will be one of your happy moments in life."

He stopped the reading and collected the cards off the bed. He looked up at me and said, "You never stop thinking, Sky. You repress hurt feelings." I didn't say anything. "Sky," Felo waved his hand in my face to bring me back. "What are you thinking about?"

"Nothing." I couldn't get up fast enough. The smell of his feet was like kicking a bag of wet garbage around.

As I stepped out he called me back in. "Hey!" I poked my head up and held my breath. "Wait for me in the kitchen. I'm going to prepare something to help open your mind for you to understand those dreams. You're gifted. You just need help to see them clearly."

"You're not going to kill any animals are you?" I asked with disgust.

Felo gave me the impression he was grossly addicted to evil associations. He had carved the number 666 on his arm and had a large picture on his wall of a giant that was part human and part demon.

"No," he answered, "I'm going to prepare it in front of you." I sat in the kitchen and watched him concoct a mixture of liquids.

He brought me a round fish bowl with holy water in it. He added three pinches of Florida water, three kernels of corn, three pieces of camphor, and strange oils. Then he instructed me to pull out an eye lash from each eye. I did, and then dropped them inside the bowl.

"Put this behind your bed. Light a blue candle beside it every night for nine days. Dip your middle finger inside and wipe it against your forehead three times, every night before going to bed. Ask for your dreams to become clear and ask to understand them. This will open your eyes in your dreams."

"What exactly am I suppose to say?"

"I'll write it down for you." Felo grabbed a pen and paper and wrote down the prayer for me. "Simple. Just recite: With this I enter in the waters of the sky. From the moment I sleep to the moment I rise. May the universe and its powers reveal to me, every message and truth I see in my dreams."

It seemed harmless. A bowl of water and oils with a pinch of my eye lashes. At least there was no animal sacrificing or anything of a bloody nature. I took the fish bowl with a few blue candles and brought it up to my bedroom. I didn't know then, that this kind of spiritual work exposed my psyche to a deeper level of intuition making me more sensitive to spirits.

CALVIN'S FIRST READING

Calvin and I were in my room fooling around on my bed. I asked him if he believed in voodoo. He looked at me like I was crazy. I told him how my cousin Felo specialized in readings and how cool it would be for him to get one.

He wacked his hand on the pillow. "Fuck no!"

"Why not?"

"I don't believe in that shit; it freaks me out." He wasn't a believer of that sort of thing. He preferred to live not knowing what was ahead; whether good or bad.

"Did you put a hex on me, Sky? Is that the reason I love you so much?"

I laughed. "No!" Calvin leaned in and started kissing me on my neck. "Just do it for me."

"Do what?" he asked.

I pushed him off me. "Let my cousin give you a reading."

At that point, Calvin was so horny he would have agreed to anything just to get me to shut up and have sex with him.

"Come here," he unzipped his pants and pressed my head down. "Let me think about it while you go down on me."

I gave him head play. After I was done, I called Felo to see if he was available to give Calvin a reading. Felo agreed to do it.

He welcomed Calvin into the attic. It was hot and smelly, as usual. It felt like we were locked in a dumpster in broiling summer. Calvin turned to me and gave me a dirty look. Clearly, he was mad for letting me talk him into doing it. I could tell he was miserable at the sight of Felo's altar and disgusted at the stink of it. Felo pulled a stool out for him to sit on, while I sat on the edge of the bed.

Felo lit a cigar and kneeled down in front of his altar with his back turned to us. He prayed to the saints that were before him. Felo then stood up, took off one of his sneakers, stomped his right foot three times near the doorway and put the sneaker back on. Calvin's spooked face worried me. He had never been exposed to something like this and I felt he was going to chew me up for making him go.

Felo walked over to us and spoke slowly. The tobacco was strong, causing him to become lightheaded. "Don't be afraid." Felo said. "I'm only going to tell you what the cards reveal to me."

Calvin shuffled the cards and divided the stack in three. Felo proceeded to turn the cards over and align them in rows. Felo studied the layout of the cards. My heart was thumping from the anticipation.

"Who's the woman with red hair?"

Calvin balked. "I don't know."

"Have you ever been in jail?" Felo asked. I squirmed at the uncomfortable vibe between the three of us.

"No."

Felo paused again. "The cards reveal to me that you're going to be arrested. Your case involves this woman in some way. She could be your attorney or the reason you land behind bars. I don't know her role in this, but I see her beside you and she definitely has red hair."

Calvin was uneasy with what he was hearing, but Felo was confident. "I see you traveling back and forth to New York. Be careful with the one who travels with you."

"Is your mother ill?" Calvin shrugged. "I see your mother in the hospital. There's something wrong with her back, but she will be okay." Felo ended the reading and collected his cards. "Do you have any questions?"

Calvin nodded no.

Felo went over to a statue from his altar and handed Calvin some beads he said were previously blessed. The statue was of an

Indian man dressed in animal print fur and carrying a bow and arrow.

"Take this; it's an Ochosi Statue. He will keep you safe from the law. He represents reason and justice. Keep him in a safe place. These blue and yellow beads have also been blessed to protect the one who wears them."

Calvin handed me the statue and beads. He had no interest in these objects. We stood up and left. Calvin didn't want to go back to my house. He was upset with his reading—and at me.

"Keep that voodoo shit to yourself. Let it be the first and last time you ever talk me into something stupid like that."

He got in his car and pulled out the driveway. I sat on the porch steps staring at the Ochosi statue and the beads. If the reading was absurd to him, why did he become upset with it? I sat there until the sun set, thinking about everything I heard. Felo came down and found me sitting there with regret.

He sat next to me and apologized. "I'm sorry Sky, but I only read what I saw. The only thing I didn't mention was that I saw you pregnant by him." His face was saddened than I ever knew.

I looked at him and asked, "Why didn't you?"

"Because I didn't see the baby." He turned away and walked back in the house.

THE NIGHTLY VISITANT

That night, I placed the Ochosi statue on my closet shelf along with the beads. I had a hard time falling asleep. Every time I closed my eyes, I was nervous. As if something was standing at the end of my bed, about to place a clammy hand upon my foot. I tossed and turned from one side to another. Then a tap on my window made me jump up out of bed. Calvin.

"What are you doing?" I let him in through the back door.

He asked, "Why do you always have the lights on?"

"I just do." I turned off the lights but turned up the television high enough to cover our voices.

"I'm not going to lie; your cousin had me paranoid in the devil's den." I could smell the alcohol in his breath.

"Why don't you take the beads? They're blessed to protect you." I tried convincing him to wear the beads but he refused. He wasn't a believer and wearing it would be a constant reminder of the fear the reading brought him.

We both fell asleep. During the night I got up to turn off the television and tried to get some rest in the dark with him. I pulled the covers over me and turned to lie on my stomach. After a few minutes of closing my eyes there was a demonic screech in my ear. It sounded like a wild animal was being tortured. My body was paralyzed from something holding me down on the bed. That sound! It brought me back to my childhood back in Florida. I thought oh Jesus help me! The screech faded away, but I continued to tremble.

"Calvin," I whispered, "Calvin." He was in a deep sleep. I moved closer to him and wrapped my arms around him, with my face pressed against his chest.

Calvin got up earlier than usual. I remember him kissing me on my forehead and asking me before he left, "Sky, what's the matter?"

"Huh?"

"Your heart was beating really fast during the night. What's the matter?"

I just shrugged. There was no way I was going to tell him about my night terrors. I turned the other way and went back to sleep.

AM I DREAMING?

While slumbering, I felt awake in a world that had the qualities of a dream. A group of young smiling children played in a park that was unfamiliar to me. The children ran around, carefree and innocent. Mentally, I became aware that I was truly dreaming. I was then struck by a sense of exhilaration. I, too, wanted to be carefree like these children. They were showing me that this dreamscape was my personal playground. Now it was up to me to figure out how to use this powerful mental ability to gain insight on my fears and desires.

"Where do I begin?" I wanted to explore this new mind skill.

"Ask for anything or anyone you'd like to see," said a blonde boy with piercing blue eyes. "You have full control on how you wish to expand your reality here."

"All right, I want to fly."

The boy threw his ball up. As I reached up for it, my body lifted into the air. I was floating with my legs straight out, holding the ball against my chest. Wow. I was gliding across the park and over a river, without letting go of the ball. This was freedom! There were no boundaries in what I can do or accomplish.

"I want to go higher!"

As I said that, the ball was released from my grasp and my body elevated higher into the air, faster. I was now flying in superman style; high in the sky just below the clouds, admiring the landscape below me.

"Take me back to the park." My body descended back to where I started. When my feet hit the ground I expected to see the same children playing at the park. I walked around but I found no children. Where is the boy? I left the park and entered a busy downtown area.

A building looked like a museum. I wanted to continue exploring my dream so I entered it. The inside appeared to be a monastery. It was a little dark and cold, but I wasn't afraid. The entrance was a vast expanse of rectangular space. The walls were painted with mythical creatures like beasts and guardian angels, all flying through beautifully shaped clouds. I continued to walk down a long hallway and stopped in front of a Buddha statue. As I stopped to admire its mysterious smile, I turned around to look, and saw the boy with blue eyes standing at the top of a set of stairs.

"There you are; I've been looking for you!"

The boy just stared at me and I stared back. When I tried approaching him, a tall shadowy figure appeared behind him. It was difficult to see its face but I didn't run away.

"It's your turn," the figure snarled at me.

For the first time, I didn't fear the figure that always haunted me. It was now in my dream where I had complete control. I was still on that superman power high and spoke to the dark figure with authority, "Get away from him!" I raised my hand and used my mind power to push it away as I moved towards it, "I order you to leave now!"

It faded away.

Once the dark figure vanished, my body pulled away from this state of dreaming to waking up. Before I opened my eyes, I heard a faint echo go into my ear, "Wake up." My eyes opened wide but my body remained paralyzed in the bed. I stayed there for over an hour, overanalyzing that entire experience.

HOLIDAY FUN

As the holidays were approaching, my mother and I were a little bummed that Sonia and Felo moved back to Florida. Sonia reconciled with Felo's father and wanted to give their relationship another chance.

In an effort to cheer us up, Andre decided to throw a big dinner party on Thanksgiving. He also wanted to honor Michael Kirsch winning the election as the new Mayor of the city Andre worked in. Andre was good friends with the mayor and donated an undisclosed amount of money towards the campaign. He invited a few of his fellow co-workers of the force, the committee that helped with Kirsch's campaign, and a few other important people. Surprisingly, my mother liked the idea, as long as everyone brought a dish. This Thanksgiving Dinner was going to be a feast and I was looking forward to it.

Andre gave me permission to invite a few of my friends to this dinner party. I asked Jade, Xavier, and Calvin to come as my guests. The night of Thanksgiving, everyone showed up. The house was filled with happy people—drunk people.

Jade and Xavier arrived. We brought our dinner plates to my bedroom and ate there. We were laughing and cracking jokes about the adults who were buzzed out of their minds. I paged Calvin numerous times, but he didn't callback. Was he avoiding us? It bothered me inside but I didn't show it. I continued to laugh with Jade and Xavier.

Xavier entertained himself by looking through my closet. "You have a huge collection of sneakers!"

I paid him no attention even though he pried through my things. My focus was on Calvin not returning my pages.

That's when Xavier pulled out the blackmail box I build in woodworking class. "What is this shit?" He grimaced at it until he saw all the money stashed inside.

I jumped from the bed, snatched it from his hands, and hid it in my dirty laundry. "Nothing. I keep my allowance in there."

"Why does it say BLACKMAIL BOX?"

"It's a black...mailbox."

Xavier was confused. I suggested we go to the kitchen and bring back some special punch that only the adults were supposed to drink; "Let's sneak in some of Andre's jungle juice!"

Jade innocently asked, "What's jungle juice?"

Xavier and I giggled maliciously. He knew what I was talking about and he was all in. As we were leaving my room, the phone rang. It was Calvin. He was on his way from his aunt's house.

The three of us gathered in the kitchen trying hard not to appear suspicious. I secretly passed Xavier a thermo bottle. Jade was the lookout guard as I made Calvin a plate of food while covering Xavier. The guests were so wasted that no one noticed him pouring the spiked punch into the bottle. We all went back to my room giddy, like we all got away with a misdemeanor.

We filled our cups with punch. Jade sipped hers, while Xavier and I competed in a chugging match. "Ready," he lifted his cup, "Set, go!" We guzzled the punch in no time. After we finished, Xavier gave me a high five. I looked over at Jade, at the jealous look in her eyes.

"Calvin should be here any minute. I'm going to wait for him outside. Stay out my closet X!"

Xavier poured the last of the punch into our cups and handed me back the bottle; "Your turn to refill it."

I held the bottle and stood there, contemplating how I was going to get more punch without anyone noticing. I secretly took out a twenty dollar bill from the blackmail box and headed outside to wait for Calvin.

As soon as I stepped on the porch Calvin arrived. He hugged me tight and kissed me, till his cologne surrounded us both. He handed me his leather jacket when we entered the house. He was handsome in his red Polo shirt, khaki pants, and black Timberland boots. As I walked through the house, I got a good feel on who would be my best distraction. The drunkest man there was Senator Alan Thompson. I walked up to him and discreetly tossed the twenty dollar bill near his feet.

I pointed to the floor. "Someone dropped their money."

The Senator picked it up and held it in his hand. He yelled out, "Who here is missing Jackson?"

While everyone turned their attention to claim the bill, I hurried to pour the punch in the bottle.

Calvin and I walked to my room but before we entered, he pinned me to the wall in the back corridor to kiss me again. He placed his hands in between my legs and massaged me. The thermo bottle and jacket were clutched in my hands, making it rather difficult to break away. He was reluctant to tell me why he didn't answer my pages sooner. It was irritating me. Calvin just wiped his bottom lip with his thumb, giving me a cold stare. Gingerly, I slid over and opened my bedroom door.

"Well it's about time." Jade worried. "We were scared you got caught."

"Cheers to us!" I lifted the container and gloated.

Jade drank only half the cup from the first round. Calvin didn't want any punch, leaving Xaxier and I to finish drinking the rest of it. As the alcohol started to set in, we decided to take our private party to the upstairs apartment.

Jade and Xavier locked themselves in Sonia's old bedroom while Calvin and I chose to make out in the living room. Calvin wasted no time in sucking and biting my neck. Even though he disliked rushing foreplay, he unzipped my pants quickly. His

100

fingertips stroked my clitoris. My heavy breathing turned him on even more. He tore my shirt off and pinched my nipples.

His untamed drive was making me a little nervous. He stood up and pulled his pants down. I sat up on the couch just waiting for his next move. He started ramming his penis in my mouth to the point of discomfort. This unusual aggressive act was pleasing him so I continued without a whimper.

Finally, he turned me around, pushed me down on my knees and he entered from behind. His thrusts were hard and fast. I picked up the pace; lifting my hips up to meet his thrusts. In the final seconds before he climaxed, he tugged on my hair and whispered in my ear; "I'm about to cum inside you." I was so wrapped up in the moment, I allowed him to shoot streams of his hot seed inside me.

We lay there on the couch catching our breaths. He bit the back of my shoulder and told me he loved me. He pulled out and ran to the bathroom. I went in behind him. After we washed up we rushed back to the living room to put our clothes back on. Xavier and Jade came out the room shortly after. Since Calvin ripped my shirt, it had no buttons left on it, so I held it together and had Jade go downstairs to bring me back a shirt. We all left the house shamelessly through my back door. The party was still going on, yet again, no one noticed us.

Jade complained that her stomach was upset and she needed to go home. Calvin's pager wouldn't stop going off and he was anxious to leave. I asked him to take Jade home. Xavier stayed behind to party some more. It bothered Jade that Xavier decided to stick around. She just couldn't let go of how well Xavier and I got along. Calvin never seemed to mind that Xavier and I were close; he was secure of himself in our relationship. I only wanted to be friends with him, but Xavier made it hard for her to accept that, since he spent a lot of time with me.

By the time the party ended, Andre and my mother were in bed, tanked. Xavier and I sneaked into the attic to smoke a joint. I hadn't been up there since Felo left, so I was a little nervous of the attic's condition. Luckily the window had been cracked open which allowed his foot odor to fade. The only things left were the bed and an empty altar.

"Sky, do you consider me a good friend?"

"Of course I do." I knew more questions were heading my direction. Questions I didn't care to answer.

"Can you tell me something?"

Considering that this Thanksgiving party was a blast and I was stoned, I was willing to let him in to my personal space—just this once—I thought. "Make it simple, X."

"Why do you have all that money inside that black box? Does Calvin have you selling drugs?"

"No, fool." I laughed. "I told you, it's my allowance."

He continued his interrogation. "Okay, can you tell me why you're hiding that Indian statue in your closet?"

"I told you to stay out my closet!"

"Calm down, I saw the statue when I brought down the black box. I didn't want to say anything in front of Jade, that's why I'm asking you now."

At least he waited to ask me in private. It didn't feel right to lie to him. Without holding back any more, I explained everything from how I wad extorted money from Andre to Calvin's spine chilling reading.

"Wow!" Xavier was so shocked that he kept smoking the joint longer than he should have. He forgot the three puffs and pass rule. "My aunt Reynalda is a Santera. She's really good. If you ever want to meet her, I would be glad to take you to her. She would be pleased to finally meet you."

I tilted my head. "What did you say?"

102

He confessed that Reynalda was curious to meet me because I always showed up in his readings. We shared the same beliefs and traditions of Santeria. But I knew there was more to that story, so I agreed to go with him to meet her.

REYNALDA, THE BEAUTIFUL SANTERA

A week went by and Xavier called me to tell me his aunt Reynalda was expecting us. I got dressed and met him at his building. It was a cold and windy morning. The threat of snow was in the air, but that didn't stop us from going to his aunt's house. The cold wind made my flesh pucker with goose bumps as we hiked to Stony Brook, which was a thirty minute trip from the complex.

She lived on Mozart Park, in a huge, fenced in three-family home. I didn't want her to be anything like Jade's godmother. I wouldn't be able to get out of my reading as easily.

When we arrived at the house, his aunt greeted us at the door. She was young and beautiful, short with curly honey hair, and dark eyes.

"Come in and make yourself comfortable. I'll be with you in a moment." She left us waiting in the parlor.

She created a good vibe. I sat back on the couch and drew a deep breath and let it out slowly. Relief. She seemed benign. I looked over at Xavier and he just smiled at me.

Reynalda came out, "Follow me, child." She escorted me to a back room.

It was extremely small but bright with one window overlooking her backyard. She had three tables circling the room. Two tables made up her altar, covered with statues, artifacts, and candles. The third table was where she conducted her readings. It was strange for me to see how bright the room was. Usually people who practiced this kept the rooms dim.

I sat across from her at the reading table with my hands on my lap, waiting for her to begin. First, she examined me as she lit a cigarette.

104

"When you come to see me, don't come dressed in black because it becomes difficult for me to read you." She blew out the cigarette smoke without taking her eyes off me and continued. "I asked my nephew to bring you so that I could finally meet you. You are always present in his readings." I lowered my eyes towards the cards on the table, nervous of what she was going to say next. "Xavier loves you a lot. He tells me all the time. I say leave that girl alone, she doesn't want you." She laughed. "But one thing I know for sure is that you will always be there for him, and that matters the most to me."

It felt good to know she understood my feelings and didn't try to force voodoo on me to change my heart.

She shuffled the cards. "He described you as a doll. And from where I'm sitting, he's right."

I just gave her a timid grin. She smiled back as she inhaled her cigarette. She put the cards in the middle of the table; told me to state my name and break them into three. She picked up each stack and spoke, "For you, for the present, and for what is to come." She then flipped the cards one by one and placed them next to each other in rows. She read, "Are you pregnant?"

My eyes flared. "No."

"Here; I see that you're pregnant and visiting a doctor. If you're not expecting now, you will be soon. Take care of your health, I see you very sick." All I thought was how my mother would wring my neck if I came home pregnant. She despised Calvin.

"Who is the young man with a medium brown complexion and a few inches taller than you?"

"My boyfriend."

"He loves you and does everything to make you happy." I smiled hard. But that smile faded as she continued. "But I see an ugly break up. This will be heartbreaking for both of you. He truly cares about you, so I don't understand the reason for the separation. I also see him in prison. I think the breakup has to do with him going to jail. You're a young girl with a bright future ahead of you. You can do better than a drug dealer." She waited for a response but I didn't give one. "I see you changing jobs, moving into a new apartment and attending college."

She paused. "There's an older woman who appears in my cards who lives far from here and does what I do. Who is she?"

"My grandmother."

"She watches over you. She placed a seal of protection around you. You are always in her thoughts. Go visit her, she misses you. There are many beautiful things in your future. You will give birth to a beautiful baby boy, by a wealthy man who will travel a lot for business."

She shuffled the cards again and had me divide them in two. She picked up the stack and read, "My saints tell me that you will return to see me. There's a girl here with black hair, a little fuller than you in size, who envies you. She pretends to be your friend but deep down inside, she hates you. Be careful with her, she wants what you have." I had a hunch that it was Jade, but what do I have that she wants? Xavier's love?

"Be careful." She put out her cigarette and waited for me to ask her questions.

I didn't ask her anything. I was processing everything she told me. I left the room and told Xavier I was ready to leave. He stood up and kissed Reynalda goodbye.

"Remember Sky, my doors are always open for you."

"Thank you."

The afternoon brought a lovely dusting of snow, covering the tips of the tree branches and blanketing the sidewalk like powdery sugar. Even with this lovely scene, I felt the urge to cry. Calvin was going to prison and breaking up with me? All this brought me down.

"Are you okay Sky? You're awfully quiet."

"I'll be fine."

Right when I struggled to hold back the pain, my tears couldn't stay in any longer. I assumed that with the snow falling, Xavier wouldn't notice. But the snowflakes clung to my eyelashes, bringing attention to him anyways. He just wiped the tears and snow from my eyes without saying a word.

A NEW YEAR

Calvin and I decided to spend First Night at the Boston Common. We went to see the ice sculptures, watch a live band, and trumpet in the New Year together. While we strolled around admiring the ice sculptures glow, he held my hand and told me his New Year's resolution. He wanted to invest his money, start his own car repair shop, and get out the drug business before the consequences of it caught up with him. Listening to him speak about his aspirations made me happy. It was the thought of him going to prison that worried me. But I didn't tell him that. Instead, I said I was looking forward to watching his dream unfold.

Soon after that, I told him my period was a week late. The look on his face said he was not thrilled about the news. That conversation didn't go as smoothly as I had wanted to. He let go of my hand and placed it over his head.

"If you're pregnant Sky, you're not keeping it."

"Why not?"

"We're too young. I'm not ready to be a father; you're definitely not ready for motherhood. You need to buy a pregnancy test, tomorrow!" He kept rambling nervously, "Damn, I should have pulled out. You should be on birth control. Why aren't you taking anything? Are you sure it's late?"

I stopped him, "Shut up already. I get it. You don't want a baby right now. I understand." But I didn't understand. Who was this guy?

We stood with the crowd waiting anxiously for midnight to come. I started to see a different side to him. He looked at his watch; one minute left to midnight. He reached for my hand again but I pulled away to adjust my scarf and hat. Then I tucked my hands in my coat pockets to avoid holding his. He ended up throwing his arm around me.

"Happy New Year!" The crowd shouted. I just held back my tears as Calvin hugged me.

It was a silent ride back home. I was itching to get out his car. Once he pulled inside my driveway, he shut off the engine.

"What's wrong with you now, Sky? I can tell you're upset." He tried to hold my arm, but I pulled away and unlocked the door. He yanked me back in the seat. "What's wrong with you?"

I gave him a dirty look. "Nothing!" I stormed out and slammed the car door so hard, I flinched.

I waited a couple of days before buying a pregnancy test, giving my period time to arrive. It had never been late before, therefore I worried. I read the instructions on the box: I had to urinate in a small cup and dip the stick inside it for ten seconds. After three minutes I would see one blue line if I wasn't pregnant or two blue lines if I was. As I waited for the results, I thought what Reynalda had told me in my reading has come to pass. Three minutes was awfully long as I stared at the stick. Shit! I wrapped it in toilet paper when I finished. I paged Calvin and waited for his call.

The phone rang once and I answered it. "Hello."

"What was the result?"

"Two blue lines."

"What does that mean?"

"It means I'm pregnant," I said in a soft voice.

"Well you already know what to do." He insisted I abort it. I clamped my teeth down and hung up. He called back but I turned the ringer off.

I threw myself on the bed and stared at the ceiling. My struggle was silent and terrible. How on Earth would I end this pregnancy or even tell my mother? I also questioned Calvin's love.

Any man who truly loves a woman wouldn't ask her to abort his first seed, or at least that's what ran through my head.

On the morning of my 18th birthday, I woke up vomiting. I didn't know what to do to stop the nausea. Because of it, I didn't go to school. I was in bed most of the day—sick and depressed.

Late afternoon I called the clinic, searching for information on terminating my pregnancy. I was given an appointment for two weeks, at an abortion facility in Brighton, Massachusetts. The receptionist was helpful in answering all my questions regarding the process. She sensed the nervousness and shame through my voice. She assured me that the doctors at the facility were professional and everything would be all right. It sounded as if she had been through this herself.

ABORTION

My mother was in the kitchen washing dishes. I slowly approached her and leaned against the wall. "I have to tell you something."

She stopped. "Are you pregnant?"

Oh no...she knew! I looked down at the floor and mumbled, "I'm not keeping it."

She wiped her hands with the towel. "What? What do you mean you're not keeping it?"

"I'm getting an abortion." My eyes flushed with tears.

"No Sky, you don't want to do that. Please don't do that!"

I turned away and walked back to my bedroom. I laid in bed, rubbing my stomach. Even I couldn't believe I was going to commit such a horrid act. I thought of everything to convince myself that it was the right thing to do. But nothing made me feel right. Calvin had a point: neither one of us was ready to become parents.

January 27, 1996 arrived. I woke up that Saturday with more tears in my eyes. Calvin waited for me outside my yard to drive me to Crittenton Hasting House and Clinic, which was an abortion facility. I sat in the car quiet, and somber. My hands were on my lap. Calvin reached over and placed his hand over mine. I didn't move.

When we approached the clinic, a few silent protesters held picket signs in the parking lot. They didn't speak. They just held their signs up to me. I passed them with my head hanging low.

I checked in at 7:03am. We sat in a waiting area...and waited. I was scared. "Cecilia Pino," a heavy set black woman called me in. I had to speak with her before the procedure to make sure I was certain about my decision. After the counseling session I went back

111

to the waiting area. Calvin wasn't there. I felt more alone and terrified.

"Cecilia Pino." My name was called again, this time by a petite blonde nurse.

When I got to the entrance of the room, I stood irresolute. My head ached horribly; my chest was on fire, my heart, which had been fluttering, gave a great leap, trying to force itself out of my chest.

"We can't waste any time now," said the male doctor.

Slowly I made it in the room. I was lightly sedated. Next thing I knew, I was on a bed and my baby was being sucked out of me via a vacuum. I lifted my torso against the cramping pain in my stomach. The nurse instructed me to stay still or the process would be done improperly if the vacuum missed the fetus. Afterwards I was placed in a room to recuperate. I was given ginger ale soda and saltine crackers, but I pushed it aside. I just closed my heavy eyes and rested. The rest of the day was a blur.

The following morning, I woke up weak. My whole body racked and wrenched with an insupportable anguish. The only time I left my room was to use the bathroom. Calvin hadn't called me and it made me feel worse. I paged him over and over again. I still didn't get a call back. Where the hell was he?

There was a knock on my door. "Come in."

Andre walked in with a bowl of chicken soup and crackers. I sat up but barely looked at him. I was too ashamed to face anyone. He put the bowl of soup on my night stand.

"Your mother went to class and I'm heading to work. There's plenty of crackers and ginger ale for you," he said and left.

COMPOSURE FAILURE

I struggled out of bed and threw on sweat pants and a hooded sweatshirt. Calvin wasn't going to ignore me. I stole Andre's car keys and went into the heavy snow and cold. The garage door slowly opened. I stared at Andre's Volvo hoping nothing would happen to it in this foul weather. I carefully got in and took off to where he spent a lot of time making his money.

I drove around Chestnut Hill until I spotted his Passat in someone's driveway. I parked across the street. When I stepped out the car, a young woman with reddish hair pulled up in the blue Mercedes. My heart rate became erratic and my stomach felt hollow in a way that had nothing to do with hunger. I stood next to the car and waited for her to step out. She got out with a bag of takeout food. I had an uneasy feeling about this girl.

"Is Calvin here?" I asked her.

She looked at me rather strange. "Who are you?"

"His girlfriend."

"Girlfriend?"

My voice got a little louder, "Yes. Is he inside?"

"Excuse me?" she locked the door to the Mercedes. "What do you want? Do you need something?"

She must have thought I was a fiend looking for a fix because I looked ghastly after the abortion. "I just told you, I'm looking for Calvin. Is he here?"

Calvin came out the house in basketball shorts and a t-shirt. "What are you doing here?"

"Why haven't you answered my pages?"

The girl interrupted and asked, "Who is this, Calvin?"

I turned to her and said, "Are you deaf? I told you, I'm his girlfriend."

She laughed. "Oh really! That's hilarious because I've been his girlfriend for the past four years."

I froze. We all just stood there puzzled. My stomach felt like it had been punched. I folded my arms and looked at him. He hurried down the stairs, off the porch, and grabbed me by my arm. He pulled me towards the street. I resisted and pushed back with the little strength I had.

"Sky, don't do this here!"

"Do what, Calvin? Is she your girlfriend? Really?" I broke away from his grasp but he grabbed me again and pulled me towards the Volvo. "Get the fuck off me!"

He pushed me against the car and said, "Stop it, Sky, you're not in the projects. They'll call the police around here."

That comment struck a nerve with me. "Get your filthy hands off me!" I bawled and broke free from his grip.

I turned back towards the young woman but she had disappeared inside the house. "Tell me this isn't true Calvin. Please, tell me this isn't true."

He put his head down and said, "Go home, Sky."

"What?"

The sharp pain in my stomach grew stronger, making it difficult to remain standing. I wiped my tears from my face as a big snowflake floated past the tip of my nose. He wouldn't look at me. I wanted to choke him, but my arms were disconnected from my brain. I fell back against the car; just leaning on it for support. He opened the door to the Volvo and told me to get in.

I cried in the car during my ride back home. The snow was thickening, swirling wildly around the car, causing me to swerve a few times before I arrived. Fortunately, I made it home safe, but I was still bawling. I ran to my room and threw myself on my knees.

"Why? Why?" I wept.

I crawled to the side of my bed and continued to cry. The phone rang. I pulled the cord off the wall causing my phone to crash on the floor. I got up and went to my mother's medicine cabinet. I looked through her bottle of pills. What if I took them all and never woke up? No one would miss me. I took the bottles in my hand, reading each one. In reality, I didn't have the courage to end my life.

I heard someone in the apartment. I put the bottles back in the cabinet as fast as I could and washed my face with cold water. When I came out to see who it was, no one was there.

"Mah? Andre?" No answer from either of them.

I searched through every room in the house. Someone definitely passed by the bathroom. But who? And where did they go? I ran into my room, pressed my face against my pillow, and screamed inside of it.

My mother barged in my bedroom, "What's going on?"

She pulled the pillow from underneath my face. I was mortified she caught me screaming. I snatched the pillow back from her and lied back on my bed. She left my room, but I could hear her in the kitchen calling an ambulance asking them to provide a section 12 for me. No, no, no. I threw on my winter coat and snuck out the back door. I quietly went inside the garage to sit inside Andre's Volvo. I turned on the engine to keep myself warm while I waited for the ambulance to arrive; then leave the house. They left after discovering that the girl interrupted was nowhere in sight.

BREAK UP

My phone remained unplugged for days. I chose to be in complete solitude. Even during school hours, I pretended to read my text books in order to hide my tears and avoid the outside world. It was necessary to shake the thought of Calvin—of his cruelty.

Complexity ran deep inside me. I didn't have an answer to any of my questions. How could he have two girlfriends at the same time? Did he really love me? How did he get away with sleeping with me almost every night? What other lies did he tell me? Why does it hurt this bad? Did Xavier know all along? Who was this other girl? What did she have that I didn't?

I remembered what my cousin Felo predicted in Calvin's reading about a young woman with red hair. It ripped me apart thinking I was lied to for two years, lost my virginity to him, and forced to abort our baby.

I started to take a different route after school. I would sneak out a side door and walk to Back Bay Station and take the 39 bus. The path was longer, but I didn't mind because I needed to be alone. Everyone else walked in the other direction to take the orange line train at New England Medical Center. If Calvin tried to pick me up or look for me, he wouldn't find me. The 39 bus drove by the complex but I would get off three stops before it, at the Eliot Sq. Monument and then take the back streets to my house.

After a week of playing ninja, while shaking through one of the back streets, a car pulled up on me. I sensed it was Calvin so I continued without looking to my left.

"Sky!"

It was Xavier; but he was riding with Calvin. I ignored them. The car was riding slowly to my speed. I took a left on Custer Street because it was a one way and I thought Calvin wouldn't make that illegal turn. I was wrong.

He turned the car and I could hear Xavier yelling at him, "What are you doing fool, this is a one way street!" I couldn't hear what Calvin said to him but Xavier continued yelling at him, "I'm dirty! I have an ounce of weed on me!"

Lucky for them, Custer was a short street and we made it to Jamaica Street without an incoming car—or worse, the police.

"Sky!" Xavier called me.

"Don't speak to me."

"What did I do?" Xavier asked me.

The car was still driving at my walking pace. "It's not what you did. It's what you didn't do!"

He jumped out the car. "Hold up!"

I stopped with my arms folded against my chest. "You knew Calvin had a girlfriend and never told me."

He spun around towards Calvin who had parked the car and was running to catch up to us. When Calvin got closer, Xavier asked, "You have another girlfriend, C?"

Calvin scooted up to me and said, "Xavier doesn't know anything. Can we talk in private?"

"No!"

THE TALK

I was eating dinner in the living room when there was a knock on my door. Andre opened it and I heard Xavier's voice, "Is Sky home?"

Andre let him in. "She's in the parlor, go right in."

I rolled my eyes at Xavier as he stood in the living room. "What do you want?"

"Why are you mad at me?"

I didn't want anyone in the house, especially my mother, to know what went down between Calvin and me. In an effort to change the subject I said, "It bothers me that my boyfriend of two years isn't allowed in this house but you're welcomed in at anytime. What's up with that?"

He smiled. "I'm smooth like that."

Andre walked in, uninvited. "Where are your manners, Sky? Have a seat, Xavier." Andre pointed his finger to the sofa. "Would you like something to drink?"

"No thanks, sir."

"Could you bring this to the kitchen for me, Andre?" I handed him my empty dinner plate.

As soon as he was out of sight, I leaned forward to get closer to Xavier, and whispered in a sarcastic tone, "No thanks, sir. Really?"

Xavier sat back and changed the television channel as if he were in his own house. "I told you I'm smooth."

"X, be honest with me. Did you know all along?" I asked him.

"Know what?"

I turned off the television to get his attention. "That Calvin had another girlfriend."

He stumbled with his words. "I don't....I um...well...I suppose so."

"I thought we were friends, X?"

"Let's take a walk," he suggested.

"In this damn cold?"

"You want to have this conversation here," he jerked his thumb behind him, towards the kitchen where Andre and my mother were.

I grabbed my coat and we headed out the door.

Dusk brought with it a harsh cold breeze. Xavier walked passed me down the stairs. I stopped at the porch, shivering. He looked back at me and asked, "What's wrong?"

"It's freezing."

"Come on! Sean let me borrow a ride," he said, pulling a screwdriver halfway out his back pocket.

We got in a white 1993 Nissan Maxima. Xavier started the car up by inserting the screwdriver inside the popped ignition and turning it like a key. The engine hummed and we drove off to Jamaica Pond.

We sat in the car and Xavier rolled a joint. "Calvin's been with Nicole since he was seventeen. She's the one who got Calvin involved in the drug game through her older brother Brian. I honestly didn't know he was still with her. He never mentions her unless it's about money. When she went away to college Calvin started fooling around with you. I thought they were done. If he wasn't making his money, he was with you."

He passed the joint to me. I inhaled. I exhaled. I did this a few times without saying a word. That sharp pain in my stomach came back.

"Are you okay, Sky?" Xavier asked, tugging on my elbow. "If you're upset because I never mentioned it, you shouldn't be. Calvin and I are like brothers."

119

I remained quiet. I inhaled. I exhaled. Her name went through my head repeatedly. Nicole. Nicole. Nicole. I passed the joint and asked, "How old is she?"

"She's a year older than Calvin." He took another drag from the joint. "I don't know what he's going to do now that you both found out about him playing around, but honestly, I doubt he's going to leave her. Calvin loves money and Nicole is his drug connection. She knows that too. My advice to you is to leave him alone and move on."

ULTIMATUM

It was a stupid Valentine's Day: I was consumed with doubt and despair and Calvin. We hadn't spoken about what took place in front of Nicole's house and my phone was still off the hook. Andre and my mother had left for the evening and planned on staying out all night.

I ended up locking myself in my bedroom to roll up a joint and turned up the beat of Guns and Roses to the tracks that included Welcome To The Jungle and Paradise City. The music was playing loudly in order to drown out the voices in my head. I bobbed my head and sang the lyrics. That's when I heard a loud tap on my window. I snuffed out the joint and turned down the stereo. I shut off the lights to my room to get a better view outside the window. Calvin.

I walked out to the back door and unlocked it. He followed me back to my bedroom. I raised my eyebrows with that questioning look. "What are you doing here?"

"We need to talk."

"I have absolutely nothing to say to you." I lied. I just didn't know where to begin.

"Let me explain." He stood in front of me and grabbed my hands.

"I want the truth...the whole truth." I pulled my hands away and sat on the edge of my bed.

"I'm sorry I lied to you, Sky. We weren't supposed to be together. Nicole and I had been broken up for a few months because she decided to live on campus and I was against it. I thought for sure it was final. When you came around, Xavier was always telling us how he was going to make you his girl. He wanted you, not me. I had no interest in you until you started coming around us and I saw how cool and genuine you were. You became a distraction for me and slowly I started to fall in love with you. I didn't know you were a virgin until the night you gave yourself to me. Believe me babe, I never felt so terrible in my life for taking advantage of you. Nicole came back to me after you and I were already together. I didn't know what to do."

I cut him off, "Really? So who are you going to stay with now?"

"You."

I didn't believe him. He omitted the fact that she was his drug connection. I knew he worked things out with her and now he was trying to make good with me. I knew he was going to continue playing both of us.

Angry tears ran down my face. "You selfish bastard! You think you can come here and give me a sorry ass excuse that you didn't mean to take advantage of me. That we weren't meant to be together? You felt terrible? You don't feel shit; not a damn thing."

"Sky, believe me. I really do love you, but..."

"But what Calvin?" I interjected again, "You love how she helps keep money in your pocket."

"Xavier told you?"

"No, I put two and two together. All your customers live in that area with the exception of a few in the complex. Your drug connection, Brian, looks just like Nicole, so they must be related. I'm not having that, so you either quit the game and stay with me or continue making your money with her."

Tears appeared in his eyes, as well from pain and confusion. I stood up to ask him, "Did you ever really love me?"

"Yes babe. I still do."

"Then why is it hard for you to let go of her?"

"Give me time. Let me finish making the last of my money to start up my repair shop. Then I promise; it will be you and me." He kissed me on my forehead and then on my lips.

"Where's my Valentine's present? You came here with an apology empty handed?"

"Never." He reached for his back pocket and pulled out a long jewelry box.

My eyes pulsed with excitement. I opened the box: a stylish gold and diamond cut Cuban Link necklace.

"A Cuban Link for my Cuban princess." He put the necklace on me and kissed me.

I turned to the mirror to look at this vibrant piece of jewelry around my neck. Through the mirror I caught him checking his pager behind my back. I knew I would never be able to trust him again.

UNLUCKY BREAK

My father was undergoing a liver transplant back in Florida. I flew out to be by his side during my school break in April. Without delay, I left the airport and went directly to the hospital to see him. He told me in that hospital bed he had been saving money for a rainy day. If for any reason, he didn't come out alive from the surgery, he requested a simple funeral service and the balance of his money was to be divided between his sister and me. This made me worry he wasn't going to make it. Fortunately, his surgery was successful and I decided to stay a couple more days with him.

"How do you feel, dad?"

"Like a million bucks now that you're here with me."

"Are you aware that your liver came from a 22 year old man?"

"In that case, I'm going to find me a young girlfriend." We both laughed.

After he separated from my mother, my father never settled down with another woman. I'm sure he had a few flings during the years, but no one ever captured his heart as my mother did. He believed my grandmother put a hex on him so that he would never find love again.

Dad told me how proud he was that I would be graduating high school. He wanted me to attend college in Florida. I was convinced it was the right move considering my relationship with Calvin was a wreck and I was at a legal age to leave home.

"Will you be able to go to my graduation?"

"I wouldn't miss it for the world!"

"Is it going to be awkward for you to see mah with Andre? I haven't invited them but I'm sure they'll be there."

"I'll be focusing on you. It's your day."

"Dad, you have to wear a shirt and a tie."

"Anything for you."

"I can't wait. What are you getting me for graduating?"

"What do you want?"

"Surprise me. I don't care what you get me; just make sure you come, please." I hugged him. He smiled and kissed me on my forehead.

I was scheduled to fly back to Boston the following morning. On my way to the airport my aunt expressed her concerns about my father flying up north to attend my graduation. He was physically unfit to travel and needed to be monitored around the clock. I ignored her. I wouldn't be attending my graduation without my father present, so she was going to have to kiss that idea goodbye.

PROM

Three days before my prom and I still didn't have a dress to wear. I was too concerned with Calvin leaving Nicole. Prom was meaningless because he made it clear we weren't going together. That was difficult for me to accept. I didn't want to go to prom alone. I cried myself to sleep because he was no longer staying with me. He rarely phoned me. How things had changed between us! I missed his company and his late night creeps. Our separation infuriated me; the wound was too deep for me to cope with.

Xavier offered to take both Jade and me to prom, but it wasn't fair for Jade to share her date with me. Besides, I wasn't going to be the lonely third wheel. I declined. I was going to buy me a fabulous dress and make going to prom alone look bad ass.

Andre and my mother pitched in to help purchase a pretty short cream dress for me. I didn't want the traditional long gown. My legs were one of my best assets and I intended to show them off that night. When I got home from shopping, I went straight to my room. I closed the door and locked it behind me, throwing my bag on the bed and taking off my sneakers. I checked my caller I.D. and saw that Calvin had been trying to reach me. He left me two messages, so I paged him.

"Where the hell have you've been? I tried calling you all day."

"I was buying my prom dress and some other things for my move to Florida."

"What? What move to Florida?"

"I'm moving with my father after I graduate to attend college out there." Even though that decision wasn't final, I figured if he thought I was leaving soon, he'd get his act together and leave Nicole.

"When were you planning on telling me?"

126

"I wasn't. It looks to me like you made up your mind on who you're going to stay with, and I've made up my mind to leave."

"What time you get home from prom?"

"I don't know."

"What do you mean you don't know?"

"I...don't...know!"

"I'll talk to you later, because you're acting stupid right now." He hung up. I slammed the phone down and turned to my pillow to cry.

The day of my prom my depression overpowered me. My mind was tired from thinking of Calvin. Jade called me early so we could go to the salon and get our hair done. Now that I had my driver's license, my mother allowed me to drive her Chevy Tahoe; sometimes. I picked up Jade and we went to the salon. I was slowly starting to get out my funk or at least I was disguising it well.

Calvin called me at the salon, but his bad attitude made everything worse. "What time is prom over?"

"Why, Calvin? Why do you insist on knowing what time prom is over?"

"We need to talk."

"Pick me up at 10:00pm at Anthony's Pier 4."

"All right, I'll see you at ten."

Xavier and Jade arrived at my door. Why? I chose to go to prom alone. But they were there and looked amazing together. Jealousy flooded over me.

"What are you guys doing here?"

Xavier and Andre just looked at each other and smiled. There was something suspicious going on but I just played along.

My mother began to take pictures of us. Then she flipped her wrist to check her watch. "Where's the limo? It should be here by now."

"We're getting a limo?" I was surprised.

Calvin and Andre got together to rent us a limo. I didn't even want to know whose idea it was, since Andre and Calvin didn't vibe well. The three of us jumped in and rode off. I sat by the door staring out the window. I wanted to cry.

We arrived at Anthony's Pier 4 in Downtown Boston, right on the Harbor. You couldn't miss the place with the huge banner in front that read Class of 1996. The place was lovely: silver, gold, and black balloons. Strands of lights provided a subtle glow to mimic a starry night. We walked to the photographer and took pictures. I stood alone for mine, but I saw Xavier talk to the photographer as he was finishing up with me. When I walked off the photo set, the photographer asked me to take one more with the handsome gentleman who talked him into taking one with me. How sweet of him! Xavier was trying to make this night memorable for me. He knew I was hurting, being there without Calvin.

Overall, prom wasn't bad. I convinced myself that I was the niftiest gal in that place. I strolled around the pier and made being dateless look cool. Some couples looked miserable, others were ridiculous together, and a few looked great. Winning prom queen would have made my night but unfortunately I didn't. I grew anxious to leave. I wanted desperately to take off the dress, throw on some sweat pants, and pick my hair up in a ponytail. I kept looking at the time, anticipating 10:00 pm to arrive.

At a quarter to ten, I told Xavier that Calvin was on his way to pick me up. I wanted him and Jade to enjoy the limo without my presence. Xavier was good with that. He gave me a high five. That's when I decided to walk out to the deck to listen to the ocean wave, swish, and splash until Calvin arrived.

When I left the pier, Calvin was waiting for me out front. I stepped in the car with a fake smile. He flashed a smile of his own.

"Thanks for the limo service. So you and Andre were in cahoots?"

128

Without answering me, his mouth covered mine and I could taste the Hennessey on his tongue. I almost pulled away from the kiss but he tasted good. I missed his kisses and how he nibbled and sucked on my bottom lip. I passionately kissed him back.

At last we ended the kiss and he asked, "Are you really moving to Florida?"

I remained silent as he pulled off from the front of the pier.

"Well...are you?"

"Yes Calvin. My father wants me to go live with him. So I'm leaving."

"Just like that?"

"What do you want me to do, Calvin, stay here and play the waiting game with you?" I raised my voice.

"I'm not a fan of your yelling!" He swung round a corner abruptly causing me to bump my head on the passenger door window.

"Slow down, will you!" I rubbed the side of my head.

He slowed down. The ride was quiet for about three minutes when I noticed he wasn't driving me home.

"Where are you going?" I still had an attitude.

"I got us a hotel room."

Being with Calvin was certainly a test to my will power. I didn't want to continue sleeping with him until he was completely done with Nicole. I almost opened my mouth to argue against going but I wanted him.

The minute we got inside the room he undressed me. He lunged at me, tossing me down on my back. The bed bounced as he pinned me beneath him. I lost myself with him. I was falling in love all over again. The euphoria didn't last. His pager buzzed. He got up from the bed and disappeared in the bathroom. I was still catching my breath when I thought: Nicole is paging him.

129

He burst out the bathroom. "Get dressed, we have to leave." My stomach churned as I grabbed his tank top to wipe the cum from my thighs, and threw it at him, missing his face. We were leaving because she paged him. I knew she did. He picked up his tank top and tossed it in the trash barrel. Without speaking, I stormed out the hotel room with my shoes and purse in hand.

I opted to take the stairs on my way out the door; to avoid taking the elevator with him. Damn him! I ran out the hotel. My heart was pulsating as I dashed down the street without a clue on how to get home. A taxi cab slowly drove by me. I picked up my speed to get close enough to get the driver's attention. He stopped for me and I jumped in.

"23... St. Rose Street...please."

23 St. Rose Street was next to the complex two streets down from Jamaica Street. When the cab pulled up to the address, I kindly told the driver that I lived in the blue house on the corner and that I had to get the money from my mother. I opened the cab door and felt my stomach tense up as I broke into a run. I pulled back on the fence to the blue house and jumped over it. I went down, flapping my arms as I landed on my ass and fell back on my head; ripping my dress. I got up, rubbed my head, and sprinted through the yard towards the back of the house. I took refuge under a tree in the alley that lead to the complex. My head sustained a minor bump but it hurt like hell.

After I caught my breath, I hurried home. I made it to the top of Jamaica Street to my house where Calvin was sitting on my back porch with a disgruntled look on his face. He stood up and grabbed my arm.

"Don't touch me!"

"How did you get here?"

"None of your business."

"Why is your dress dirty?"

I ignored him and walked up the stairs to open my back door, but before entering, I turned and said, "Do us both a favor, and stay out of my life. You made your decision to stay with that white bitch and I've made my decision to leave to Florida." Then I locked the door behind me.

In the coming days, Calvin sat on my front porch waiting for me to talk to him. I would just walk pass him and pretend he wasn't there. He wouldn't say a word; he would just sit there and wait to see if I would give in. But I refused to say anything. Some evenings, I would discreetly watch him behind my living room curtains, to see how long he would wait there. It looked like nothing was going to stop him from coming around.

LEAVING PEACEFULLY

It was 4:00 pm on a Wednesday, the first day Calvin didn't sit on my house steps. Instead I found Andre standing there. I figured Andre must have played the cop role and told him to leave. But even if he had, it was not like Andre to stand out on the porch doing nothing. With a puzzled look on my face, I asked him if he was alright.

"Your mother needs to speak to you."

I found my mom in the kitchen with tears in her eyes. Something was terribly wrong.

"Something wrong, mah?"

"You're father's body is rejecting the new liver and the doctor's are giving him less than a week to live."

"What? Can't they just get him another liver?" I didn't think it was true.

The sadness with which she responded, "I'm sorry, Sky, he's not going to make it," convinced me it was over for him. "I'm getting the time off work and you and I will fly out Friday."

Without a reply I turned away and ran to my room. I threw myself on my bed and cried uncontrollably. Not only did all my crying sap the energy out of me but it made it impossible to sleep. I tossed about for hours, and then, for the sake of variety, I went to the living room looking for sleep. I couldn't.

As soon as we landed in Florida that Friday afternoon, my father passed away. When I learned this, I was pounded by waves of ache. In fact, a part of me died with him that day. I never got a chance to say goodbye. It was the biggest blow my heart had ever received.

My aunt let my mother and me stay with her for the duration of the funeral as well as allowing me to choose his casket. After she paid for his service she took out a bank check with the remaining balance.

"This is your half of what he left."

I stared at it. I would have preferred nothing in exchange for a few more years with him.

When we walked in the funeral home, the day of his wake, everyone was lined up to hug us. I met a lot of family members I didn't know I had. Meanwhile, my emotions were distorted when I finally dared to see him in the casket. All I could do was put my head down and cry.

"He went peacefully," my aunt whispered to me while I stood by his body. I said nothing. I couldn't take my eyes off him. Tears were tumbling down my face. Even though it was hard to believe he was gone; it was comforting for me to know that he left peacefully.

The church filled slowly. I sat alone in the last row observing the crowd and watching the slide show that played clips of his life. When the slide show played a picture of me sitting on his lap when I was an infant, I sobbed for the rest of the ceremony. Everything hurt because he was a vital part of my world.

Finally my father was buried on the same day of my graduation. Instead of walking down the aisle with the rest of the Boston High School Seniors, and waving at my father from Mathew's Arena; I was at a cemetery field, saying my last goodbye by tossing a rose at his gravesite.

The following morning, my mother and I flew back to Boston. Andre picked us up from Logan Airport. Given that I was mourning the death of my father, Andre and my mother refrained from speaking in the car. When I arrived home I noticed a black Honda Civic in our driveway. I picked my head up. It was the car I had been saving to buy. When I got out Andre's car, I walked to the driveway to get a closer look at the Civic. At the same time, Andre stood next to me and gave me the keys to the car.

"This won't alleviate your pain and it won't make up for your loss, but your mother and I bought it as a graduation present."

"Thanks." I opened the car door and sat inside. It was exactly how I wanted it: a 5-speed hatchback, with black interior and power windows. The car was only two years old.

"The car is fairly new, but if you want anything else done to it just let me know."

"No, it's perfect. Thanks."

I went straight to my room to check my voice mail messages. I had many messages from my classmates, my teachers, my principal, and my closest friends. My grandmother left me a message asking me to call her, but I didn't. I only called Calvin.

"Hey..." I could barely speak.

"How are you feeling?"

"Like death."

"I'm so sorry for your loss and everything you're going through, baby...I want to see you."

"Come pick me up."

"Can I take you out to dinner?"

"A quiet dinner?"

"Is that what you want?"

"Yeah."

"Okay, I'll be there in an hour."

Calvin took me to the Golden Temple on Beacon Street. He also granted me the quiet dinner I wanted and needed. I barely touched my food but it didn't bother him. The only thing he was concerned with was comforting me. Before he paid for dinner, he dug inside his pocket and pulled out a small gift box.

"I bought this for you. A graduation gift."

I slowly reached for the box and opened it. They were a pair of onyx and diamond yin yang earrings. Stunning. I gently rubbed the earrings with my right pointer finger as I admired its radiance.

"They're beautiful."

"The onyx is a powerful and protective stone. The jeweler told me that it represents emotional stability, while the diamond is the most precious and strong stone there is; which complements the onyx."

"Is that right?" I couldn't stop my tears.

"I'm really sorry, Sky."

"Stop apologizing!"

"It hurts me to see you like this."

I lost my composure. I felt the urge to throw the earrings at him but I liked them too much. "It hurts you? Does it really hurt you? Does it hurt you when you're fucking Nicole? Does it hurt you that I aborted your baby?"

"Calm down, I said I'm sorry." He remained calm, unlike me.

"Your apologies aren't going to change how I feel about what you did to me."

He said no more. He called the waiter over and asked for the check. He paid for dinner and left the restaurant. I trailed behind him, me and my stupid tears. The hostess stopped me and offered me a napkin to wipe my face. She also handed me a fortune cookie. I gave her a weak grin, thanked her, and left. Before I sat in the car I opened the fortune cookie. It read: If the cake is bad, what good is the frosting?

Secretly I felt like an asshole for my outburst in the restaurant. With the death of my father and Nicole still in the picture, I didn't know how to act. Calvin didn't say anything to me because he didn't know what else to do to make things right between us. He quietly drove me home.

135

As he began to drive, he inserted a CD in the car radio and turned up the volume to this particular song: Don't Leave Me by Blackstreet. Calvin was dedicating this song to me; his way of expressing his feelings, I guess. Too late, though. I was emotionally damaged.

BEST FRIENDS

I missed my bed. I crawled into it and pulled the covers over my head, still hoping to wake up and find all this to be a bad dream. Unfortunately, this wasn't going to happen. Andre came in my room and told me I had a visitor. At first, I was tempted to be rude because I wasn't up for visitors. But I was curious. As soon as I came out, I found Xavier sitting in my living room holding flowers and a card. He stood up and hugged me. I broke down and wailed. He just held me tight. He was the only one that could relate to the pain of losing a parent. His presence was a great solace for me.

After releasing me from this act of affection, he stepped back with a smile and pointed to our driveway. "I hear that's your new ride." He wiped my tears with his thumbs.

"Yes it is."

"Are we going to bless it?"

"Huh?"

Xavier put his fingers near his mouth and inhaled deeply—a sign of smoke.

"Oh, bless it! Sure."

We took my new car out for a test drive. If I had any idea that Andre and my mother were going to purchase a car for me; I would have circled all the BMWs on the Auto Hunter instead of the Hondas. But nevertheless, I was grateful.

Xavier had me park in front of the complex while he ran indoors. Ten minutes later, he came back with weed and a CD.

"I'm not listening to that heavy metal shit you like," Xavier put a CD in my radio. "Strictly Tupac when I'm in this ride."

I just laughed as I pulled off and drove to Jamaica Pond, our usual spot for smoking sessions.

137

"Amazingly, State Police has never caught us smoking up here," I said as I looked through my rear view mirror; on guard while Xavier rolled the joint.

He shot me a mean look, with a little heat behind it. "Don't jinx us." He licked the joint and turned up my radio.

We ended up strolling around the pond while we smoked the joint. We didn't even care that a couple passed us. It was dark; it was our freedom.

NEAR AND FAR

July: hot and rainy. I was in my room listening to Toni Braxton, Unbreak My Heart, while the rain lashed against my window. My room was unlit and gloomy. The strain of my breakup and the death of my father eroded the last threads of heartiness I possessed.

I called Reynalda on the phone to ask if she would give me a reading. She agreed. I didn't bother calling Xavier to go with me. I felt comfortable enough visiting Reynalda alone.

Soon after arriving at Reynalda's house, a storm accompanied the rain. This made the atmosphere in the entire house dark and muggy. Reynalda lit a white candle on the reading table. And unlike the last time she read them to me, she rang a little butler bell right before she began.

"He's coming back...I see you guys living together." She was referring to Calvin.

"The problem here is that he's not leaving the other girl. He's confused. His heart is torn between the both of you. Reason being, he loves money more than anything... and this other girl gives him that." She paused.

"I see him behind bars. And while he's away you will finish school and move on with your life. There's no need for me to work a love spell on him, because you're not destined to be with him."

Listening to her, made me feel sad, but our trust was gone. We weren't ever going to be the same whether Nicole was in the picture or not.

"I see two tall gentlemen you'll be interested in; one more than the other. But I see here, you'll be involved with both of them. And this guy you're with now will be a thing of the past."

She collected the cards and had me shuffle them again. Only this time the reading was shorter. "You will be taking a trip to Cuba by the end of this year or the beginning of next. After this trip, your life will change dramatically. So just keep in mind, I will be here whenever you need me."

SASHA: THE OTHER TWIN

Now that I was out of school, working at the Federal Reserve Bank became full-time. Sometimes Jade's twin, Sasha, would join us for lunch. She was much more outgoing and down to earth than her sister. They were definitely different. Sasha was coming around so much that by the end of the summer, she and I got closer, while Jade and I grew apart.

One day, Sasha and I were window shopping around Downtown after work. Jade had left work early that day because she had to take care of some things. Sasha looked peeved. She told me she knew exactly why Jade left work early: Jade was visiting her godmother, Iris. I pretended not to know Iris. Sasha expressed how much she was against Jade visiting this woman.

"Iris is a Santera. When we were younger, our mother would bring us with her to see Iris. My mother knew I didn't like going but I was forced to go anyway and wait in the living room while my mother got a consultation." She stopped to stare at a dress on a mannequin. "I can't comprehend why Jade trusts that woman. Yes she's known us since we were little girls, but she is wicked."

I cleared my throat. "Don't you get curious to know what lies ahead of you?"

Sasha scoffed, "Not at all. I believe what's going to happen is meant to happen. We have no right to seek ways to change our destiny or hurt others in the process to benefit ourselves."

"What if you need a little financial help? That's not hurting anyone."

"Sky, you can seek financial help without going to a voodooist. I rather be poor and happy than to turn to some underground, ghetto cult, practiced by uneducated people to get me a few dollars. Last time Jade visited her, I found out that Iris told her I was going to get married young, then have affairs because I was going to be miserable with my husband. I was livid. I told Jade never to tell me anything again."

"Why does Jade believe in that sort of thing?"

"Believe in it? She lives and breathes it! Iris somehow got into her head when Jade was younger; making her believe that she had the means to help Jade with whatever she wanted. Iris told Jade she would help her get a better position in this bullshit job at the bank. Don't say anything Sky...Jade had Iris work a spell on Xavier to make him stay, when supposedly he was going to leave my sister after he slept with her."

Listening to Sasha made me understand why Xavier and Jade were off and on. Iris was luring Xavier back to Jade because Xavier was known for playing around, then leaving. But he did stay with Jade longer than any other girl. It only made sense that she had him spellbound.

NEW HOUSE RULES

Andre and my mother wanted to rent out the second floor apartment. Why not rent it out to me? Although they both agreed that me living alone upstairs was absurd, they'd give it some thought.

"The Federal Reserve is encouraging me to take up financing classes in order to qualify for future promotions," I explained over breakfast.

"What do you think, Andre?" My mother asked politely. "Can we afford to send her to college?"

Andre just sat at the dining table stuffing his face with scrambled eggs and bacon while he dazed off thinking how to answer my mother. After a few lazy bites he agreed to pay my tuition and let me stay in the apartment upstairs—as long as I maintained a B average. One thing I purposely failed to mention to them was that the bank would reimburse me 80% of the tuition. So I decided to pocket the money.

When I was accepted to Northeastern University for the upcoming fall semester, I began to move my things to the upstairs apartment. Although inside I felt hollow, my life was at a good turning point now that I was starting my independency.

A few days before school started, I sat in my mother's kitchen eating fried chicken and rice. My mother was lecturing me about living on my own and how she was expecting me to be responsible. Andre didn't say much except that he didn't want the apartment to turn into a frat house. I just sat there eating my dinner without letting them know that I didn't care what they had to say.

During their lecture, our door bell rang. While Andre went to see who it was, I put my plate in the sink and washed my hands. He entered the kitchen with a displeasing look on his face. "Calvin is on the porch asking for you."

I ran out to meet him, thinking he wanted to see my new place I had been bragging about. But he stood there looking worried.

"I need a favor," he stared down at the duffle bag he was holding.

"Come inside." We went up to my apartment.

He unzipped the side of the bag, pulled out cash, and dropped the duffle bag on the floor.

"Could you hold on to this until Monday?" I took the money from him and counted it: $9,000.

I didn't ask him anything about the money because I suspected he was leaving to New York again. He had moved up in the drug game and was now taking trips there to pick up large amounts of cocaine. And now that I had my own place, he probably felt entitled to come and leave his goods behind.

I had him follow me to the attic where I had a statue of La Caridad del Cobre (Our Lady of Charity) guarding the entrance. Caridad, in the customs of Santeria, controls love, sexuality, and money matters. Her role is to help her followers with human pleasures. And this is why I had her standing guard with cinnamon, coconuts, and honey as my offerings to her.

On the other side of the attic, I set up a small altar with candles, a statue of Saint Michael, the Ochosi statue, a picture frame of my late father, and pink roses all around. It was my first altar, ever.

As Calvin stood at the entrance, I searched for the sacred beads that my cousin Felo had given him in the past. Once I found

144

them, I placed them around his neck, and then I wet his forehead with Florida water.

I looked him straight in the eyes and said, "Saint Michael will protect you."

He kissed me and told me he loved me; then left the house. I opened the duffle bag. I couldn't believe my eyes. It was his dirty laundry. I placed my hands over my head as a sign of relief. I thought the bag had drugs inside. He had some nerve to expect me to do his laundry, but he knew me well enough that it would get done.

Andre walked in immediately after Calvin drove off. "What did Calvin want?" The police officer in him became present.

I responded without making eye contact. "A favor."

"I hope you're not holding any drugs in my house!"

"I'm not holding drugs!" I sat on my bed waiting for him to leave.

"Then what are you holding?" He was annoying me with his questions. "What's in the duffle bag?"

I pushed it towards him with my foot. "Check for yourself."

He searched the bag like he had a warrant for it. Luckily, I had stashed the money in the attic next to my altar. After he searched inside, thoroughly, he said nothing and left.

To take my mind off things, I called Sasha to go out. We headed out to a friend's party in Franklin Field. Even though we were out, appearing to have a good time, I didn't tell anyone how sad I felt inside. I wasn't the same person after the abortion. Not a day went by without thinking about my baby or what it would have been like to keep it. By this time, I would have given birth to my unborn, but instead I was at a house party pretending everything was all right with me.

145

SO MANY TEARS

My first semester at Northeastern was ending. Surprisingly, I made the dean's list. Andre and my mother wanted to reward me by sending me to Cuba to visit my grandmother. We took out a passport for me to travel there. When I spoke to my grandmother over the phone, she sounded weak. Her voice was low and her laughter was faint. We both knew her days were few and she wanted to see me one last time.

But the Federal Reserve Bank didn't approve of me taking three weeks off. They said I would have to resign if I chose to leave. Leaving the bank wasn't a bad idea; working there was boring. My mother agreed that I should resign and go visit my grandmother, then focus on school full time when I got back. I didn't bother leaving the bank on good terms, I simply quit.

On the morning of December 22nd, the day before I flew out to Cuba, I climbed up to the attic and knelt in front of my altar. I held the picture of my father and cried. My mind wasn't filled with images of holiday lights, brightly wrapped presents, reindeers and sleighs, nor was the sounds in my ears of Christmas carols. Instead it was filled with darkness, emptiness, hurt feelings, and confusion.

"Watch over me, dad. I'm scared and I don't know who to turn to. My life is changing. And the more it changes the more depressed I become. What's wrong with me? I killed my baby, dad. I didn't want to but I did. Do you see my baby in heaven? I wish I could turn back time. I would have spent more time with you. I'm so sorry, dad."

I cried myself to sleep on the attic floor with my father's picture still in my hand. When I woke up, I wiped the drool from the side of my mouth and went downstairs. It was noon so I packed a couple suitcases and called Sasha to say goodbye.

The following day I flew to Cuba to visit my grandmother. Seven years had passed since we were together. It upset me to find how her body had debilitated from years of using it to communicate with spirits. My first week there, I partied at Carnivals in different towns with my cousins all day and night. I hardly slept or saw my grandmother. By the second week I was exhausted. All I did was sleep.

Three days before my time in Cuba came to an end, I woke up to roosters crowing early morning. But I stayed in bed. I didn't mind their cock-a-doodle-doo, but that wasn't enough to get me up. My grandmother walked in and asked, "Cielo, when is your birthday again?"

"Tomorrow, grandma." I attempted to go back to sleep.

"Come to my room when you get up. I need to read your cards." She had some strength in her voice. "I had a dream about you and my saints are calling. I need clarity."

Well who needs the enduring blare of roosters crowing to wake me up, when I had spirits in my grandma's ear? I unwillingly got out of bed to wash up. I dragged my feet as I headed to her bedroom. She wasn't even there. Great. She was probably in the back yard slaughtering goats. But I found her in the back of the house feeding the dogs.

"Are you ready?" she asked.

"Yes," I mumbled.

I followed her back to the dark room she was now using for her card readings. Her altar was smaller than I remembered it, but she still had the big Indian Statue I used to stare at as a child. She also had candles and other spiritual artifacts around the room. I sat at the table across from her. She pulled out the cards and stared at me as she shuffled the deck.

147

"You are becoming a beautiful young woman," she said with a smile, "Just like I was at your age."

She passed the cards over and instructed me to divide them in three. Slowly she put the cards facing up, side by side, and began to read them.

"There will be many changes as soon as you step foot off this island. I see you working at a new job, but you will encounter many difficulties there. So keep both feet grounded because this place will try to take you down." She let out a short laugh and said, "They won't be able to, though. You have a fighting spirit." She examined the cards. "I don't like what I see. You're surrounded by dark clouds and you have tears in your eyes. You look unhappy and broken hearted." She stopped to look up at me. "Your father's spirit followed you here, but he refuses to come inside my house. It looks like he's waiting for you to leave. He looks after you." She took the cards and shuffled them again. "Break them in two."

I divided the deck in two and placed them on the table. "I see a lot of traveling. Things come easily to you; especially money." She pointed at a few cards with coins on them, "You see...money. You radiate self sufficiency and this will attract men that need protection and guidance. You serve as a comforter. Try not to fall victim to failed relationships and heartache. You'll meet a man later in life, who is tall, handsome, with Indian colored skin," she pointed at the card with a prince on it. "But you are here," she then pointed to the card above the prince with a female figure on it. "That means you will love him more than he will love you. That's not a good sign. His card should be on top of yours; not the other way around."

I thought of how I never wanted to fall in love again.

"Who's your friend with the dark hair and light skin?" she asked. I shrugged. "You know exactly who it is."

"Probably my friend Jade, grandma."

148

"Yeah, be careful with those you call friends, especially her. She's a whore! And she's jealous of you. There was some work done on her behalf to separate you from someone, but it didn't work. She likes to sleep around. So stop hanging with her."

Jade was quiet and reserved. She was physically attractive, but had a personality of a wall. I remember a conversation I had with Xavier about his suspicions that she was cheating on him. So he showed up at her house and saw a guy leaving. Xavier almost caused a scene outside her house but he says they both denied being intimate so he stopped himself from going off. Then another time he was over her house, the phone rang. She picked up the call in the kitchen. Xavier then picked up the phone in her room and eavesdropped on the conversation. According to him, it was another guy and he later admitted to being involved with Jade. He broke up with her for a few months but ended up getting back together. I guess it's true when they say, be careful with the quiet ones.

"I see a baby boy. Oh the joy this child will bring to your life! He will be big and healthy. God bless him. Too bad I won't be around to see him. But I can see him here—beautiful. Before this child is born you will be involved in something major and you will succeed at it. There will be new beginnings, strong alliances, and you will rise to the top."

She stopped to study the cards again. Only this time she let out a loud scream, "Poison! Oh dear God. I see someone trying to poison you." My heart almost stopped. Her eyes moved back and forth from one card to another. "I need to work on you before you go back to the States." My grandmother stood up to light a few candles in her altar and with her back still towards me, she said, "We're done now, Cielo."

I left the room for the patio. I sat on a rusty metal rocking chair for the rest of the morning. My mind was now chained by a horrid thought of someone trying to end my life. As I rocked back and forth, I mumbled the lyrics of So Many Tears by Tupac.

"Ah!" I was startled by my grandmother who joined me on the patio.

"I'm going to the shopping plaza to pick up a few things. You think you'll be fine alone?"

"Yeah, I guess."

"Don't worry about what I saw in your cards. We're going to stop whatever negative force comes against you." She waved her finger at the fence in front of her yard. "You're father is over there, I can hear him telling you he loves you."

After she left to the shopping plaza, I slowly made my way to the front of the house. Tearfully, I whispered, "I love you too, dad."

TWISTED BIRTHDAY

The morning of my 19th birthday, my grandmother handed me an all white dress. "I have to perform a spiritual cleansing on you today. Wear this dress with all white undergarments. No jewelry, no shoes, and no questions."

My grandmother, who was also draped in white, was preparing to do something to me, on my birthday, and I couldn't question her. That made me nervous. I put on the white dress and walked barefooted to her reading room. She had removed the table and chairs, leaving only her altar. I noticed an outdated radio on the corner of the floor. She turned on the tape player to the sounds of Caribbean music, with a woman chanting in a high pitch voice. Then, she handed me a bottle of dark rum and told me to take three swigs. After I guzzled down the three sips of liquor, I watched her dance around with a lit cigar to the beat of the music. She carefully placed three candles on her altar and then turned to face me.

"Ask for whatever you desire as you light each one."

I stood at the altar deciding my first wish. I spoke in a low tone, allowing the intricate rhythm of the drums to play over my voice so my grandmother wouldn't hear my crazy wishes.

"Give me a man who's successful, handsome, and nothing like Calvin. I want Calvin to feel the jealousy and pain that I felt when I caught him cheating." The first candle was lit.

The second wish coincided with my reading in becoming wealthy. "I want to be rich and live a comfortable lifestyle where I don't ever have to worry about money." The second candle was lit.

I couldn't think of a third wish. My thoughts were a junkyard, piled together with unnecessary things. As I rushed to think of something, my grandmother asked me was I ready. That's when the death of my father popped in my head. If Andre never came in to the picture, my father would have probably still been alive. My third wish was for Andre to disappear.

After lighting all three candles, I faced my grandmother. Without warning, she spun me around in circles, until I became dizzy. Once she stopped spinning me, she grabbed a bucket full of scented water with flower buds inside, and poured it over my head. I was soaked. She was doing everything so fast I was caught off guard. The water went up my nose and in my mouth causing me to choke.

My grandmother's body shuddered to a halt, while her eyes rolled in the back of her head. She then started speaking in tongues with a raspy voice. I closed my eyes in fear, listening to this spirit that possessed her body, "Don't be afraid," she demanded. Still I flinched at this scary voice. She covered my head with a white mantle making me more nervous. Now I couldn't see, so I had my head down looking at her feet moving around me and blowing cigar smoke. I coughed from the thick smoke penetrating through the white veil.

She started to speak to me as she continued circling around me. I was so shaken up that I couldn't comprehend what she was saying at first. She stood behind me for a moment too long.

She surprised me by wrapping her arm around my neck and bringing me down to the floor slowly. I let out a screech.

"Don't be afraid, trust me," she said. She pressed her hand on my forehead as I laid flat on my back. The mantle was still covering my face, making it difficult for me to breathe.

I screamed, "Stop! Stop! That's enough!" I sat up, uncovered my head, breathing profusely and crying. When I attempted to stand up, she forced me back down with incredible strength. I remained sitting, with my head down weeping. The raspy voice pushed at me, "Stop that crying, little girl. I am not here to hurt you." I closed my eyes, waiting for this ritual to end.

"Please hurry up," I begged.

She walked over to the altar and pulled out a machete from behind the Indian Statue. This is insane!

"This is it. I'm going to die." I closed my eyes tight.

Without letting go of the machete, she swung it from behind me, hitting the floor on my left side. I flinched. Sill standing behind me, she separated my legs further apart with the tip of the machete. She was making enough room between my legs to hit the floor a second time with it. I jumped every time that thing came swinging down. After she hit my right side of the floor, she ordered me to stand up. I couldn't have stood up any faster.

She showed me six colored handkerchiefs: pink, white, orange, yellow, blue and red. "Pick two," she said.

I chose red and blue. She took the red one from my hand and held it in my face. "Money and power corrupts. Don't let the riches of the world change you."

She began pacing and thinking before she spoke again. "Do not eat or drink from people you do not know. That way your body will evade the poison."

She stopped pacing and stood still facing me. "You have the ability to foresee things in your dreams." She tapped the side of my temples, "Listen to your dreams, for they speak to you." Then she tapped my chest where my heart lays and said, "Your intuition is strong and will never fail you. When you make a decision, stick to it. If it's the wrong one, you will know. Just reassess the plan and never hesitate to start over."

She then took the blue one and held it up to me, "You will step on his head. He will try to run but you will squash him like a bug. You will not let him make fun of you. His life is in your hands."

Who was she talking about? Calvin? Andre? Someone I hadn't met yet? I didn't bother asking. I just wanted her to be done with this ritual.

153

The spirit left her body. My grandmother became weak, almost fainting, she held on to me. I grabbed her, to lift her back up. Her eyes rolled in the back of her head again.

"Grandma!"

She became present. "Bring me to the bathroom." She was still holding on to me.

I helped her frail body to the bathroom. She knelt in front of the toilet and vomited. I shut the door to give her some privacy. Then I went to my room to change into some dry clothes and pack my suitcases for my flight back to Boston. I stayed in bed for the rest of the day. It was impossible to wipe out of my head what took place in that room.

Exhausted, I fell asleep early. At some point in the night, while in deep sleep, my upper body convulsed and I gasped for air. I thought it was the midnight visitant making its presence known. But there was nothing there. My heart was racing from my body coming up from my sleep so abruptly. The room was dark, lit only by a candle, with the image of Santa Anaisa (Saint Anna) on the glass jar. She is the spiritual queen of love. She dresses herself in yellow and gold. She loves to dance, laugh, drink and smoke.

I looked in the yellow light of the Santa Anaisa candle for a glimmer of hope for a lonely girl like me. The candle was suddenly extinguished, leaving all in profound darkness. There was no sleep for me after that. I turned to my side and placed the pillow over my head to wait for the sun to rise.

Before leaving Cuba, my grandmother came into my room to check on me. She gave me a notebook with different spells she wrote up herself and a couple of candles. Then she gave me a white cloth pouch she hand stitched, to carry with me as an amulet.

All these items were given to me to help me in my next stage in life. But the most interesting thing was a baby food jar sealed with black candle wax. She told me it was the most powerful magic powder she prepared after my cleansing ritual.

"Don't use this on just anyone who upsets you," she said, "use it on the one who tries to hurt you in the worst way. Just be careful because this formula is destructive and will ruin their life."

I had to unpack half of my suitcase again to wrap it tightly in a black t-shirt, then a pair of jeans, to smuggle it safely back home. The thought of getting caught with the jar in customs at the airport frightened me.

"You write the person's name on a piece of paper five times. Then you write five things you want to happen to them over their name. Put the paper underneath the jar. Light a black candle over the jar for three days and repeat the prayer in this notebook. After the third day, unseal the jar and pour the powder wherever they step foot."

UNDER A SHELL

I arrived in Boston the following evening looking like a hobo. My mother picked me up at Logan Airport, appalled at my down in the dumps appearance. In a hurry to leave Cuba, I wore old wrinkled clothes. I had such a massive headache, that I wore a loose ponytail without brushing my hair. The more I tried to make sense of that horrible ritual, the more the headache intensified. It was frustrating not being able to tell anyone how this spiritual cleansing ironically left me feeling heavy and oppressed.

Anxious to get home and take a long hot bath, my mother nagged about my appearance. I didn't see the point of explaining my situation to her; she never gave a damn about anything but herself. She was more concerned at the outward appearance than what was really going on inside me. I couldn't wait to get home. Before she could even turn off her car, I opened the door, rushed out, and dragged my suitcases across the lawn. She called me but I paid no mind. When I reached the porch, she got out her car and demanded, "Sky, do not ignore me!" I continued to ignore her. I hurried up the stairs to my apartment and locked myself in my bedroom.

The following months were spent alone in igloo isolation from everyone except Calvin. I put all my time into school in order to ignore all the pain and confusion that was sinking in. As I attended school full-time, Calvin would periodically stay with me, slowly moving things in. By the time I finished my final exams, he had moved in completely. The move was so gradual, it was hard to detect until I was done with the semester. He took care of all my bills, though. He also put food on the table and kept a chill atmosphere for me to study. Everything was right except the romantic side of our relationship. Our sex life had fizzled. It turned into a routine where I would just roll over, do it, and roll back into my corner of the bed.

From time to time, thoughts of that ritual back in Cuba crawled through my mind. My body would still jump sometimes out of the blue. If I didn't hear Calvin turn his key and walk in, I'd scream when he entered. I blamed it on the stress of school, but in reality my nerves were unsettled from years of spiritual sensitivity.

It would infuriate me when he laughed at me. Especially when he made fun of me still sleeping with the hallway lights on. I would threaten to put a hex on him to shut him up or worse, stop holding his drugs. He would stop joking around immediately because he didn't play when it came down to his business. Even though he hated going to the attic, he believed it was the safest place for him to stash all his dirty money and drugs. So he would always apologize with a hug and a kiss whenever I got upset at his ridicules.

The attention Calvin gave me during that time wasn't reciprocated. He complained how different I had become, but I always reminded him it was his fault I was giving him the cold shoulder. My feelings were on ice. This was how I turned out and how things would remain; either he had to accept it or see his way out the door. I believe he was trying to compensate from the guilt of lying to me those years we were together. Whatever his reason was, I made it clear to him that I was never going to be the girl I use to be no matter what he did. But he continuously tried.

After finishing all my classes and finals, I spent three weeks in bed or on the couch. What began as melancholy because of my father's death anniversary, ended up in major depression. I missed him deeply. My mental state was so overwhelming to Calvin that he would stay away for days at a time. Although that spring brought beautiful warm weather, I huddled under the covers and cried every day. I wouldn't take a shower for up to two to three days at a time.

Only when Calvin would show up, I'd get in the shower to avoid hearing his mouth.

One night Calvin offered to take me to the movies to watch Face Off starring John Travolta and Nicolas Cage. I'll admit: I appreciated that he was trying to pull me out this emotional shell. So I got dressed and let my hair out that night. Yet when he met me outside the driveway, he didn't look too happy.

"What's wrong?" I pretended to be concerned.

"My mother has to have back surgery."

"Back surgery? Why?"

"She has some sort of spinal instability and has been complaining of back pain for over six months."

"Oh...damn." I didn't know what to say to console him. I really didn't care about his mother or her spinal problem.

"I guess your fagot ass cousin was right. There was something wrong with my mother's back. Remember?"

"Wow, I forgot all about that."

"Not me. In fact I told her to leave UPS and find another job, but she wouldn't listen. All that heavy lifting affected her back. But what do I know? I should have told her a gay psychic told me."

"Stop calling my cousin gay."

"He's gay, Sky. Don't act like he's not."

We drove to Revere Showcase Cinema for the late show. I was looking forward to watching John Travolta in this new movie. On our drive Calvin allowed me to smoke a joint in his car. So I lounged in the passenger seat and was zoning to the radio. He played a Jay Z CD all the way there.

"You all right?" Calvin placed his hand on my lap.

"Yeah."

"You got all quiet on me."

"Just listening to the music." I was super high.

"How's that weed?"

"I'm feeling it!" We both laughed because *I'm feeling it* was the hook to the rap song that was playing.

Everything turned out well that night. The movie was great, we had plenty of weed, and Calvin drove to Revere Beach to order delicious shrimp plates from Kelley's Roast Beef. We sat out on the beach and ate. The ocean breeze triggered memories of my childhood by the docks in Cuba. I started to reminisce with Calvin about how much I loved sitting on the dock and how I got my nickname Sky. He had heard the story before but he listened as if it were the first time. I appreciated that.

SOUND AND FURY

When I came out from the dark place that possessed me, I walked to the complex looking for Xavier. After so many months of drowning myself in my school work, our friendship took a back seat. He had finally graduated from high school and I wanted to catch up with him.

"Congratulations!" I was proud of him for finishing school in spite of the many times he had wanted to drop out.

"Thank you. Thank you. I couldn't have done it without you and Jade."

"Oh stop it. Yes you would have."

"How you been? I tried calling you a few times but you ignored my calls. Now that you're in college, you think you're too good to hang out with me."

While I played off the humor in what he said, I was also peeved at his remark. "It was my father's anniversary of his passing, so you know..."

"Oh that's right, Sky. I'm sorry, baby girl. It's nothing but love here for you."

Initially, I visited the complex just to see Xavier for a hot second. But it turned out that he wanted to hang out that night. He asked me if I would order the Mike Tyson and Evander Holyfield fight at my house since his cable had been shut off. I agreed to have him and a few others over for a simple kick back to watch the fight. Calvin had left to New York earlier that day, so I figured it would be nice to have friends over while he wasn't there. Calvin never liked having company and I had picked up on that. But one time seemed harmless. It would be like the good old days.

Later that night, everyone who was invited showed up to my apartment. Sasha, Sasha's friend Angela, Xavier, Xavier's older brother Miguel, and Rodney, who I hadn't seen in a long time, all were there ready to watch the big fight. The guys were in the parlor rolling up weed buds inside cigar leaves, while the girls and I were in the kitchen setting up the chips, dips, and drinks.

Rodney, Xavier and I went into my spare bedroom to blow clouds of weed. In the same fashion, Sasha, Angela, and Miguel were in the living room drinking Bacardi and Coke; so I thought. Shortly after, we were all back together in the living room anticipating the fighting match to begin. I noticed Angela and I were the only ones without a drink in our hands. She appeared a bit sheepish until I motioned her to follow me to the kitchen. That's when I pulled out Calvin's bottle of Bailey's Irish whiskey.

He had it in my refrigerator since Valentine's Day, when I had no interest in commemorating the occasion; which explains why it was still there. This day being different from February, I decided it was a good time to enjoy it. I poured the Bailey's in two cups of ice and sprinkled cinnamon over it.

"Here you go. I can't have you sober in this house." I grinned and handed her one of the cups.

"Girl, I'm so glad you have this because I don't like white liquor." She sipped the Irish whiskey. "I get crazy and start seeing white spirits." She laughed nervously.

I assumed there was some truth to what she said and of course I believed her, but I didn't bother entertaining that conversation. Rather, I grabbed the Bailey's bottle and returned to the living room.

The boxing match was about to start. I sat on the floor next to Xavier, up close to the television. He was ecstatic that his idol, Mike Tyson, was in the ring. His energy was truly magnetic; it caused

161

my mood to exhilarate as well. But unlike Xavier who displayed his emotions, I kept mine under wrap.

The fight began! We were sitting on edge watching Holyfield dominate the first two rounds of the match, landing powerful body shots on Tyson and opening a cut over his eye from an accidental head butting. This wasn't looking good for Tyson.

"Come on Ty!" Xavier shouted, "Show this fool what you got!"

"I don't tink eem going to win!" Rodney chimed in.

"Yo Rod, get off Holyfield's nuts! Xavier yelled back.

"Tyson is nutten but a pussyclot tha hits hard!" Rodney laughed just to antagonize Xavier.

Just seconds into the third round, Tyson bit Holyfield's ear! "Oh shit!" I screamed. I couldn't believe my eyes. I didn't know much about boxing except for what I had learned from listening to Xavier, but I knew biting wasn't a part of the sport. I remember all of us shouting in disbelief, especially Xavier.

"No fucking way! I can't fucking believe this shit! Tell me that didn't just happen!" Xavier was now on his feet, pivoting and clutching his head with both hands.

The fight was stopped as referee Mills Lane debated on whether to disqualify Tyson or continue despite the Dracula move. According to the boxing commentators, the ringside doctor overruled the decision to stop the fight. Instead, Tyson was deducted two points.

Shockingly the fight resumed. As a result, Holyfield slammed Tyson. Seconds before the third round came to an end; Tyson once again brought his head above Holyfield's shoulder and bit another piece of his other ear. As if that wasn't gruesome enough, he spit out the piece of cartilage on the ring floor.

It was unbelievable. I remember being in shock when I heard one of the boxing commentators say, "I'm nothing short of shock. I have no response for what I just witnessed." It was exactly how I felt watching that awful display. In an instant, there was a fiasco in the ring, with people rushing in. Tyson lost his temper and threw swings at everyone who was in his way. Security had to hold him back and that's when his bodyguard started fighting security. It was wild, yet entertaining.

Even though Tyson lost his reason, at that moment boxing became my favorite sport. It wasn't to say that I agreed with Tyson for resorting to such a brutal act, but I saw how violence and controversy came together at the same time, and the complexity of that ran deep inside me.

With all the commotion inside my apartment, it was hard to hear the knock at my door. I was on my third cup of Bailey's when Andre barged into my apartment in his police uniform. The entire room stood still.

"Come out here for a minute." He ordered. I followed him to the hallway. "I made it clear that I didn't want any parties in my house. I stood out there for five minutes knocking on that door and you didn't answer it. So I walk in to find that not only did you disobey my order, but you have all types of illegal activity going on under my roof; disturbance, drugs, and underage drinking. Your guests have ten minutes to leave the premise, or I'll be forced to have them arrested." My face grew heated with embarrassment because he said it loud enough to scare everyone.

When I came in the living room, everyone was standing against the wall ready to leave. "I'm sorry guys, party over." I frowned as everyone walked out one by one.

Rodney got close to me, "I lef yuh some ganja in deh room. Tanks, star." (I left you some weed in the room. Thanks girl.) He gave me a hug.

"Thanks Rodney." I shut the door behind him.

163

Next thing I knew, the toilet flushed and I walked to the bathroom to see who was in there. I smiled when I saw Xavier coming out.

I asked, "You want to toke a last one before you leave?"

"After tonight's fight and your punk ass step-father threatening us, I need to smoke more than one." He whispered.

"Call him my step-father again and I'll pull a Tyson move on you!"

"I'm crashing right here on your couch tonight."

I shrugged. "Roll it up then."

With this in mind, I made sure the deadbolt lock was on and I shut off most of the house lights. We sat in my spare room and placed a folded towel underneath the door to prevent the smoke from escaping. We sat there smoking and talking about everything that happened that night.

Hours later, I grabbed an extra pillow and sheet for Xavier to stay the night. We both lounged on the couch watching music videos until we fell asleep.

At 6:41 am, half asleep, I shut off the television. Xavier was passed out on his stomach with his left arm hanging off the couch, touching one of his sneakers, and the pillow over his head. I tip toed into my bedroom to avoid disturbing him. After I got in bed, I pulled the covers over my head. That's when I heard a tapping noise at my door. I stopped to listen, thinking Xavier wanted to come in. But he never did. After a few more minutes, there was another tap at my door.

"Come in," I grumbled. Still no answer.

Eventually, I got up to open the door, but no one was there. I assumed Xavier went back to the couch, so I left my bedroom door open in case he returned. I tossed around in the bed trying to get comfortable. Impossible. My room became extremely cold, sending chills down my back. This was definitely a ghostly presence. Scared out of my mind, I jumped to my feet and hurried into the living room. Xavier hadn't moved. He was sleeping in the same position. To be sure, it wasn't him pulling a prank on me; I attempted to wake him up. But he was sound asleep, so I left him alone. In the meantime, I went to take a shower since there was no possibility of me getting any rest.

I turned the shower on and let it heat up. I climbed in and felt an instant relief from the soothing water on my body. As I closed my eyes, I imagined Calvin pressing up against me from behind, like he once did; rubbing the lathered sponge against my wet body. I started sliding the sponge around the bottom of my breast and then back on top, sending shivers down to my core. I couldn't wait for him to get home from New York to have sex with him. I hadn't felt like that in a long time. While I rinsed the soap off my body, again, came a light knock at my door.

"Go away!" I shouted.

"Not until I use the bathroom." The door opened slightly.

I peeked out the shower curtain. "Oh, it's you. Get out! I'll be done in a minute."

"Who else would it be? And I'm not waiting. Stay your ass in there while I piss." He just walked in, lifted the toilet seat, and peed. I didn't take my eyes off him until I was sure he was out the bathroom.

"You have no shame!"

He tilted his head back. "A little silence please."

"Just hurry up so I can get out."

"What do you have to eat? I'm hungry."

"Help yourself and fix me a plate too." I motioned for him to leave with my hand.

I threw on my bathrobe and padded down the hallway to my bedroom. As I was getting dressed I could smell the bacon from the kitchen. This made my stomach growl and so I rushed out the room. I sat at the table and watched Xavier measure and prepare the pancake batter. After the bacon was cooked to a crisp, he set it aside.

"Did you hear my son knocking on your door this morning?" He laughed.

"What?" Something inside me didn't want to hear what he was about to say.

"There's a spirit of a baby that follows me." Xavier paused to pour the pancake batter in the frying pan. "He's been by my side for a few years now, but he only makes his presence known when I stay over a girl's house."

"Why does he follow you? And how do you know it's a baby's spirit?" I stood up to help him set up the table and took out the orange juice from the refrigerator.

"When I was sixteen, I was seeing this older girl named Natalie who had a one year old son named Jacob." He sat at the table and served breakfast. "I used to sleep at her house a lot and Jacob used to tap on her bedroom door every morning for a bottle of cold milk. She wouldn't get up, well at least when I was there. Instead I would get up to make him a bottle." Xavier took a bite of the pancake and a big gulp of orange juice. I could tell he had stopped to hold back his tears. "Then he would climb in the bed between his mother and me to drink his bottle. He had a habit of putting his cold hands on my bare back to watch me jump from the chills. It made him laugh every time. When he didn't do this, I would turn around and grab whichever hand he was holding the bottle with and place it on his stomach so he could jump from the chills too. He loved playing with me like that. He was such a cool baby."

"What happened to Jacob?"

"He died in his sleep, holding his bottle. But I wasn't there that day. Natalie came to the door crying and told me he passed away." His voice was broken by emotion. That's when he stuffed his

166

mouth with more bacon and pancake. "You're the only girl I've ever told. Shit, you're the only one who's ever heard him, besides me."

"How do you know I heard him?" It freaked me out that he knew I heard the spirit of this child roaming in my house.

"I'm the only one who can hear him tapping on doors. No girl I've ever slept with has ever heard him. Most times, these girls think I'm crazy because I never explain to them why I open their bedroom door in the early hours of the morning. But today was different. I heard him knocking at your door. Strange...I heard you say something and then he knocked again and then you opened the door. You must have left it open, because I heard you jump out your bed, cursing, like you were scared. Then you came running in here to check on me. I was too tired to wake up and tell you not to worry—he likes you."

It was heartbreaking listening to Xavier recount the life of this child and his spirit. I couldn't help but avert my eyes and sip my orange juice, hoping that was the last I was going to hear about this baby's life. Xavier knew me well enough to stop.

For the next hour we chatted aimlessly about boxing; nothing unusual there. He was strongly considering moving to New York to start his career as a professional fighter. My initial reaction was to talk him out of going, but that would have been selfish of me. He was going to enjoy the last of those summer days in Boston before leaving.

"I support you under one condition."

He smiled. "What's that?"

"You won't forget me when you become rich and famous."

"Forget you? Never! I'll make you a part of my team."

"So what's your plan?"

"First, I'm moving back into our old house. Then I'll start working with my uncle who is well connected out there."

167

"That's cool. What are the odds of you moving back to your old house, huh?"

"My mother owned the house so I'll stay there with my uncle who rents it from my dad."

That explained why Xavier's father didn't work. He collected Social Security from the state and received rent money from the house his late wife, owned in New York. The poor man fell into a deep depression that he never stepped foot in that house after she passed away. He chose to move to Boston because he wanted his sons to be close to their aunt Reynalda now that their mother was gone.

After breakfast, Xavier helped me clean the house. I was expecting Calvin to come home that day so I didn't want any evidence of our little party. At the same time I didn't want Xavier to find out that Calvin was living with me, so I had him throw out my trash to get him out my apartment. I went back to bed when he left, to catch up on the sleep I missed that night.

The sound of my stereo playing Smile by Scarface and Tupac, drifted through from the next room, slowly waking me up from my nap. It wasn't loud, but enough to let me know Calvin was home. A warm feeling came over me when he quietly walked in the room. I could tell he didn't want to disrupt me but I turned to stare at him and smile.

Suddenly the sky turned gray, making my room dark, and a surprise rainstorm came rushing down. Calvin took off his sneakers and got under the covers with me. As he pressed his chest against my back, he slid his hands under my shirt, rubbing my breast, making my sexual juices flow. Sensing that I couldn't take much more of this, I turned on my back and took off my shirt. Calvin slowly moved on top of me, bringing the sheet cover over us. We were now face to face and his trail of kisses were moving down to my stomach and up again, driving me crazy.

He finally went all the way down. "That feels so good," I whispered. I closed my eyes as he continued to work his mouth on me. His soft lips fit there perfectly. When his tongue reached the side of my clitoris that brought the most intense feeling down there, I placed my hands on his head to hold it in place. I couldn't help but thrust to the rhythm of his tongue working me to climax. It was a good feeling before I let out a loud moan and came.

CAN'T GO FOR THAT

The summer drew on, and it was time to search for a job. I spent a couple days driving around the city filling out applications at hospitals, banks, airlines, and even the Boston Herald establishment. Many of the jobs I applied to called me back for an interview. The problem was most of these jobs were offering me minimum wage because I was a young college student. I constantly told myself, "I can't go for that," forcing me to turn down every opportunity.

After two weeks of turning down jobs, I walked downstairs to my mother's apartment to ask her for a referral at Beth Israel Hospital. She was reluctant to refer me after I quit the Federal Reserve, saying I wasn't responsible enough and she didn't want her name tarnished if I pulled another stunt like that. I tried convincing her that I wouldn't do that again, but her attitude was incredibly off-putting. Andre overheard me pleading with my mother over it and walked into the kitchen. He suggested I go to the city and apply for a civilian job with the police force. Precinct F was looking to hire an administrative clerk for the detectives. I sat at the table and poured me a bowl of Frosted Flakes cereal, listening intently.

"There you go, Sky. You have your referral now." She grabbed her keys, kissed Andre goodbye, and rushed out the door.

"In case you decide to apply, let me know, I'll speak to the captain there," he said to me, "Just keep in mind you may get drug tested and have to pass a typing test." That was his way of warning me to stop smoking marijuana.

I finished my cereal and left the house. I drove to the City Police Headquarters to apply for that detective's clerk position. I wrote down Andre's name as reference on the application to sway personnel in hiring me.

While I sat and waited to hear my results of the typing test, the woman looking over my application said, "You did really well on your typing test; would you be interested in applying for the 911 operator position? The Communication Center is also hiring. You seem like an ideal candidate based on your resume and typing test."

I filled out another application for the 911 operator position. The woman told me all I had to do then was wait to be called for an interview from both captains of The Communication Center and Precinct F. I left feeling confident I was going to be hired but nervous about a drug test. Even though personnel didn't mention anything about drug testing, I called Calvin and asked him what I needed to do to clean out my system. He told me to buy some cleansing tablets called Golden Seals.

Once I bought the bottle of Golden Seals, I read the instructions thoroughly. The label said I had to take three tablets, three times a day with a glass of water for two weeks. Also, in order to get clean results, I had to stop smoking marijuana.

After two weeks of not smoking and taking the Golden seals tablets, I didn't hear back from the City Police Department. Instead, I received a letter from American Airlines hiring me after an interview I did a month prior. It seemed a major recruitment was underway for flight attendants and if I was interested, I had to attend an orientation at the Hilton Hotel near Logan Airport. In the meantime I accepted the position; even if it meant dropping out of college.

The day before my orientation with American Airlines, the City Police gave me a call with great news. Captain Jeff Cole from Precinct F wanted to interview me; so did Captain John McDowell from the 911 Communication Center. I scheduled the interviews one day after the other for the following week, to be well prepared for each one.

Since I wore the same clothes to all my interviews that summer, Calvin gave me money to buy new ones. I ended up going on a frantic shopping spree with Sasha for a couple new dress suits. Even though American Airlines offered a higher salary, I wanted to look my best and interview well with both captains before deciding if I should work with the airlines or the police.

Despite my nervousness, my interview went well with Captain Cole from Precinct F. Since Andre knew Captain Cole, he gave him a call. Captain Cole had confessed to Andre that he didn't want to give me the opportunity because I was still in school for finance and that meant I wasn't going to be around for the long run. He suggested that when I interview for the 911 position, not to mention that I was a student and he would put in a good word for me on Andre's behalf. To my complete amazement, it worked, I was hired for the 911 operator position, and I was never drug tested.

After receiving such exciting news, I had to carefully consider my next direction. Was I going to drop out of college and travel the world with American Airlines or further my education while working for the City Police Department? With a hard choice and an indecisive state of mind, I called my grandmother in Cuba for some advice.

"Yes Sky, I saw a lot of traveling in your future, but remember what I told you: always listen and trust the voice within you. No matter what you decide to do, your choice will be the right one. Either you will travel the world as a stewardess or you will take vacations to different places. My advice to you is to sleep on it and you will wake up to your decision."

"I love you Grandma. Thank you."

That night, I went to my attic and lit a few candles in the name of all my saints who were there; to help me wake up to the right choice. That night I had a vivid dream: I was driving on Centre Street and caught Calvin walking with Nicole. Enraged with the sight of them wandering arm in arm, I looked for a parking space to get out my car and confront them. As I drove around the corner, to turn back around, the scenery changed from Centre Street to a children's playground I had never seen before. I went from driving a car to walking alongside the park. As I looked around, feeling lost, I noticed a large crowd of people running and screaming. I followed the crowd to an empty lot where I saw smoke and fire coming out of a jet plane that had crashed. That's when I woke up from the dream and decided I was much safer behind a desk than up in the sky.

The following morning my mother asked me to drop her off at work because Andre had came home from working a double shift that night and fell fast asleep. Her truck was at the mechanics and she didn't want to ride the bus. I agreed to take her only if I could drive Andre's new Volvo. She didn't care as long as she made it to work on time.

The minute I started the engine, the speakers blared Hall & Oates, I Can't Go For That. I turned down the volume to a few decibels while I waited for my mother. As I sat in the car waiting, listening to the music, I reflected on the dream I had with the plane crash. At that moment, when I tuned in to the chorus, I got my second confirmation in regards to my decision. No coincidence there. After my mother sat in the car, lecturing me to drive Andre's new car carefully, she asked me if I had made a decision between the two job offers. I lied by saying no and changed the subject by asking for Chinese take-out for dinner that night.

Why did my dream include Calvin and Nicole together? The thought of them sent a sharp pain to my stomach. Rather than assume the worst, it was easier for me to try and overlook the meaning of the dream. Deep down I knew he was still seeing her; but I needed to believe he was completely done with that relationship. Yet how could I catch them this time around? Calvin always covered his tracks. Every move he made involved making money. Some nights I would secretly drive by her house to see if his car was parked in her driveway, and other nights I chose to ignore my suspicious thoughts because I didn't want to face another painful episode.

173

At six o'clock the next evening, my mother called me to tell me Mayor Kirsch and his wife were going to join us for dinner. When I walked downstairs at a quarter to eight, I was pleased to find Chinese take-out at the table. I sat down to eat when I noticed that sitting before me were half empty glasses, each containing some type of liquor in them. That was a sign that it was going to be a long night.

Everybody was buzzed and obnoxious, asking me, "What's the matter? Why aren't you smiling?"

"I'm just tired. It's been a long day and the thought of starting work and school next week is worrying me." I lied. The thought of Calvin and Nicole in my dream was bothering me. And the jealousy was overpowering my thoughts.

My mother asked, "So you're going with the police department?"

"Yeah, I start training Monday."

When I told them the good news, they encouraged me and were proud I had chosen to work there. Since they were all in good spirits, after having a few drinks and hearing the good news, I managed to throw in a little money request for new wardrobe. How could they deny me cash under a happy state of mind? Andre got up and went to his office. I stood at the door and watched him open a safe he had in the closet. I tried peaking inside to see what he had in there but it was too dark. He pulled out three hundred dollars and told me not to go crazy with the money.

THAT WASN'T THE CASE

On Thursday, I invited Sasha to go to the mall. We always had fun shopping together. She would mock snobby people by giving store attendants a hard time about their prices or how they arranged their clothes. That day she pulled a mini skirt off the rack and told me she was tempted to go into work with it, wearing fishnet stockings, and a pair of red pumps. Our cackle was so loud, it sounded liked project hallway laughter.

"Can you imagine the look on your boss' face if you walked in like that?" I said.

Sasha began telling me how she was earning good money at Fidelity Investments but she was miserable. Everyone she worked with was uptight. It didn't fit her style. She was full of spunk and energy. Being an Accountant Assistant was weighing down on her.

"Talking about work makes me want to go out and get drunk. I always look forward to my weekends. Sometimes I go out to the clubs on Thursday nights, without giving a damn that I have to work the next day. Speaking of Thursdays, let's go to Roxy's tonight, Sky. It's Latin Night!" She did a little Salsa step with her feet and waved her hands in mid air.

"Okay, but I need something to wear," I said.

She grabbed the mini skirt again and laughed. I snatched it out her hand and placed it back on the rack.

I rolled my eyes. "Help me find something more tasteful."

The night was hot and humid. However, that didn't stop Sasha from wanting to hit the nightlife. This was my first time going to a nightclub so I was excited. Besides, hanging with Sasha was always a good time.

"We are going to have fun," she exclaimed.

I picked her up at her friend Angela's house. They both jumped in my car, reeking of alcohol. Angela was 22 years old and had her own place. That's why Sasha had me pick her up over there. They were pre-gaming with a few shots of God knows what.

We drove by the Roxy's on Tremont Street in Downtown. Sasha swore she saw Xavier working the line. For a moment, I thought the alcohol impaired her vision. Yet she assured me it was him. After we parked the car, I handed my keys to Sasha to hold in her clutch. We walked towards the long line of people waiting to get in to the club.

Sasha, in an effort to prove to me she saw Xavier, went to the front of the line to find him. Indeed, she found Xavier working security at the door. She let him know we were in the back. So, he spoke to head of security, who let us in.

Xavier whispered to wait for him at the bar where his brother Miguel was bartending. I waited with excitement as the girls and I checked out everyone coming in. Xavier came over to me and discreetly gave me a wristband that the club used to identify the patrons who were 21 and over.

"Put it on in the bathroom," Xavier said.

"You know I don't like to drink that much!"

"Girl, you're in a club. I told my brother to take care of you. Enjoy a free drink or two," he said and kissed me on the cheek. "And don't borrow any trouble!" He laughed and left. That was his thing to say ever since he heard Andre say it to me.

I went to the Ladies room to put on the wristband. When I came out, Sasha and Angela sashayed off to the dance floor. I stood at the bar chatting with Miguel.

"What would you like to drink, Sky?" Miguel asked me.

"I don't know. What do you recommend?"

"How about a Sex On The Beach?" He winked.

"Sex On The Beach," I giggled, "Okay."

176

I sipped on my drink as I stood by the bar. It was the first time I was drinking in public, so I tried to play cool. I looked around at everyone at the club. I checked out the way they were drinking, standing, and dancing. After about 20 minutes Xavier came up behind me.

"Take it easy on that drink, killer! I don't want to carry you out of here," he said in my ear.

I turned around and gave him a big smile.

"Where's Sasha?" he asked. I jerked my thumb behind me towards the dance floor.

"Why aren't you dancing?" He snuggled me by my waist.

I just shrugged and continued drinking.

"I have to go. Slow down with those, you hear me. I'll be back to check on you." As soon as I turned back around, Sasha made her way back to me from the dance floor—smiling and sweating.

"This ugly guy just gave me his number." She chuckled at the napkin he used to write his number on.

"What ugly guy?"

"He's standing with Xavier near the restrooms, with the gray dress shirt." She pointed at their direction.

"He's not ugly, Sasha. He's just short."

"Short and ugly!" We both laughed. Miguel handed me another drink.

Within an hour and a half, I started to feel dizzy from all the drinks I had consumed. My body felt a little numb. Sasha and I had the giggles. We both laughed at everything we said. But I didn't enjoy this dizziness. Being drunk was making me feel sick to my stomach.

"I was meaning to tell you, I saw Calvin a few days ago with his girl."

I raised an eyebrow. "His girl?"

"I think it was Nicole. She had long red hair."

177

"Where did you see them?" I was noticeably upset and Sasha knew she said a foolish thing.

The nervous pain in my stomach took a hold on me. Why would Sasha bring that up at the night club? She claimed she had forgotten to mention it to me before. Just when I was going to confess that we were still together, someone approached me and politely grabbed my hand to dance. I rudely pulled away from him. The stranger apologized and walked away. It wasn't my intention to react that way but he came over at the wrong time. Sasha was a bit embarrassed at how I turned him down. She felt bad for the guy but couldn't care less about my feelings.

Desperately needing to go to the bathroom and relieve my system of all the alcohol, I scurried off. I sat on the stool with my hands holding my face, waiting for the moment to vomit. I wanted the drunken feeling to be gone. All of a sudden there was a firm knock on the bathroom stall.

"Are you okay in there?" said an unfamiliar voice.

"Yeah, I'm fine." I flushed the toilet and walked out.

Three girls were fixing their hair and makeup in front of the mirror. One said, "Xavier had the balls to come and talk to me. I told him to fuck off!" I'm thinking; here's goes another one. "He's lucky Rick didn't catch him talking to me or else he would have lost it!"

My stomach crunched. I sensed trouble. Women were going to be the death of Xavier if he kept fooling around with so many of them.

I left the ladies room staggering around the club looking for Xavier to warn him about what I had heard in the ladies room. Shortly after, I saw a crowd running and gathering at the exit door. I pushed through the crowd and found Xavier fighting a dark skinned Hispanic man. It had to be this Rick character. The guy was a beast. He had Xavier in a head lock, punching him in his face. I panicked. Without hesitating I took off one of my shoes and clocked the guy on his

178

head. Then Xavier body slammed him against the wall. When I tried to strike him again, I felt someone pull me off and yank my arm. That's when I dropped my shoe. The guy holding my arm was the ugly short guy who gave Sasha his number. I wrestled to get out of his grip but when that didn't work, I bit his hand as hard as I could until he let me go. I pushed through the crowd again, back to the fight. Xavier now had the guy underneath him, pounding him. Before I knew it, the girl from the bathroom tried jumping in, but security subdued her. In a flash, more guards rushed in to separate the fight. While security attempted to help Xavier, I took one good swing at the girl, slamming my left fist on her mouth. Then I grabbed her by the hair and brought her down. That's when someone held me from behind. Holding me gave me the advantage to stomp on her head, twice.

The short ugly man shouted, "Get her out!"

Security apprehended me until the police came upstairs. The guy Xavier fought was covered with blood and his shirt was torn. I tried escaping but I was pressed in a corner. Then the police arrived.

I was placed under arrest on the spot. Being handcuffed sent my anxiety through the roof. When the cop shoved me in the back of the patrol wagon, I brought my hands underneath me and forced one handcuff off with my foot. I couldn't bear being in restraints. As we rode to the station, I stuck my finger in the back of my throat and forced the vomit out. What better way to release it than in the back of a paddy wagon.

I was transported to Downtown for booking. I was allowed a phone call at 2:45 am. I dialed my house, hoping Calvin was there. Shockingly, he picked up.

"I've been arrested."

"What the fuck for?" No surprise, he sounded upset.

I tapped my fingers on the officer's desk. "I'm in Downtown. Can you please come and bail me out?"

179

"I'm coming."

By the time Calvin bailed me out and drove me home, I had to shower and get dressed to appear at Suffolk Superior Court. I was charged with assault and battery with a dangerous weapon, shod foot. I appeared in court alone and sick. Not a good look. The girl who I assaulted also showed up in court. She walked in with a bruised forehead, her boyfriend Rick, and an older woman. I assumed it was her mother. Once again I found myself in trouble for fighting. Coincidentally this mess revolved around Xavier, like always.

My stomach was nauseous. It felt worse every time I heard someone else's name before mine. At about 1:20pm I was called. After being there most of the day, the judge gave me another court date to come back.

When I arrived home, I called Sasha to apologize. She told me that Xavier drove her home in my car. No one answered when I called Xavier's phone, so I decided to worry about the car later. I needed to rest.

After my nap, Calvin walked through the door. I stayed in bed. I wasn't sure how to confront him about Nicole. He came over to the bed and tapped me on my shoulder.

"What?" I asked.

"Wake up."

"I'm up. What do you want?"

"Are you fucking Xavier?"

"What?" I bolted up, angry and awake.

"Tell me why all your fights are tied to Xavier?" Even I couldn't explain the reason behind these brawls.

I raised my voice, "Where do you come off accusing me of sleeping with Xavier, when you-"

"Calm down," he interrupted.

"No! No, you're not going to-" I didn't stop shouting until he covered my mouth with his hand and shoved me back down on the bed.

"I said calm down!"

I forced his hand from my mouth and stormed out the room. He followed me to the bathroom. I tried closing the door behind me but he stuck his foot in the doorway.

"Calvin...move!" I struggled to kick his foot out the way.

"Come here," he grabbed my arm. He pulled me back into the bedroom and shut the door. "I'm not trying to argue with you. I just want a straight answer."

I stood before him. "No! That's not the case. X is my friend and I wasn't going to let anyone hurt him. I don't go starting trouble with any of these bitches. And if I remember correctly your punk ass cousin fought me over *her* infatuation with X. Does that answer your question?"

"You all are too close. You don't see it? I see it! Everyone sees it! He likes you—always has. How do I know he's never tried anything with you after we had our fall out? He didn't even know I was still in the picture when I spoke to him earlier today—in your car!" Calvin paused to wait for a response; with his face still up against mine. "Why didn't you tell him we were still together? Huh? And why didn't you tell me that you had a few heads up in here watching the Tyson fight, when I was in New York." I pushed back some. "Why the big secret? You two are fucking around, I don't care what you say."

"Oh my God, Calvin! Your body is going to come up missing you keep accusing me of cheating. I swear on my father's grave, Xavier and I are just friends. The only reason you have a problem believing that is because you're still fucking around with Nicole. And you're judging me based on what you're doing behind my back." I pointed my finger at him and waited to see his expression. Guilt was written all over his face. He just stared at me without uttering a word.

181

"Cat got your tongue, player? I can't hear you!" I glared at him. "Am I lying?"

"I do business with her brother. I can't control when she comes around."

"Don't give me that...don't even go there because it's played out! Are you still fucking around with Nicole? Why don't *you* give me a straight answer?"

"Don't start this again!"

"Oh, now I can't speak. Let me remind you that you started this. And on top of that, I can have any company I want. This is my fucking house. Now move!" I pushed him out my way and left the house to go find my car.

EARLY TERMINATION

Training for 911 started at 4:00pm sharp. I arrived at Police Headquarters 20 minutes early. A sergeant checked me in, gave me a pair of headphones, and had me wait for my trainer, Robert Cournoyer. Meanwhile, I got a tour around the entire department. I was introduced to everyone and shown the different sections that made up the Communication Center. One of the sections was a separate area called the Support Room.

Robert broke it down to me. "This is the Towing Unit. Here is where we authorize all the towed vehicles in the city, both private and police ordered."

My trainer began showing me what to write in the log sheet, how to verify license plate numbers with the Registry of Motor Vehicles, and then how to enter it into the database.

I watched how he collected the information and entered it into the system. He assured me it was a piece of cake and I wouldn't have a problem because everyone in the Support Room looked after each other.

"This is the Stolen Car Unit. When someone reports their car stolen at the precinct, the officer will call in the information to us so we can enter it." He showed me how to make out the report and where to file it.

I followed him to another section. "This is the Base Channel. This radio system communicates with officers on the streets through their radios when they need to check for warrants, do a criminal background inquiry, run license plates, or a driver's license status."

Robert had the elderly woman sitting on the Base Channel show me how to look up information by running my name in the system as an example. When she typed in my name, the system displayed my felony charge at Suffolk Superior Court. Robert read it closely and blurted out, "Does the department know you have an open case?" Everyone in the room stopped to stare. I was flushed with embarrassment.

The woman who was sitting on the Base Channel kindly whispered to me, "Any time an employee gets in trouble like this, they have to report it to the department. I'm sorry Robert didn't use tact when telling you this."

I went downstairs to Human Resources to report what had happened. I explained that I caught the case just days after being hired. The woman shook her head and said, "I have to run this by my director and your captain."

All I could say was, "All right."

I went back upstairs and sat with Robert, listening to him take 911 calls while I waited to hear back from Human Resource. After an hour sitting on barbed wire, a sergeant walked over to me.

"Pino, come with me," he addressed me by my last name in a cold manner, "Bring your headsets."

I followed him to the captain's office. Where I knew nothing good was going to come out of this. I was ready to lie and twist that fight story around. But I wasn't given a chance to speak.

"Please sit down," said the captain, "It was brought to my attention that you have a felony charge pending on your record and that is grounds for termination. When and if you beat the case, you can reapply with us. However, in all honesty, I don't think you'll be rehired. Leave your headsets here…and thank you for your time."

I placed the equipment on his desk. Without saying a word, I left Headquarters with my head hung low. I called Andre when I arrived to the house. After I told him everything that happened, he was furious that I was terminated. I was expecting him to be more upset at my offense but it didn't come as a surprise to him that I was arrested for fighting. He told me not to worry about it because the

184

department wrongfully terminated me and he was going to try and reverse it.

Later that evening, Andre knocked on my door. He came in and said, "You can go back to work on Wednesday. They're going to make you write out a Form 86, which is a report where you explain the situation. Write a brief summary stating that a fight broke out in front of you as you were leaving the club. The crowd became violent and you were trying to protect yourself by pushing your way out the ruckus. Your charges are accusations, not facts. That's it. You got it?"

I nodded. "Yes, I got it."

"Let me know when your next court date is. I called an attorney who's a good friend of mine and he's going to represent you." He got to my door and before leaving my apartment said, "And Sky, don't borrow trouble with the department. You don't want to become a household name."

202 (TWO-O-TWO)

Puzzled faces stared at me all around the 911 Comm Center when I returned to work. I was given a number—Operator 202. And so every day, I walked in at a quarter to four in the afternoon, checked in with a supervisor, sat with my big mouthed trainer, and plugged in my headpiece to take 911 calls. That was my nightly routine.

Things didn't start off so well with the yackety-yak behind my arrest and coming back after being fired the first day; those were two strikes against me. And to make matters worse, I was given Fridays and Saturdays off, which seemed to piss off a lot of people. All thanks to Robert Cournoyer, who exposed the situation fully. But I pretended not to be sensitive to all the criticism floating around. So, I filled up my time in between 911 calls, studying and doing homework.

After a rocky start and my six month probationary period ending, I started to feel more comfortable. I befriended a couple of girls, Massiel and Frances. Massiel was Puerto Rican, in her mid twenties, who had two years in with the department and Frances was an Italian American police cadet, who was twenty one, with a year and a half in herself. Any time I had questions or trouble on a call, Massiel was always willing to help. She was pretty genuine. Frances was a bit reserved but very close to Massiel.

"People get hostile over the phone sometimes, but it's never personal." Massiel told me. "You just take it with a grain of salt and send those help. This department will target you all the time if they don't like you. They can push a button on their console to hear your calls, just to find you making an error and have a reason to write you up."

"Thanks. I'll keep that in mind." I threw my legs up on the desk. "You're wicked cool."

"Oh girl, don't sweat it. We have to look out for each other...especially as Latinas. That's why it's smart to do the right thing all the time and keep your nose clean. That way, you give them no reason to come after you."

Going to school, then going to work was a grind. But there was nothing better than work in which you assist in helping save lives and still have some down time to do homework. I almost had a romantic flair for what I did even though I was working day and night without breaks. As corny as it may sound, I loved my job.

By the time I got home at midnight, I would smoke a little and watch television before turning in. On rare occasions, Calvin took the night off from hustling, and joined me. I enjoyed those moments. I would focus hard on the television, and he would smoothly lean in and just kiss me all over my face, to distract me.

He was a good kisser but a poor listener. I hated talking about work to him because he didn't care to hear about it. Sometimes I'd wish Xavier was there instead to hear my 911 stories. Boy did I miss him. But he was off conquering the world of boxing in New York.

It was cold and snowy on this particular evening late February, when I was assigned to the Towing Unit with Massiel. The first hour was hectic, with calls flooding the phone line. Then I got a call that caught my attention.

"Police Tow Unit."

"This is Roadrunner with a tow."

"Reason for the tow?"

"Snow emergency."

"Year, make, and color."

"93' Mercedes, blue."

"License plate."

"6-7-2-0 Harry Robert"

When I ran the plate in the system, it came back registered to Nicole Maher from Chestnut Hill. Something told me Calvin was behind that wheel before it was towed. Furious, I entered the information in the database. I then turned to Massiel and told her if anyone called looking for that Mercedes, place the call on hold for me speak to them.

For the next hour, we were watchful to see who would call looking for that car; Nicole or Calvin. Massiel had a hunch on what was going on without me having to run down the story. She just had my back like that. As I waited for the call, a sergeant came into the Support Room.

"Pino, are you Operator 202?"

"Yes, sir." My voice trembled. Anytime a supervisor came looking for me, I worried.

"Come with me." He turned around and walked off. I stared at Massiel with wide eyes, afraid I was in trouble.

I followed him to the supervisors' desk and he handed me an envelope. "This is a commendation letter from the Chief. His nanny called 911 last week for a medical emergency. His son was having a seizure and she told him Operator 202 did a great job translating for EMS and eased her nerves. He wants to grant you a day off for an outstanding job."

My heart leapt with relief. As rewarding as it was to be recognized by the Chief for a job well done, I couldn't erase that Mercedes being towed. As I hurried to get back to the Towing Unit, Massiel told me a man called looking for the car. She put him on hold for me, but he hung up.

My eyebrow quirked, "You're shitting me!"

188

BAT AWAY

A few nights later, Nicole was sitting in her Mercedes, out front of my house. Slightly dismayed, I walked over to her car to find out what the hell she was doing there. She stepped out wearing sneakers and a ponytail as if she was ready to throw down with me. I stood there without batting an eye and crossed arms.

"Can we talk?"

"I don't have anything to say to you."

"I'm not here to start trouble. I just want to know what the story is between you and Calvin. It's not fair that he's still playing these games...going back and forth. He needs to decide which one of us he's going to stay with."

"Where is he now?"

"I'm not sure."

Without taking my eyes off her I said, "Exactly! He's on his way home, which is here with me."

She scoffed, "Then why are his shoes still under my bed?"

I thought of beating the snot out of her, but I was holding myself under rigid control. "You know what Nicole? Don't come to my house with that bullshit that you're still with Calvin and expect to avoid trouble." I reached the handle of her car door and jerked it open. "You should leave while you're still safe, because I swear on everything I love, I'm going to fuck you up if you don't!"

She slammed the car door shut without getting inside. "I'm not scared of you and I'm not leaving until Calvin gets here."

The girl had cojones! She was determined to wait for him and confront him about choosing one of us. That's when I couldn't control myself any longer. "All right bitch!" I turned around and ran inside the house. Within the few minutes it took me to grab a metal

189

bat out the basement, Andre pulled up in the driveway in his police cruiser. As I rushed out the house, I saw Andre speaking with Nicole. He must have sensed something wasn't right when he saw her in the Mercedes Calvin use to come around in.

As soon as he saw me approaching her car with both hands holding the bat over my shoulder, he jumped in front of me. "Give me the bat, Sky." He lunged at me to take the bat away.

"You're lucky, bitch!" Andre blocked me from getting near her. "Don't ever come to my house again!" She was laughing making me angrier. "I swear Nicole, you're going to catch a bad hit!"

"Sky! Be quiet!" Andre pushed me towards the house then turned to Nicole and said, "You need to leave my property young lady before I have you arrested for trespassing."

Nicole complied with his order and left.

Andre came upstairs, raging. "I shouldn't have to come home to find you screaming to catch another case. Wrestle to control that temper of yours." He wiped his face and rubbed his eyes. "I can't continue sticking my neck out there for you every time you feel the need to fight. And if all this is over Calvin, then he needs to leave this house. I've had it up to here already with your shit!" He pointed at his neck and left my apartment.

When Calvin got home, I unleashed my anger. It was another serious rift about Nicole that exploded into an exchange of bitter words followed by weeks of silence between us.

Eventually Calvin moved out, but his money and drugs remained in my attic. He believed in the saints' protection and good fortune, so he asked to keep his stash there. I allowed him to. From the time he took his first trip to New York after I gave him the sacred beads to wear, he professed that everything was paying off in spades. And what's good for the goose, was definitely good for me, because I was on that payroll stacking as well.

190

CARMEN, THE LAUGHING SANTERA

Now that Calvin was gone, I spent a lot of time on my own, weeping bitterly in my bedroom. I cried nearly every day. Even when I was at work, I was withdrawn—quietly shedding tears. Massiel and Frances always invited me out but I continuously turned them down. I wanted to be left alone to assess the situation. Recognizing what was wrong and admitting to it was a battle. Although things were painful after our fight, I wanted to believe that there was something gentle and comforting somewhere for me. I just hadn't found it yet.

One day, in late spring, I wanted pizza from the best pizzeria in Boston, Same Old Place. When I stepped outside my house the weather was nice and warm. Instead of taking my car, I put my hair in a bun, shaded my eyes, and strolled down Centre Street.

When I got to Same Old Place, I noticed an older, but attractive woman, wearing a lot of gold chains, waiting for her order. Something about her presence was strong, making it hard to keep me from staring. She smiled at me and complimented my ying yang earrings that Calvin had given me. I smiled back and thanked her.

After I finished my slice of pizza and Pepsi, I decided to continue walking down Centre Street towards Highland Square. A little distance from the block, I spotted the woman from Same Old Place sweeping the sidewalk. I took my sunglasses off to get a better view of what I was looking at. Never had I noticed that there was a botanica on Centre Street. That prompted me to stop and speak to the woman.

"Do you give consultations?"

She stopped sweeping. "Yes, I do."

"Are you available now to give me one?"

"Sure. Come inside." She led me into the shop.

I followed her inside and stood by the doorway. The shop was cozy with hardwood floors that needed polishing. One side of the wall was filled with candles of all sorts and across from it was a register with different perfumed potions on the counter.

"Come with me, my child." She had me follow her to a tiny room in the basement.

I sat at the table across from her with my legs crossed. She shuffled the cards and ordered me to uncross my legs and state my name.

"Cecilia Pino."

"Cecilia Pino," she repeated and rang a cow bell. "Cut them."

I divided the deck of cards in three and placed them on the table. She scooped the cards and placed them faced up, until she covered the entire table with each card.

"An old worry is haunting you and you're not sure if you handled it properly." The only thing that haunted me was the abortion I had two years back. My biggest regret.

"The past is gone, dear child, don't worry over something that already happened." She pointed at a card and asked, "Who's the tall, fair skin guy I see here?"

I shrugged.

"He lives far from here but he thinks about you all the time." She let out a loud laugh. "He's very flirty and is surrounded by many women."

I guessed she was referring to Xavier. "He's my friend."

"There's a girl in his life who did some spell work to separate him from you. That's why he moved away. Where does he live?"

"New York."

"Yes, I see it here. Things aren't going too well for him out there but he won't tell you that because he doesn't want you to worry. You're going to take a trip out there one day. Why don't you give him a chance? I see he's a good kid." She let out a short laugh.

"We're just friends."

"Oh...but he loves you more than that, dear. That love is spirited and solid. It's so strong that he'd give his life for you. Don't be foolish." She let out another loud laugh. "So who's the short dark skin guy?"

I don't know what bothered me more, the questions or her amusement. "My ex," I mumbled.

"You need to let go of him. He's no good. I see there's another woman beside him and they're going to have a child together."

This reading was too negative, I thought.

"I see you talking to a lawyer about some legal matters. Do you have a law suit against someone?"

"No, it's just a charge I picked up last year."

"You don't have to worry about that. The case will go in your favor."

The Santera sat back in her seat, placing both hands on her stomach. I questioned what she saw because she looked at the cards intently.

"Do you plan on moving?"

"No."

I was comfortable living upstairs from my mother despite the few intrusions by Andre. But I remembered my cousin Felo saying our house will no longer be there.

"I see you moving to a new apartment. So come see me when you do. This place appears cold. I'll give you something to bring warmth to it. And stop crying over your ex-boyfriend. He's just an asshole with a lot of money. There are plenty of men out here. You're young and pretty. Cutting your losses will be a smart move on your part. The longer you hold on, the longer you will suffer." She let out a chuckle. "Go out and party. Distraction will allow you to meet people. Get rid of everything that reminds you of him, even furniture. Once you do, you will be in a much better space. You know in your bones that it's time for a change. You just don't know where to begin. Besides, the man you will marry will have ten times the money this little asshole has."

"Oh damn!" We both laughed.

"You have a friend who will have a weak pregnancy and miscarry. But she'll become pregnant again and give birth to a girl. You will be asked to be the godmother. Do you have any questions for me?"

I nodded. "How much do I owe you?"

"Fifteen dollars."

I paid her the money and walked up Centre Street back home. Her reading sent me on a mind trip and left me feeling the same; if not worse. I worried about Xavier and how he was doing in New York. It didn't come as a surprise when I heard Jade was still doing voodoo on him. Moving out there was probably the result of the spell. What was wrong with Jade? I couldn't understand how pulling him away from me was going to pull him closer to her.

194

COURT HEARING

Standing outside the courtroom of Suffolk Superior with my mother by my side, I nervously scanned the hallway for my lawyer. I tried my best to pull myself together but my mother's jitters annoyed me. After waiting some time, my lawyer, Jared Conroy, brusquely marched in with his usual confident pace.

"Ready, Cecilia?"

"I'm ready, Mr. Conroy." I sounded less certain than I really was.

"The victim in this case met with the director of Consumers Affairs and Licensing to discuss the mismanagement at the Roxy Club which permitted underage drinking which led to the violent brawl that sent him to the hospital. He's going after the club and doesn't want to pursue the charges against you. The judge wants to slap you with probation but I'm going to convince her that you're willing to seek anger management since it's your first offense."

"So that's it?" my mother asked.

"That's what I'm shooting for, Mrs. Medeiros. No need to be nervous."

"Nervous is one thing. Vomitous is another." My mother exaggerated.

"Well, if it makes you feel any better, this judge is fair, and I personally know her. I'm sure your daughter will get anger management, then the case gets dismissed."

The three of us walked into the courtroom. No sooner than taking our seats, the clerk announced, "All rise! The Honorable Claire Stewart presiding." The judge took the bench and motioned for everyone to be seated.

The prosecutor pulled out a brown, accordion folder and called on me first, "Case number 97-H395 Valentin vs. Pino." I approached the table on the left hand side of the room near the judge. There I stood in front of her, staring down at the floor. My lawyer and the judge were jabbering away so rapidly among themselves that I could not understand what they were saying.

All I knew was that there would be a motion to dismiss all charges after I completed a ten week anger management program. According to the judge, I didn't deserve a slap on the wrist after taking a look at the pictures of my victim's wounds. But she believed in second chances and warned me to never step foot in her courtroom again.

At precisely 12:00 o'clock in the afternoon, after my court hearing, my mother and I arrived to the house with hunger pains. I flew up the stairs to remove my dress clothes and invade my refrigerator. I inserted my apartment key and unlocked the top lock. When I turned the door knob to open the door, I discovered it was still locked. Andre must have entered my apartment because I never used the bottom lock and he was the only one with the spare key.

While I was in my apartment heating up some leftovers, I picked up the yellow pages and searched for my new therapist. I chose a clinic in Cambridge, near the Galleria Mall to make my commute to Northeastern University a lot easier. And if I had time to spare in between the two, I would be able to sneak in a little shopping.

Relieved that my belly was full, I went to my room to put on something comfortable. Then there was a firm knock on my door. Only one person had a knock designed to alarm. Andre. As I rushed to pull my sweatpants up, I heard a more insistent knock at the door.

"Wait a minute!" I hollered.

I hurried out my room to open the door. Andre barged in like the policeman that he was and grabbed me by the back of my neck.

"What the…fuck?" My heart thumped unevenly.

With his hand strongly gripped on my neck, he brought me to the kitchen, pulled out a chair, and slammed me down on it. "Call your half breed boyfriend and have him come get his money and coke out this house immediately!" I found it hard to believe Andre was that aggressive with me. I guess the cop job possessed him even after quitting time. "There's enough cocaine up here to send you to jail for a life term. Are you fucking stupid or what?"

I couldn't say anything to excuse myself for allowing Calvin to keep his stash in the attic. Andre would have never understood what I made in a week, with Calvin, surpassed twice as much what the city paid me—before taxes. What could I have said? Nothing—the money was that good.

After Andre left my apartment, I called Calvin. "You need to come over, like, now!"

"I can't. I'm in the middle of something." He had an indignant tone of voice.

"Andre was here and he was livid at the attic's *condition.* He told me to tell you that you need to get over here and *pick up* your mess."

"Shit! Are you serious?" His tone changed as he realized what I was talking about.

"As serious as he was."

"All right, can you do me a favor?"

"What?"

"Can you bring me the *laundry?*"

"Where to?"

"Meet me at the carwash on Amory Street at 3:00 o'clock."

"Done."

Andre, returning moments later, gave me the devastating news that my grandmother had passed away. It happened suddenly, although thinking about it, I realized it had been coming for some time. Her health was deteriorating faster since the last time I had seen her. One minute she was on her feet feeling hard as nails. The next minute she'd be in bed trying to regain strength.

My mother was crying uncontrollably downstairs, so Andre had to deliver the message for her. I closed my eyes, feeling the pressure of tears wanting to come. That day couldn't have gotten any worse.

Three o'clock came around and I met Calvin at the carwash on Amory Street. He got in the passenger side of my car and struck up a conversation. My instinct said, speed the fuck up and get out of here, but Calvin wasn't moving fast enough.

He glared at me, as if I were his problem. "What's wrong with you now?"

My eyes were red from constant weeping over the loss of my grandmother. I kept my head down and mouth shut because I didn't want his sympathy. I just wanted him to take the duffle bags out of my trunk and be done with it.

"You're just going to sit here and ignore what I'm asking you?"

It almost seemed that way. I just couldn't fix my mouth to tell him about the devastating news. It was still shocking to me.

"I don't have all day, Sky."

I leaned forward and pulled the trunk release button. My head rested on the steering wheel with my eyes closed. I just wanted him to take the duffle bags out—fast. Once he got the message, he stepped out the car and removed them. As soon as I heard my trunk slam shut, I started to drive out of the carwash.

A second later a police cruiser pulled in the carwash. Nervous as hell for Calvin, who still had one duffle bag in sight when I looked through the rear view mirror, I purposely let go of the clutch to make the car shut off and distract the police officer.

"I'm such a dope," I said timorously to the officer whose driver side was parallel to my driver side. He just smiled at me and I smiled back. I turned the ignition and watched the cruiser just drive around the carwash past Calvin and exited out behind me. What a close call.

NIGHT TERRORS

In the months that followed, my mental condition worsened. Our break up depressed me, my marijuana habit increased, and my dreams were gross and repugnant. My dreams were so intense that I'd wake up trembling, consoling myself: "It's just a dream, Sky."

I stayed in bed for days. Isolating myself from the world, just to cry and cry. Sadly this depression stole my energy and drive; I didn't see any other way out.

Sleeping with the television on didn't seem to work. One night, I drifted off into a sleep while watching the ten o'clock news in the parlor. A demonized man came on the screen and said, "Welcome..." in a gravelly voice.

The screen faded to black and then displayed a pit with scorching fire burning a multitude of people. A sea of human faces was burning and thousands of eyes all stared at me. The screen zoomed in slowly and when I looked closely at the monitor, a lost soul in a pit called out to me.

"Cielo, salvate!" It was my grandmother screaming out to me: Sky, save yourself!

I could hear the fire crackling in the pit. She was in hell with her skin searing, leaving bloody red muscle underneath; chained like a slave inside the pit of fire. "Please no! This can't be happening! I woke up in a cold sweat crying, "Grandma!"

Another night, I dreamed that while I sat at my mother's dining table with Andre and other guests I'd never met. We were all sitting there waiting for dinner to be served. My mother threw a butcher knife on the floor. I saw the knife land on the back of a rat. I hid my reaction because I struggled to speak. She picked up the injured rat with both hands and pulled its head from the rest of its body. Its bloody spine was left dangling. Andre watched her with a bemused smile, but the smile faded as he looked at me. My mother then lifted the lid off her slow cooker and places the rat's body inside. No one else seemed to be disturbed at this besides me. I then shot up in bed. My face was covered in sweat and the room was silent. I whispered, "It's just a dream, Sky...just a dream."

By this time, I had developed a doctor and patient relationship with Dr. Roman Wesley in anger management. I was anxious to get my report that stated I completed the program in order to get my case dismissed. When I arrived to his office, he greeted me with a warm smile, "How are you today, Sky?"

Half of me wanted to say, *everything under the sky torments me and makes me sad;* while the other half wanted to say, *just give me that damn report so you don't have to see my face ever again.*

"I'm cool, Dr. Wesley."

"Could I ask you something, off the record?" He looked intently at me.

"Sure."

"Is there anything you would like to share with me that I can help you with, aside from this court paper? You see, anger usually leads to depression and you show signs of someone that may have difficulty dealing with depressive moods."

"Are you asking me to submit to more therapy?"

"Well if it's not court ordered you may feel a little differently about coming here by choice. Again, it's totally up to you."

I sat and thought of where I should begin. Here was a man, a professional, who knew I was controlled by rage and wanted to help me deal with my wounds. Now that it was my choice and confidential, I would give it a try.

"I'm corrupted by sorrow." My hands glided over my lap. "It's like I live in this dark place where even the sun's rays can't get through. God, it's dark! All I do is cry. No one ever sees those tears but I don't want to cry anymore, Dr. Wesley..."

He prescribed me Trazodone for my depression and aggressive behavior. I accepted the prescription but I wasn't sure about taking them. It's not that I minded trying the medicine; I just didn't want to be like my mother.

CHANGES

A year had passed and brought a few changes in my life. I graduated from Northeastern University with my associates, I found solace in therapy, and Police Headquarters relocated to a newly constructed building. Among these changes, Calvin opened up an auto repair shop like he had wanted. And although our relationship had ended, he made it a point to stay in contact. Occasionally, I slept with him, but those rendezvous were few and far between.

It was December of 1999 and the frigid winter air came rushing as I got inside my car to start it up. On my way to work a rattling noise came from under the hood. I called Calvin to have it checked out. But he told me I was better off setting up a false car theft and letting the insurance pay me for a total loss. So I agreed with the plan.

It was Monday morning, dark, cold, and windy. I waited for Calvin to come through with our plan. I left him several messages but he never returned any of my calls. Enraged at him for ignoring me, I drove to his shop on Dorchester Avenue. When I arrived at the shop, I barged in to the office bitching, "I need to speak with Calvin! Where is he?"

"Calvin who?" said an older black gentleman wearing a mechanic's jumpsuit, raising his eyebrow, annoyed at my snippy attitude.

"The...owner?" I suspected I was in the wrong place. Bad move.

"The owner here is Keith Matthews, young lady. Ain't no Calvin running this shop." He had a southern accent.

I scratched my head. Keith was Calvin's uncle. Why would Calvin tell me it was his shop? I guess he felt some entitlement since he was investing his dirty money there.

"Oh my God! I am terribly sorry for intruding like this." I turned away.

I hurried out the door to avoid any more embarrassment. I'd deal with Calvin later. On my way home, Sasha called me on my cell phone, crying.

"Do you work today?"

"Yeah. I'm on my way home to get ready now. What's wrong?"

"I need a ride to the hospital." Her voice was weak.

"What's wrong with you?"

She sobbed. "I think I'm having a miscarriage."

"Miscarriage? I didn't know you were expecting."

"I've been having complications since I found out, so I didn't want to tell anyone. But I've been bleeding since this morning and my doctor told me to go the emergency room."

"I'll be over in a few...hang in there." I ran to my car, started up the engine and slammed on the gas pedal to get there as quickly as possible. Meanwhile I called out sick from work to be by Sasha's side.

Sasha got in my car looking pale and sickly. I didn't want to ask her anything. I just drove her to the emergency room, silently. Tears streamed down her face on our way to the hospital while she held her midsection. It broke my heart.

Just as I was pulling up to Brigham and Woman's Hospital, my phone rang numerous times. Calvin. I had to ignore him because Sasha was in agony and I didn't want him to know what was going on.

"Oh God, it hurts!" Her voice was almost a shriek. I watched in horror as the blood seeped through her jeans.

I fumbled through my purse for money to pay the valet attendant. To my surprise I found a bottle of prescription drugs that belonged to my mother and a crap load of cash I didn't usually carry. The pocket book wasn't mine. My mother and I both had a black Coach bag that was similar in design. Somehow I confused the two the last time I visited her.

In the event of getting Sasha settled in her room, I forgot to return Calvin's call. Instead, I sat down to read the prescription bottle. They were called Klonopins. When I asked a nurse what they were, she said it was medication for anxiety. I had never taken any prescription drugs but I needed something to bring me down from this tension. Without thinking, I threw back a pill.

Within minutes, I dozed off in the waiting area. While I slept, I dreamed Sasha was standing in the hospital corridor, with a baby girl in her arms. I wanted to hold the baby but every time I moved towards her, she moved further away from me. A ripping pain shot through my stomach bringing me to my knees. Then with a swiftness that is only possible in dreams, Sasha was gone.

"Sky..." whispered Sasha.

I woke up slowly, glancing around the waiting room as my eyes adjusted to the light-and to Sasha, who was in a Johnny gown.

"Sky, the doctor is going to perform a D & C on me. Could you go get me some clean clothes?" She looked drawn and tired.

"Perform what on you?" I sounded out of it.

"They're going to clean out my uterus."

"All right. Call Jade and tell her to have your clothes ready when I get there. I don't want to go inside your house." Her mother was never too fond of my friendship with her daughters. In her eyes, I was a bad influence.

205

I.A.D. (INNOCENT AND DISTURBED)

After I dropped off Sasha at her house, I smoked a joint in my car. The rattling engine bugged me even more when I was high. I tried to phone Calvin, but my battery had died. *Oh fuck it.* I just wanted to get home under the warm covers anyways. I was drowsy from the downers.

The sound of keys opening my front door awoke me at 1:00am. Calvin snuck his head in my room but I pretended to be deep in my sleep. I could hear him pacing all around the house. I sensed something was wrong when he didn't come back to my room. In the middle of the night I got up to use the bathroom. The living room was dark, except for some light flickering out of the television set. I saw Calvin sitting on the couch with his head thrown back, staring at the ceiling. He didn't even turn to look at me. I didn't bother asking him what the matter was. I was too tired to be concerned.

The following day I woke up at noon. Calvin was gone and so was my car. I assumed he was bringing it to the shop to start the insurance job, but he didn't say anything to me about the plan. I ended up borrowing my mother's Chevy Tahoe and headed to work. After my shift ended, I tried calling him but his phone was off. When he didn't show up to my house that night, I worried. Something was wrong.

A day later a detective from the Internal Affairs Division showed up at the Communication Center. My sergeant took me off the phones and escorted me back to an office along with the Detective. The Internal Affairs Department wanted to bring me in for questions but they advised me to get a union representative. Clueless and nervous, I called Andre on his cell phone.

"A detective is here from IAD. He wants to interrogate me but he's telling me I need a union rep. I don't know what to do or what's going on."

"Let me make a few calls. Don't go in there alone."

"Ok."

I sat at the supervisor's office waiting for Andre to get back to me to figure out what all the mystery was about. Finally Andre walked in to the Communication Center with a union rep to accompany me to Internal Affairs.

Calvin had a warrant out for his arrest. Nicole's brother, Brian, and he got into an altercation over stolen drugs. The argument escalated when Brian accused Calvin's mother of stealing the drugs to support her cocaine habit. A scuffle broke out between the two and Calvin pulled out his gun and shot Brian in the stomach. Calvin ran off. As the story unfolded, I discovered the day he shot Brian was the night he last stayed at my place. My problem here was Calvin had been arrested in my car and officers confiscated 20 grams of coke. That didn't sound like Calvin. He didn't deal nickels and dimes. It was the amount Brian allegedly stole from him. Somehow it turned up after their feud. However, the weapon used in the assault wasn't found. Now my car and I were under a series of investigations. That alone was enough for me to panic.

Andre asked to speak to the union rep in private. Looking at me like he could either wreck me or rescue me. The union rep and I stepped in the hallway with him to discuss what we had just learned.

"What do you know about this incident?" asked the union rep.

"Nothing. I was in the emergency room with my friend Sasha two days ago. The car was making a rattling noise so I called Calvin to take it to his uncle's shop to have it looked at. He came the next morning to pick up the car and I haven't heard from him ever since."

The union rep excused himself from us to make a call. Andre cornered me in the hallway and with a stern and low voice asked, "What shit did you get yourself into this time?"

"Nothing!"

"Where's the gun?"

"I don't know!"

"You don't know?"

"Oh my God, Andre, why don't you believe me?"

"You are as stealthy as they come."

"Then why are you helping me if you don't believe me?"

"Oh, I'm not helping you. I'm trying to save your mother the aggravation of finding out the things her daughter does underneath her nose."

"I have nothing to do with this, I swear."

"So you're not holding anything?"

I growled. "No."

"The less you say in there the better you're off."

"I don't have anything to hide."

"Really? My attic didn't seem to look that way once upon a time."

"How much trouble is Calvin in?"

"Calvin? You should be worried about how much trouble you're in."

"I didn't do shit!"

"Let's hope not, because last I checked, you two had enough blow in my house to pay my salary for a year. And I do a lot of overtime. So, I'm only going to say this once: if you're hiding that gun, get rid off it!"

The union rep came back and we spoke briefly about the matter. Andre left us to go to work, while the union rep and I walked inside Internal Affairs. The two detectives doing the investigation were waiting for us. I took a seat in a small bright interview room with no windows and a tape recorder in the middle of a round table. The two detectives questioned my relationship with Calvin and what was he doing with my car. I took deep breaths and tried not to appear nervous.

"What's your relationship with Mr. Matthews?" one detective asked.

My union rep interrupted. "Is Ms. Pino being charged with anything?"

"We're just interviewing her because her vehicle was confiscated during an arrest. Now if you'll excuse me, I'm asking her the questions."

"If she's not being charged with anything then this interview is over."

"Are you aware that the man arrested in her car was involved in a shooting?"

"No. Let's go Ms. Pino, this interview is over." The union rep stood up from the table.

"Now wait a minute, this interview isn't over. I need her statement!"

"Charge her with something and we'll have your statement. Until then, you have nothing. Let's go, Ms. Pino."

The detectives were livid. Moments later, a sergeant came out to the door as we were walking out. He carried a folder and glared at me.

"We will be touching base with you again. Next time you're in here we will determine your charges and punishment based on all facts and circumstances surrounding the incident and you." He had a way of spitting when he spoke. It was gross.

Why the fuck was I going to be punished? I had nothing to do with that. But I wasn't going to speak, and risk pissing off any of these Detectives.

I called Andre to let him know how it went. He was going to work on getting my car back with the promise that I would leave Calvin alone indefinitely. He didn't want my mother to become suspicious for using her car so he let me borrow his Volvo until then. I swore to him from that day forward, I would have nothing else to do with Calvin.

In the face of humiliation over my business being exposed, I found superiors watching me like I was a big red dot. In this police environment you were automatically guilty until proven otherwise.

Whenever I took a break, I was timed and scolded if they felt I took too long. One lieutenant told me that I needed to let him know when I got up to go to the restroom. Others would go out for long periods of time to smoke a cigarette but never were spoken to. One time, someone in the Support Room was drunk as hell. The supervisors had him sent home in a police cruiser. During the ride home, the guy, extremely inebriated, jumped out the cruiser and ran off. The situation was on the hush for political reasons. But whenever I answered back to some foolish reprimand, I got pulled into the office for suspension.

Another time I was called to work overtime on 911 on the day shift. I refused it and went back to sleep. Thirty minutes later I was called again and hired on overtime to work in the office as the supervisor's clerk. I accepted it and drove in to work early morning. When I arrived, a sergeant decided to put me on 911instead. I explained to him that I was hired to clerk in the office, not to do 911. He decided to scream at me because I simply refused to do overtime on 911. And that meant they had to hire someone else. I walked away to leave, but he yelled at me, and ordered me to come back. He continued to go off.

"Are you done?" I asked condescendingly.

A screaming match broke out between the two of us. Then the lieutenant from that shift decided to argue with me also. I was later written up and the lieutenant pushed for a suspension for disrespectful treatment. The fucker even had the audacity to lie in the Deputy's face at a hearing to appeal the suspension. He said the sergeant never raised his voice at me and I was the only one shouting. After that I accepted all other suspensions that came my way. It was useless to fight these bullies. They all stuck together with their lies.

During that time, we had another lieutenant who gave out an incentive for those who took the most 911 calls the first two hours of our shift. He would let two people go at 8:00pm. That was half a shift. Some days I would have the most calls but I was never given the eight o'clock go. Why would he? In everyone's eyes, I was a bull headed troublemaker.

It didn't matter that I was ambitious and worked hard. If I wasn't liked by one, I was picked by all. Now my attitude towards work was changing. I looked at the telephone system like a crummy machine with annoying buttons on it. My conversations with callers were becoming abrupt and my questions were short and clipped.

I didn't have a sympathetic voice anymore—it was robotic. People would get upset when they had to repeat an address to me. Sometimes the public was reluctant to answer any questions. I would try to gather as much information as I was required to but it was irritating so I would just put in a half ass call into the system.

"You're a good operator, Sky." Massiel sounded concerned. "What's happening to you?"

"Everyone wants an immediate response but no one wants to help give all the information needed. Then they want to yell: fuck the police! Shit, try working for them. These supervisors don't know shit about this position but yet they want to tell you how to handle these ignorant ass callers. I chose this job, but I didn't choose to be undermined!"

211

"Breathe, girl!" Massiel laughed, "Take a break so you can cool off that hot head of yours. Anyways, Frances is graduating from the police academy in June, so we've been invited to her surprise party, if you're up for it."

"That's fine. Count me in," I said, still feeling crabby.

I waited for my lunch hour to leave the building. As I walked pass my mailbox I thought of emptying it out. It had piles of unread department notices I couldn't care any less for. As I walked out the doors of the department, with a large amount of mail, I looked through it and saw a closed envelope from IAD. The investigative report concluded that I didn't violate any of the department's rules and regulations. I was cleared from that situation.

DON'T SPEAK

The winter finally passed away, and early in the spring of 2000, I secretly decided to visit Calvin. He was a detainee at The County Jail awaiting trial. It was visiting day for him and I wanted to arrive early to avoid running into Nicole if she showed up. I drove to a nearby parking garage and paid to park the car for a few hours.

In the jail lobby, I filled out a visitor's sheet and handed over my driver's license. The officer at the counter checked the computer to see if Calvin could receive any visitors. She approved the visit and told me to have a seat and wait to be called. I sat there shot to pieces, with a million thoughts racing through my mind. I longed to end this confusion in our relationship. I also wondered if I could ever be immune to this type of life.

My name was called after twenty minutes of waiting. They were probably running me for warrants or something. I walked through a metal detector and proceeded to take the elevator to the third floor. Once I got off, I slowly made my way down a long hallway with numbered doors, looking for the visiting room that matched my pass.

I walked into a closet-sized room with a plate-glass window that separated the inmate from the visitor. I perched on a stool and waited. Finally Calvin arrived; wearing a navy blue inmate uniform with a white long sleeve thermo shirt underneath.

Stunned at the sight of me sitting there, he asked, "What are you doing here?" It wasn't the welcome I expected.

"I wanted to see you."

After awkward silence, he put his head down, putting much thought into what he was going to say next. I just stared at him,

213

speechless. I knew nothing good was going to come out of this visit. It was written all over his face as he brought it back to meet my eyes.

"Don't come here anymore." He opened his mouth and shattered my emotions. "I'm sorry Sky for everything I've ever put you through, but I can't have you come up here to see me."

His words gripped my heart. I was at a loss for words. Even as he was telling me not to visit him anymore, I couldn't find the strength to get up from that stool to walk away. As much as we fought, as much as we held on to a broken relationship, and as much as we loved each other; this felt final.

"Don't say things you can't take back."

"I'm facing three to five."

"And?"

"And Nicole is pregnant," he confessed.

I don't know what came over me. My grief was so raw, my stomach churned and shook violently. I went apoplectic with rage: with an open hand I started attacking the window. I must have wacked it five times.

"Sky, stop!"

A corrections officer heard the commotion and opened the door on the inmate side. He ordered me to leave as he pulled Calvin out. I stormed out with a throbbing hand. My body couldn't stop shaking as I ran towards the elevator. I started to hate him. I didn't want to, but I did.

News of my outburst must have gotten to the officer at the front desk because when I passed the counter, she was on the phone, scowling me. I left the visiting pass with the locker key there and hustled off, leaving my driver's license and the contents of my locker behind. It was nothing of value. I could always pay for a duplicate license.

I scurried back to the parking garage. The farther I got from the prison the more bitterly I wept. After I picked up my car, I pulled

214

over on Merrimac Street. My head rested on the steering wheel as I listened to Kiss 108 FM play Don't Speak by No Doubt. I was breathless as I screamed and hit the radio. Once again I was left in the dark.

RAY POVEZ

Weary of all the things that dragged me down to low ebb, I went into a self imposed hiatus. I would wake up with gut pains that came in waves, causing me to call out of work a lot and stay in bed for days at a time, filling the room with my black mood. Not only was I dreading Calvin's rejection, I felt like I was also enduring some remnants of the dark period from my father's passing. His death anniversary was the most dreaded date on my calendar.

But things turned around the night Massiel called to remind me of Frances' surprise graduation party. She planned the party with the captain of Precinct G whose son had also been recruited by the City Police. I was a little hesitant about going at first. The party fell on my father's 4th year death anniversary and I would have preferred to stay home alone. However, Massiel insisted I go and promised me a good time.

Before the party, I lit a white candle in my bedroom in memory of my loving father. I placed his picture next to the candle with a 14 karat gold rosary necklace attached to it. I sat on the edge of my bed with my head down, allowing my tears to flow, giving myself time to work through all my emotions before heading out.

I walked leisurely to my car, looking up to the sky. The stars that night were gorgeous and the moon was three quarters full. I drove to the party, intending to stay there for an hour.

I arrived at Le Meridien Cambridge with a small gift box in my hand that I had Sasha neatly wrap. As I approached the door, I saw many unfamiliar faces. I looked around trying to find Massiel or Frances in that huge crowd but I couldn't, so I walked over to the bar.

"Can I have a Heineken?" I asked, untangling my hair.

216

I kept looking for Massiel while I waited for my beer, and still, she was nowhere in sight. The bartender came back with my beer and placed it behind me. When I pulled out my money to pay for it, the bartender informed me that the gentleman on the other side had paid for it. I smiled when I saw that the gentleman was an officer who worked at the front desk of Headquarters. When I walked over to him to thank him, Massiel showed up at the same time. As soon as the three of us were conversing, Frances appeared also.

"Hey! You made it!" she exclaimed.

"Congratulations." I said, pulling her into a big hug and handing over her gift box.

"Aww, thanks girl!"

Within a few minutes three more guys joined the group. Frances introduced them to me as officers who worked for the department and I shook each one's hand. We all joined in small talk as I sipped my beer. It was more of a prop in my hand than anything.

The music was blaring—a cacophony sound that I wouldn't term music even if I was high on crack. I was anxious to leave. I thought of excuses to come up with, to not appear rude. It felt strange being in a room full of happy people while I had to disguise the turmoil inside me. I started to count down the minutes until leaving time, narrowing down the different excuses I was going to use to get out.

As the night wore on, Massiel introduced me to a handsome man. Ray Povez. He was attractive, medium built, six feet tall, and broad shouldered. I was instantly attracted; drawn in by his eyes. They were light golden brown, with jet black lashes framing them.

"Sky?" he asked.

"Yes." I giggled.

"That's not your real name is it?"

"I don't use my real name as a defense mechanism. So if I ever go down for anything, it would be for my own indiscretion, not because someone brought me down."

He laughed. "Oh I see, underneath that calm demeanor is a rebel."

"It's not always obvious to outsiders, but yes, I'm a rebel at heart." I smiled and sipped my now warm beer, to play cool.

Shortly after, we joined the group again and the guys were chatting about how the former Larry Bird of the Boston Celtics mastered one of the NBA's most formidable frontcourts. It was unclear how the subject even came up, but that's men for you. They love speaking sports. I slowly backed up against the wall to get a better view of Ray and how he interacted with the other officers. He was a ray of sunshine in my dark world. My gaze kept straying when others were talking. I couldn't focus on the topic of basketball. Shit, I didn't even understand it. Not only did I stare at him fully, I noted how he bit the sides of his tongue when he laughed. I thought; am I being too obvious in my attraction? Does the rest of the group see it? Or am I being self-conscious?

Ray politely disengaged from the conversation with the others and made his way to me again. "Are you always this quiet?"

I couldn't help but smile. "I'm just a little tired; it's been a long day."

He pointed at my beer. "You want another one?"

"Sure."

Ray gently put his hand around my waist and said, "Ven conmigo." (Come with me).

We walked to the bar and Ray asked if I would take shot of Hennessey with him. I agreed to it, hoping the cognac would take the edge off. I had never felt so overwhelmed by a man's presence like I did with him. While we waited for the bartender to come over and serve us, Ray asked, "Are you seeing anyone?"

I put my hand over my forehead leaning against the counter in a dramatic pose and said, "Well, I've been trying to break up this serious relationship I have with my cable television, but we've been together for so long, it's almost impossible to let go."

"Sounds pretty serious," he played along, "I don't want to come in between that."

The bartender brought us our shots and a Heineken to chase it down.

"What do you want to toast to?" he asked.

"How about to a great summer." With plenty of adventures that hopefully includes you.

He mocked me, "Could I be included in this great summer?"

We raised our glasses and I said, "Why not," and we tapped them together.

I slammed the shot glass down on the counter and lowered my head, clutching my fist as the cognac went down my throat.

"Tell me something about you that I would never guess just by looking at you," Ray urged.

I didn't answer right away. The Hennessey was taking a while to settle in my stomach. Not to mention the question required thinking. I wasn't the type to open up that easily because my brain was a factory of violent and execrated thoughts.

"I killed a cat when I was sixteen," I confessed.

His eyes grew wide. "No you didn't."

"I most certainly did," I admitted. "Are you going to arrest me for confessing to murder?" I stuck my wrists out.

"We need another shot," he said, "this conversation is going better than I expected."

"I'm just kidding, let me start over. You would never guess that I enjoy planting flower seeds in the garden I have behind my house," I said sarcastically.

"Bullshit," he said, "I want to know how you killed a cat. Was it by accident?"

"No, it was premeditated." I told the story nonchalantly. "Its owner was a nosey old hag named Ruth Jankowski, who dropped a dime on me, while my mother and her husband were away in New York for the weekend. My mom beat the shit out me and her husband grounded me for two weeks. I felt imprisoned in that house. I had a lot of time to think. So getting Ms. Jankowski back for snitching was never going to be erased from my mind until I did something about it." I gulped my beer, "I believe in the eye for an eye ethic."

Ray passed me the second shot glass. "How did you kill it?"

After downing the cognac, I continued my confession. "My mother had prescription bottles of different types of pills. I grabbed a bunch, crushed them into powder. Then I got...um...um," I sucked my teeth and snapped my fingers trying to recall the name of the solution I used. "Anti-freeze! So I mixed the crushed pills in a peanut butter and jelly sandwich, poured the anti-freeze in milk, and waited for the cat to come out." I let out an evil laugh.

I had never told anyone I killed Ms. Jankowski's nasty cat. Now the story made me laugh at how crazy that was.

Ray's face changed, as if he were trying to remember something. "You are something else! What's your mother's husband's name?"

"Andre Medeiros. He's a lieutenant in the Motorcycle Unit. He was with the K-9 until his dog bit my ex-boyfriend on the leg and he was transferred." I was talking a little too much.

"I know Andre. He trained me when I first got on the job. You had that man paranoid for months!"

I shut down. I wasn't interested in continuing the conversation but Ray pushed it. "Did you think Andre didn't know about it?"

"How much of this story do you know?" I asked. It seemed like the joke was on me since I assumed no one else knew.

"Well, between us, Andre came in the next day and told a few of us that story. He saw someone wearing a black hooded sweatshirt creeping through the yard. He thought it was someone trying to break in to his house. I guess he recognized you by your sneakers. But anyways, he watched you from behind the blinds pull out something and feed the cat. He found it even stranger that you stood there watching it eat. Didn't you step on it or something?"

"Wow, I forgot I stepped on his neck." I almost sounded remorseful.

"We teased Andre for months: You're still alive, man? He would shake his head and laugh because he said you hated him. He thought you were going to poison him next. " Ray laughed as he recounted Andre's version.

I was now guzzling my beer. Suddenly Ray moved up against me to let someone behind him get by. I caught a whiff of his cologne and measured how much taller he was than me. I felt so short but I liked it. Ray looked down at me and chuckled. Finally I joined him in a light laughter.

He then joked. "So tell me something, did you bury the cat in your flower garden?"

"Funny!" I appreciated his sense of humor. Every time he laughed and smiled, he bit the sides of his tongue, which I found cute.

I finished my beer. I excused myself to use the restroom, and then wandered to the roof top garden to brood alone and to cool off with some fresh air. I inhaled the night wind and sighed. The party inside was in full swing but I needed a moment to myself. I leaned against the stair railing, gazing out at the moon. I thought of leaving at that moment.

221

I felt an unmistakable presence of a man behind me. "Estas bien?" (Are you all right?) Ray whispered in my ear.

"Si, solamente necesitaba un poco de aire." (Yes, I just needed some air.)

"It's a beautiful night isn't it?" He came around and stood beside me.

"Yeah, I love how you can see the craters on the moon." I lightly touched his forearm.

"Is that how you got the name Sky, from staring at celestial objects?" He chuckled.

"As a matter of fact, smart ass, I did. It's where my thoughts run to."

"Are you into astrology?"

"Ironically, I never really got into that sort of thing, but my college professor told us once that there is a powerful energy behind every new moon and it's a good time to ask for something you desire."

"Is this a new moon I caught you staring at?"

I nodded yes. For a moment we remained quiet. He probably thought I was crazy or just plain drunk.

"Is there anything you want right now in your life?" I didn't take my eyes off the moon as I asked him.

"I want a promotion."

"Now say it again and mean it."

"I just did." He chuckled.

"Don't laugh. Just say it, but be specific this time. What type of promotion do you want?" I asked dryly.

"You are the strangest girl I've ever met."

"So I've been told. Now try it."

"All jokes aside, I want to get out of Precinct G."

"Where would you rather be?"

"I took the detectives exam a couple months ago. I really want to work in the Drug Unit. And if this crazy idea you have me speaking out loud works out in my favor, I'll treat you to a nice dinner."

"And ice cream. I love mint chocolate chip."

Frances came outside. "There you go! I've been looking for you."

"What's up?" I smiled.

"Your gift is beautiful. I love it!" She hugged me again out of appreciation.

"I had it blessed by my friend's aunt to protect you now that you'll be working on the streets."

She smiled. "You're too much. I'll leave you two alone, I just wanted to say thank you again."

"What did you get her?" Ray asked.

"A gold rosary."

"Wow. That was nice of you."

"Yeah, I guess. The jeweler gave me a good deal for two. I bought one for me and one for Frances."

"Where's yours?"

"I keep it in a special place."

He didn't ask me where that special place was. Instead he waved goodbye to some party guests who were leaving and then leaned in to ask me, "So what did you ask this new moon?"

"It's a secret." I laughed.

Our conversation was playful and flirtatious but we never exchanged numbers. I thought the night was going well, the chemistry was strong, but maybe he found me a bit too eccentric.

Right before we all decided to call it a night, one of the officers who I chatted with in the beginning of the party walked up to us and said, "When you get tired of this goof troop, give me a call."

223

I scoffed at his remark. When I looked at Ray, he winked his eye at me. His confidence was attractive also. He walked me to my car. "It was nice meeting you." He said as he closed my door.

"Same here," I responded, hoping it wouldn't be the last I seen him.

DISPATCH

As the sultry days of summer heated up, so was talk about getting rid of the police dispatchers and replacing them with civilians. The entire Communication Center was subject to major changes once this plan began. Dispatching is different from call taking. Call takers gather information from 911 to pass to the dispatchers, while dispatchers directed the cops on the street via radios. Dispatching was a position that gave total power over the police officers on the streets, along with a huge step in our pay grade. The officers opposed it, but we civilians were looking forward to this change.

While all this was being argued and processed, I worked without breaking stride. Rather than crossing my fingers, I wanted to earn that promotion. I showed up to work early and took as few breaks as possible. My attendance improved and I possessed a dedication with every 911 call I took. Even in the Support Room, where there was little supervision, I wanted to prove that I had outgrown the clerical duties and was ready for more responsibility.

When the dispatch position opened, half of the Communication Center went after it. Six positions were available. I applied knowing I had all the skills that qualified me for it. Unfortunately, I was denied the position. I was livid.

Rumor was the lieutenant who suspended me in the past was in the new captain's ear bad mouthing me. This may have been true, but I knew other factors played a part in the decision. Our department was overseen by a new commanding officer, Captain Dwayne Lyons. It was when Captain Lyons appeared in the Comm Center, he began to acquire his reputation as a pervert. If you wanted something done, wearing something skimpy and showing cleavage was the way to get it. And that's putting it lightly.

Flirting with management wasn't my style nor was brown nosing. Many other women call takers were the same way. A few would bat their eyelashes and wear low cut shirts to get their way, while some just accepted when management screwed them over to avoid the battles that came with standing up for yourself.

Captain Lyons was an incompetent supervisor who was dumped in the Communication Center because no other Precinct wanted him. He was like the Deputy Barney Fife character from the Andy Griffith Show; a goof ball who couldn't make a decision to save his life. I really believed that the department gave him a gun with only one bullet that he had to keep in his shirt pocket. It's enough to say he was a stumbling idiot. God bless him, I'm surprised he had enough brain power to keep his heart pumping.

When I got home from work, upset at being turned down for the dispatch position, I walked around the complex looking to buy a few bags of some chocolate thai from Rodney. In no tranquil humor I searched for him, especially when a few knuckleheads selling drugs in the complex were trying to ask for my money up front. I was no fool to that trick. Besides, I only bought from Rodney because his bags were generously large and we always covered our exchange with a hug.

No one seemed to know where Rodney was, so I sat on the bench in front of his mother's apartment to wait. A half an hour later, Rodney walked out the apartment building with a fine young lady I can describe as a red bone: a voluptuous light skinned black girl. She had blonde highlights in her long wavy hair, a turquoise sun dress, and white sandals.

"Wah gwan, Sky?" (What's up, Sky?)

"Hey Rodney, you still have some of that chocolate thai?" I whispered.

226

"Nuh, I ha nutten right now." He frowned, "Mi a go get yuh ganja from dem eediats over deh." (I'll get you weed from those idiots over there.) He pointed at the group.

"They offered it to me earlier but I chose to wait for you."

He chuckled. "Deh druggists will box bread outta yu fast." (Those dealers will try and cut into my money fast.)

I handed my money to Rodney to go buy it for me. I didn't know any of those young fellows. He took my money and counted it. He raised three fingers up at me and I nodded yes. I wanted three bags to last me a week.

"Sky, dis is mi gyal Coco!" (Sky, this is my girlfriend Coco.)

"Hi." I lifted my hand in a quick wave but she just gave me a half ass grin without saying a word.

Coco was the possessive type. She stood there with her arms crossed against her chest as Rodney spoke to me. She was less than pleased when he told her to wait there as he walked away to get me what I needed. Her presence made me a little uneasy but as fired up as I was from work, her rude ass became tedious to me.

When Rodney came back, he pulled out his fist to drop the bags in my hand. I gave back one of the bags and told him to roll it up. I was really going to piss off Coco now. Rodney smiled and pulled out a box of Garcia Vega cigars from his back pocket.

We sat there on the bench and smoked. She played with his dreads that were now long past his shoulders. We spoke about Xavier and how he stayed in touch with him, his car thieving brother Sean, and a little history on how he met Coco. He seemed madly in love with her.

By the end of our smoking session, Rodney asked me if I still had my Civic. He asked me if I was interested in getting rid of it. Sean was working in a tow company where Coco was a dispatcher and they were staging fake car accidents to scam insurance companies out of money. I agreed to it. I had been eyeing the BMWs in the Auto Hunter for months and this scam caught my attention.

The details were simple. I would bring my Civic to the tow company where Sean would stage the accident. The collision would take place inside an enormous garage where the tow company stored their vehicles. Sean sweeps the debris from the two cars and dumps it in an intersection late night to make it look legit. The other car owner would take the blame for the accident and take the points on their driver's license, but both cars would be a total loss. Once the insurance pays us for the total loss on our vehicles, we each had to pay Sean $500 for the job.

When I agreed with the plan, Rodney suggested I include Coco as a passenger. I didn't like the sound of that because she didn't appeal to me. But when he told me she would have to pay me a thousand dollars out of her claim money—to be included as an injured party—I accepted the offer.

A week later, on a rainy night, I got a call from an unfamiliar number while at work. When I answered, I didn't recognize the voice.

"Is this Sky?" Her voice was sweet.

"Yeah, who's this?"

"It's Coco."

"What's up?"

"Can you come by the tow lot tonight so we can talk?"

"I get out close to midnight. Is that cool?"

"Perfect. I'm at Ultimate Towing on Norfolk Ave."

Her voice didn't match the attitude she displayed when I met her. She was pleasant and polite. I figured money was the factor.

When I arrived at the tow lot, Sean was there with another guy named Speedy. I looked around the place and saw how humongous the storage area was. There were three cars, two tow trucks, a flatbed, and more space to fit about three more cars.

"Suh yuh ready, crazy?" (So are you ready, crazy) Sean asked with enthusiasm. His Jamaican accent was not as thick as Rodney's.

"For?" I asked, a bit confused.

"Ah git rid of this old metal." He slammed his hand on the hood of my car.

"When?"

"Now. Yuh can watch with Coco frah the office window and she'll explain how yuh will make out the accident report to match deh story."

"How will I get home?"

Sean sucked his teeth, "Yuh tink I'd leave yuh stranded, crazy? Coco will take yuh home."

They meant business. It was a rainy night, the set up was looking perfect, and Coco was welcoming this time around.

I watched Speedy and Sean clear out the storage area by removing all the tow trucks and cars. Speedy brought a 1994 Dodge minivan inside and Sean drove my Civic. My stomach was dancing a tango. This was different from when I use to watch Sean strip cars. Sean parked my car in the center of the storage area and got out to direct Speedy, who was putting on his seatbelt in the minivan, getting ready to crash it.

Speedy waited for Sean to give him the green light and BOOM! Just like that he rammed into my Civic, damaging the driver side front quarter panel. I stood in the office with my hand covering my mouth. When I turned to look at Coco, she was laughing at me. This was normal to her because she saw this all the time.

Sean swept all the pieces that were on the ground and placed it in a large black trash bag. He and Speedy drove off in a tow truck to find an intersection to dump the debris. Coco and I stayed behind discussing what chiropractor we were going to be seeing and what we were going to do with the claim money.

229

When Sean returned, he wrote down the intersecting streets, Ruthven Avenue and Harold Street. Then he gave me all the information of the other vehicle and how the report should say the owner failed to stop; causing the accident.

HIDDEN IN THE DARK

There I was in a dark room with a night light plugged on the wall. The darkness of the room overpowered the dim light. I felt lost, with little clue as to how I got there. I wanted to walk towards the light but I felt paralyzed. My eyes roamed around but it was black with nothing else to see.

A few more night lights appeared on the wall but not enough to illuminate the room entirely. I remained standing there, confused, waiting for something to transpire.

Soon enough, I saw what appeared to be a man and a woman making out on a couch. Though neither of them noticed my presence, I made my way to them with a heavy force that made me lumber like an elephant. When I got close, I could see it was a shirtless man hovering over a naked woman; rubbing his hands up her thighs. For a while she was motionless until a sudden nerve worked her up to massage her breasts. A strange smile pulled at the corner of his mouth as he lowered his head to go down on her. Before his mouth touched her vulva, he shot up to look at me. I didn't dare to move. The man had scruffy brown hair, creepy white eyeballs that jumped out at me, and gashes around his face.

Out of nowhere he retreated back into darkness and I was now in an underground bar. There was no music playing. Everything was black: the walls, the chairs, and the drinking cups. There was a small crowd of stoners with gothic clothing standing around doing absolutely nothing. I turned around to ask the bartender where the exit was. It was Keanu Reeves, the Canadian actor. Even though it was a bit loony, I saw him as my saving grace from this mysterious place. But safety was an illusion. He had a sad look in his eyes when he told me there was no exit. Unable to think straight or breathe, I found myself again in total darkness. That's when I heard my house phone ring. Still asleep, with no image in my head, I heard a recording: "This is a collect call from an inmate at The County Jail..."

My eyes flew open, as I realized I had awakened from a strange dream. Raindrops were tapping against my window, as I reached over, a little disoriented, to my nightstand and grabbed my dream book. Darkness denoted depression and desperation. It also meant I needed to control my temper. While dreaming with a celebrity like Keanu Reeves was seen as a hero I was searching to save me.

I rose from the bed and got ready to go in to work. When I got there, Massiel had a look that said she was hiding something. An overnight change in her attitude that was telling me something was wrong. Choosing to ignore her for the time being, I plugged in my headsets to the phone system and read my Cosmopolitan magazine.

Towards the end of our shift, one of my co-workers, Rasheeda, informed me that four more persons were hired for dispatch. My blood started to boil again when she mentioned the names of those who were hired. I wasn't one of them. The four hired were Rasheeda, an operator Jamal, Massiel, and a girl Katana who came from the Licensing Unit. That explained why Massiel was acting weird towards me. She didn't know how to tell me she had been hired for the dispatch position. I thought she knew me better than to think I wouldn't be happy for her, but I figured I'd deal with that issue later.

The following day, I arrived an hour and half before my shift to speak to the captain. It didn't surprise me to catch him flirting with one of the 911 operators inside his office.

"Can I speak with you?" I said with an unpleasant tone. I wished someone had stopped me from going in that man's office with such animosity.

"Why wasn't I chosen for the dispatch position?" I demanded an explanation. He began pointing the finger at the rest of the command staff, claiming it was a collective decision and Human Resources felt the others had interviewed a little better than me. The thing that irked me the most about him was he was a lousy liar.

"I have enough time and experience than some of the applicants that were hired. That's not fair."

"You can always apply when the position comes back around, Ms. Pino."

"So you can tell me the same thing you're telling me now; that it's HR who is picking the candidates. Sure, I'll be glad to reapply. I can't wait to hear the next excuse." I stormed out his office.

Massiel and two other girls, Shawna and Rasheeda, agreed it was a wrong move to confront a captain with such disrespect, even though I should have gotten the dispatch position.

I asked. "How the fuck did someone from Licensing that has no experience with 911 whatsoever get the position?"

"It's all politics in here, Sky. You're only going to make it harder on yourself next time the position opens up if they see how pissed off you are," said Rasheeda.

"I swear, sometimes I think these supervisors get a rise from watching us get upset." I bit into my sandwich.

"Stop giving them a reason," Massiel said with a snippy tone.

"And when were you going to tell me you were hired?" I snipped back.

"I just found out my damn self."

I didn't believe her but I chose to leave it alone. She was getting on my nerves with her sudden bad attitude. For the remainder of the shift, I imagined what my callers looked like and shared my humorous descriptions with Rasheeda to make the night go by fast.

HAPPY TIMES

The summer was taking off. I extended my vacation to three weeks—from mid July to the beginning of August. Reynalda concocted a spiritual bathing potion for me. I had to pour it over my body, from head to toe and light a candle on my altar. It was a remedy to clear my path and bring me good luck. I was still secretly struggling with my breakup with Calvin. She saw that it depressed me and that my horrid dreams became more frequent and intense. Reynalda wanted to open up a new passage for love to enter and help rid the night terrors. She also told me that Xavier was going to visit us. Finally some good news, for I missed him dearly. The distance made us grow distant. But knowing he was going to visit brought joy to my soul.

The spiritual potion Reynalda prepared for me was working wonders. My mood was lifted. I was sleeping better. Andre was going to help me finance a new BMW. Coco and I became close and continued going to chiropractic therapy together to keep up the charade of being injured. The accident claim was looking safe. And Sasha and I spent our nights hanging all over Boston—carefree.

Sasha was always a trip to have around, which people enjoyed. I was a little less sociable than her but either way we always had a good time where ever we went: cookouts, parties, and bumming on the beaches. We were spending so much time together that I asked her to move in with me. Moving Sasha in, help cut the rent cost in half and she had the freedom that she lacked living at her mother's. It worked perfectly for both of us.

One summer night, in mid August, Sasha and I were going to attend a sweet sixteen celebration which her younger brother was taking part in. We were in our apartment discussing who else was going to the party. I rolled up a joint in her room while she finished blow drying her hair. I smoked more freely in the house than before. No need for me to go to the attic or smoke outdoors because Andre and my mother were always out together whenever they weren't working. Andre even hired a house cleaning lady to come once a week because they were hardly ever there. The only time they were home was on Sunday mornings when all three of us would have brunch. I usually just made myself a plate and brought it upstairs, but sometimes they asked me to join them at the table.

I turned on the music in the living room and lit up the joint. I bobbed my head as I strolled back into Sasha's room to get high. She wasn't much of a smoker, but that night was special so she joined me.

"Hold up, Sky! Let me wrap my hair with a scarf. I don't want it to smell like weed."

I ignored her and kept smoking, forcing her to wrap her hair fast. Our favorite song, Try Again by the late Aaliyah came on. We screamed with excitement because we were both huge fans of this once beautiful artist. I sang the lyrics as I sat on Sasha's bed waving my hands in the air.

We finished smoking and I slipped into the bathroom to shower. When I got out and dressed, I saw Sasha sipping on something. "Try this." She handed me the glass.

"What is it?"

"Rum and coke."

I took a sip and said, "Pour me some."

She poured me a glass and I brought it to my room to enjoy while I got dressed. I threw on a short eggshell white Cheongsam dress engraved with baby blue Tibetan flowers and pulled my hair back in a bun with chopsticks. Sasha wore an elegant red Chinese gown with gold beaming patches at the neck, the traditional dragon design around the edges and a long slit on the side. She flat ironed her hair and wore it out. We continued to drink after we dressed, waiting for her sister to pick us up. We chose to ride with Jade since we planned on getting tanked that night.

Jade was outside honking her horn. Sasha and I ran around the house grabbing everything we needed. We were so tipsy we bumped into each other. We even bowed once like Chinese people and burst into laughter.

"Hurry up, Sky, you know Jade hates waiting," Sasha reminded me.

I hadn't seen Jade in over a year and I wasn't sure if I wanted to spend an evening of festivities with her. She was probably jealous of how my friendship with her sister had evolved throughout the years. It made me wonder if she would put a hex on us too. I was still secretly holding a grudge for all the voodoo tactics she put on Xavier and me. I resented her for him moving to New York. She was determined to separate us. But that night I put my feelings to the side because Sasha and I needed a sober driver.

Outside, we found Jade in a new silver BMW 3 Series. "Wow, Jade!" Sasha shouted. "I love your new car!"

Damn it! No way was I going to sport a new BMW after Jade bought hers.

"Hi Jade, how are you?" I politely greeted her.

"I'm fine, how about yourself?"

"I'm good. Maintaining."

Sasha looked at what Jade was wearing and then opened the visor to apply her red lipstick. "Someone didn't get the memo," she commented.

Jade wore a plain yellow spaghetti strapped dress with a pair of fancy high heeled sandals. She was avoiding the Chinese theme.

We drove to Knights of Columbus function hall on Washington Street in Roslindale. The hall was full of Asian décor and Chinese caterers. Many of the girls wore Chinese dresses; it was definitely a unique sweet sixteen. The birthday girl went to a private school where the students were predominantly Chinese and she didn't want a traditional sweet sixteen party.

Sasha and I walked straight to the bar, ordered our drinks, and walked back to our assigned tables.

"Why did we get the corner table in the back?" Sasha asked.

"We can get fucked up back here and no one will notice," I replied.

Since Sasha loved being the center of attention, she switched the name cards from an empty table to our table.

"What are you doing?" I asked.

"My brother is coming out in this and we deserve to sit up front." Her lips turned up at the corners.

"This ain't a wedding, bitch." I looked over at Jade, but she just shrugged her shoulders and sat down. I followed their lead, hoping no one cared that we were switching tables.

Everything started off well: the food was delicious, the atmosphere was fun and friendly, and we even watched a traditional Chinese dragon dance. I was having a great time. After the birthday girl made her appearance with the twin's brother, the party began. The disc jockey had his eye on Sasha the entire night. No wonder— the way she moved on the dance floor made her out like a video vixen. For one song, she was the only one dancing in the middle of the floor. She danced and drank without a care in the world. It's one of the things I admired most about her.

As I looked around the room at the guests, Ray entered the hall. My stomach dropped and twirled uncontrollably. I turned my attention back to Sasha, pretending as though I didn't see him. When he made his way over to my table, I was in awe. He bent down and kissed me on my cheek.

"Hello beautiful," he captivated me with his smile.

"Hey! What are you doing here?"

"This is my niece's birthday party," he explained.

"Oh wow! What a small world."

He pulled up a chair and sat beside me, but people came up to the table to speak to him, making it difficult for us to hold a conversation. An older woman came up to him, tugged at his hand, and invited him to dance. Jade leaned over and asked me, "Who's he?"

"He's a police officer I met a couple months ago," I replied.

"He's gorgeous! Is he single?" She sounded interested.

"I'm not sure, but a man that fine can't be single."

Ray returned to his seat. "That was my aunt. She asked me if you were my date."

I just smiled. That led me to believe there was a strong possibility that he was available. Sasha came back with two drinks, handed one to me.

"Sasha, this is Ray. Ray, this is my best friend, Sasha."

Sasha shook his hand and gave me a look that said: girl, make a move! I sipped on my rum and Coke and gave her the look that said: I'm working on it. She took off her shoes and headed back to the dance floor. Ray flirted with me for the rest of the night. My thoughts reverted back to that night we met and how well we connected. The alcohol and his presence had me perspiring.

As the night went on, we noticed each table had small cards with the Chinese Zodiac written on them. Ray picked one up and read it to himself. When he finished reading, he passed it to me. According to this astrology I was a crazy horse who loved freedom.

He asked, "What's your sign?"

"What's *your* sign?" I returned the question.

"I'm the snake," he answered seductively.

"Do you bite?" I leaned back a little, as if I were scared to get close.

He whispered in my ear, "Only if you let me."

I jelled up quickly.

Before I knew it, everyone collected their purses, center pieces, and headed out the door. The party was over. Ray stood up and kissed me goodbye on the cheek. I was still seated at the table waiting for Sasha. The disc jockey was interested in her and they were exchanging numbers. Jade and I waited for her to finish. While we waited, I cracked open a fortune cookie. It read: *You can always find happiness at work on Friday.* I folded the fortune slip in half. It didn't apply to me, I thought, because Fridays were my nights off.

"Come on, Sasha," Jade grew impatient. Sasha staggered out the hall with Jade and I.

A crowd of guys were hanging out front of the function hall. "Is she all right?" one asked.

"Yeah, she's fine," I replied.

The guy then followed us to the side street where we had parked. A little nervous, I stopped to stare at him.

"What, you don't know me anymore?" he asked.

"Oh my God, Adrian!"

Adrian was unrecognizable. He was twice the size from when I last saw him five years before. His hair was cut low, almost bald. It broke my heart to see how his appearance was dirty and greasy. It was clear he was still living a hard and heavy lifestyle. Jade and Sasha glared at him with disgust before getting inside the car.

At that moment, Ray appeared out of nowhere and asked, "Is there a problem here?"

No one said anything, especially me, who acted like Adrian was a stranger. Where did Ray come from? Slightly drunk, shocked at Adrian's appearance, I just stood there. I started to hear the Twilight Zone theme in my head, do do do do...do do do do. Adrian stared Ray down, threw out his cigarette butt and walked off.

"Sky, are you okay?"

240

I became present again and responded, "Yeah…yeah, I'm fine."

"What did that guy want?"

"I don't know."

Ray thought Adrian was harassing us, but I didn't bother explaining he was an old buddy from my childhood. I was too ashamed to admit I knew someone with such a poor appearance. Yet I felt horrible for just standing there and not really acknowledging Adrian. Before I opened the car door, I handed Ray the fortune cookie I still had folded in my hand.

"Here's my number, call me." I was being sarcastic since he hadn't asked for my number.

Why? The chemistry between us was strong.

I got in the car and left. It was 1:30am and the nightclubs in Downtown were about to close. Jade said she wanted to drive around the area and watch the drunk people come out. That's not the reason: she wanted to show off her new car or maybe she was stalking someone. Sasha was passed out in the front seat but I agreed to go for the ride.

We drove by Boylston St, watching people waddle out the clubs. We stopped to watch two drunken guys ready to fist fight outside the Wang Theatre on Tremont Street. We laughed and yelled out the window, instigating the fight.

"Hit him! Don't let him talk to you like that!"

Jade dropped us off at the house at about 2:30am. Sasha was still passed out in the front seat. I opened her side of the door and woke her up. "Come on girl, we're home."

DIFFERENT COVERS

My vacation was over and it was time to go back to work. Time away helped me return refreshed. It was a hot Sunday, and unlike any other summer night in the city, 911 was quiet.

Rasheeda came and sat with me during her break from dispatch training. She was filling me in on what was going on in the department while I was away. Captain Lyons was having an affair with one of the new dispatchers. The trainer was ready to fail her but Captain Lyons was pushing for the trainer to be patient. If she continued to have a hard time, he would extend her training for another week.

Another tale was that the dispatchers and operators were going toe to toe arguing all the time. The new position had gotten to their heads; making them behave like they were superior to the call takers.

None of that interested me until she mentioned that a new order came out; which was when police officers were transferred around the force. This meant some of our supervisors were leaving the Communication Center. I was looking forward in having new sergeants and lieutenants.

I asked Rasheeda if she knew anything about why Massiel was acting indifferent to me. I was away for three weeks and she never once called me. Rasheeda opened her eyes wide. "You didn't hear?"

"Hear what?"

"She's pregnant."

"Pregnant?" I was surprised. "That explains why she was so moody with me before I left."

"Moody? The girl won't even tell anyone who got her pregnant."

"Why?"

"No one up here knows. She's been miserable since she found out. Shawna said she overheard her talking on the phone that the father of the baby doesn't want it. But Massiel is going to keep it whether he's involved or not."

"That's awful. Maybe I should talk to her." I knew what it was like to have a man force me to abort.

"No. Leave that alone. Massiel is stubborn and hates when people pry in her business. Let her figure this out on her own or wait for her to tell you."

"Okay. Now what's up with the new girl?"

"Oh, you mean Kat. That bitch is weird as hell. She doesn't talk to anyone."

"What's wrong with her?"

"Everything. She looks like she belongs with the Adam's family."

Katana Nowak was a Polish girl who was anti-social and mysterious. She was blonde with blue eyes and stood 5 feet 7 inches. She didn't look at anyone when she walked pass them and spent her breaks alone with her head down on the table. No one ever saw her eat, use the ladies room, or socialize with anyone. Rumor was she got the dispatch position because her father, Lieutenant Aaron Nowak, worked in the Anti-Corruption Unit. Some said she didn't have a good relationship with her father but everyone respected her because of him.

Her style was gothic and her fashion was punk rock. My first impression of Katana was that she was angry about something none of us could figure out. She didn't associate with anyone unless it was work related. Rasheeda also mentioned that people suspected she

243

was a racist against Blacks and Hispanics. I was warned to stay out of her way.

Towards the end of the summer, a co-worker and I traded days off. I never liked giving up my weekends, but I didn't have anything planned that Friday. Not that I ever planned half the things I did; my motto has always been: I go where ever the wind takes me. Sasha's motto was: expect the unexpected. No matter the proverb, something always came up for us to do.

At about 9:00 at night, I stepped out the office to buy a soda from the vending machine. When I opened the door to the break room, I noticed a man's raggedy old wallet on the table. No one was in there so I picked it up to see who it belonged to. Katana's ID card was inside, with her entire paycheck. What in the world was she doing with a man's wallet? That *was* strange. But anyhow, I went to go return her wallet.

I bought a can of Pepsi and made my way to the dispatch area to look for Katana. Her trainer had let her go early because she seemed upset. I asked him how he could tell she was upset since she seemed disconnected from the outside world. He jokingly said she was hissing all night. Another dispatcher chuckled and joined in to say she was frightened when Katana drew back her lips and bared her teeth like an angry cat. I walked away laughing at the jokesters to finish up my work in the office. I put the wallet in my back pack and figured I'd give it to Katana next time I saw her. Leaving a wallet full of cash with anyone else was risky, especially if money turned up missing.

Once I returned to the office, the clerk I was working with had to stay for the next shift. She told me to take the rest of the night off. She had me covered. So I grabbed my back pack and headed out the doors. When I got off the elevator in the main lobby, the front desk officer called me over.

"Someone left something here for you." He handed me a small book.

"A book?" I looked at it and laughed, "Who left this here?"

"I don't know. It was here when I came in."

"Thanks, John. Have a good night." I slowly walked away reading the cover and the back of this book.

Katana was outside the building, finishing the last of her cigarette. I approached her to give her the wallet. As I got near her, she rudely gave me her back.

"Hey Kat...Katana," I stuttered.

She turned to look at me with a mean unflickering stare. It screamed: what the fuck do you want? I quickly pulled out the wallet from my back pack and handed it to her.

"I, um, found this in the break room."

She softened the stare. "Thanks. You don't know how much I appreciate this. This wallet belonged to my grandfather before he died; it means a lot." Her eyes were glossy like she had been smoking grass or she was about to tear up.

"You're welcome." I learned how valuable something could be to someone regardless of its outer appearance. She had such a tough exterior, I would have never guessed a wallet lost could have hurt her so much.

She tried pulling out a twenty dollar bill to give me but I stopped her, "Uh uh, you don't have to."

"All right then, I'll buy you lunch tomorrow."

"Now *that*, I won't refuse." I smiled. But she didn't smile back. Instead, she thanked me again and said goodbye. She really did have a cold demeanor.

I turned to walk to my car. As I got closer to the parking lot, I opened the book again. It was Ray Povez who sent me an astrology book and wrote on the back of the front cover in big bold letters: **I'm a Scorpio and I'm free this weekend**. With it, he left his number for me to call him. It was the most original way a man had ever showed interest in me. When I opened the book to his sign, The Scorpio, he highlighted the section: How To Seduce A Scorpio, and all the traits that described him best.

According to what I read in this book, high voltage was written all over Ray. He wanted to teach me how to get close to him. Judging by the description he highlighted, I either had a lot to look forward to or much to fear.

FLIRTING WITH DANGER

Coco and I drove together to physical therapy the following morning. I brought the book with me to show her and see what she thought about it. I knew word would get back to Calvin that I was moving on, so I made sure to bring the proof for her to read.

We arrived on time to the chiropractor's office on River Street in Mattapan Square. The girl at the front desk told us the therapist was running late, so we walked to McDonalds for breakfast. We sat there eating our sandwiches and discussing Ray.

"He comes off strong, don't you think?" Coco was analyzing the highlighted sections of the book.

"I didn't see it that way, but now that you mention it, yeah, he does. You have to see him though. Coco, he's fine; like universally fine."

"What is universally fine?" She laughed.

"Every woman would agree that he's attractive even if he's not their type."

"You sound crazy."

"I am crazy...a little crazy about him."

She handed me back the book. "Have you called him?"

"No. I'm afraid to."

"Why?"

"I'm not really sure how to explain it."

My heart was afraid that it would suffer again. I wasn't completely over Calvin and I wasn't sure of Ray's intentions. Didn't how to seduce a Scorpio mean he just wanted a sexual relationship? I didn't have much experience and felt I wasn't ready to just give myself to anyone yet.

"Well if it makes you feel any better, at least you know what you're getting into with this Ray guy. He seems pretty straight forward. Call him. There has to be more to this book, I mean Ray, than just the cover," she laughed.

After physical therapy, I called Ray to thank him for the book. After about an hour of conversing, he invited me to go out with him. We made plans to go watch The Cell starring Jennifer Lopez later that evening. Before hanging up he told me he would call me to confirm our date. I was overly excited and looking forward to it.

It was still early in the afternoon when I got home. I laid my head on the pillow of the couch and felt myself drift off. I was looking for a little rest before my movie date with Ray. My eyes closed and slipped into a deep sleep.

During my nap, I found myself in a dream sweeping my attic. As I swept away I noticed my attic was dusty and full of boxes. The more I swept, the more the dust surfaced. I tried moving the boxes around but they were heavy. I thought about getting Andre to move them but then I thought he would want to know what were in them. I didn't want him policing my attic and discovering the guns. Yes, guns. Something in my spirit made me believe those were weapons that were packed away without actually looking inside.

Afterwards, I walked out the attic and my dream shifted to Star Trek's Starfleet ship. Inside the orbital office was a group of naked females, seated in the rear. They all sat there quietly like they were waiting for something. Two robotic security guards at the door and a suited gentleman sitting at the control panel were pressing buttons and speaking over a radio. The transmission was unclear but I sensed trouble for these women prisoners. I thought about saving them by distracting the guards so they could break free. I coughed uncontrollably and held my chest as I threw myself on the floor. My theatrical approach failed. No one moved to help me. The entire crew ignored my plea for medical attention. Even the women lacked emotion and ignored me.

I woke up from my dream coughing. Sasha was in the living room drinking and smoking a cigarette. I fanned the smoke out of my face.

"Cigarettes are nasty." I sounded grumpy.

"I'm sorry, Sky." She stood up to open the window.

"What's the matter with you?"

"Nothing." She was lying. Something was on her mind. "Go look at your caller ID."

"I'm too tired to get up, who called?"

"The Commonwealth of Massachusetts." She exhaled and looked at her fumes take shape, and then disappear into non-existence.

"Calvin?" I sat up on the couch. "Did you accept the call?"

"I almost did, but I wasn't sure how you would react."

I jumped up to check the caller ID. The nerves in my stomach made me run to the toilet. It made me physically ill to find out he was calling me. What did he want? Then I remembered that strange dream I had in the underground bar, where I heard the collect call coming in, before waking up. I knew there was a reason behind this call, I just couldn't figure out what it was.

I washed up in the bathroom and remembered my movie date with Ray. I went in my bedroom to roll a joint, pick out an outfit, and read my dream book to distract my mind from Calvin's collect call. The attic represented the mind. It held secrets and hidden thoughts, while the boxes were a symbol of how I boxed in a lot of my emotions. The broom was telling me to clear up my spiritual space. This all made sense because I had also neglected my saints on my altar. They were calling me.

Nothing in the book mentioned Star Trek, but I looked up spaceship and it read that I was going to face a puzzling situation that would make no sense to me. That interpretation alone was confusing. So I decided to clean my attic as I saw in my dream to give the saints on my altar some fruit and money as an offering.

I grabbed my broom out of the pantry and a rag to dust off the altar. Sasha offered to help me clean the attic because she had never been up there. I told her the attic was infested with mice to scare her. I knew how strongly she felt about mice and I didn't want her to discover my altar since she was also against Santeria. She decided to clean the living room instead, to eliminate the cigarette odor she left behind.

When I entered the attic, my heart dropped and my body trembled. There was a piece of a cotton fiber insulator in the middle of the floor. A strong wave of psychic ability came over me causing me to shake. I pictured a gun underneath that foam piece like in my dream. I had never experienced such a strong conviction like I did at that moment. With a supernatural effort, I forced my hand not to tremble as I bent down to lift the insulator off the floor. Calvin's .380 semi-automatic pistol used to shoot Brian had been concealed in the ceiling the entire time. The weight of it finally pushed through and fell out.

I cleaned the gun and set it aside. I began to sweep the floor and thought of ways to discard it. Another thought was to keep it. After I swept the floor, I dusted off the artifacts on my altar and placed three peaches on it and money as an offering to my saints. When I removed the dead flowers from its small vase, it fell backwards. I got on my knees to reach back there for the vase and felt a small box. What next? It was a box of ammunition.

250

HANDS ON OR HANDS OFF

Sasha helped me get ready for my date. As usual, I tied my hair in a bun, but she insisted on straightening it out with a flat iron. She even trimmed my ends. My hair was so long that it passed my waist when she ironed it. I didn't like makeup, but I did put on mascara and a thin black line above my eye lid with a liquid liner Sasha had. It made my eyes stand out beautifully.

Ray picked me up at nine o'clock that night. As soon as I stepped out on the porch, I caught Andre and Ray talking outside in our driveway. Because the two hadn't seen each other in so long, the conversation carried on longer than it should have. I ran back upstairs to take one last look at myself and then I ran back downstairs. They were still in a deep conversation. I interrupted them by lying to Andre, saying my mother wanted him.

I got inside Ray's car and sat quietly during the ride—extremely nervous—trying to think of something interesting to talk about. But my mind was blank.

"What's going on with you?" Ray placed his hand on my lap and rubbed it.

"Nothing."

"You look sort of out of it."

"I'm just listening to your taste in music. What is this?"

"It's Latin Freestyle."

"I kind of like it, it sounds like house music. What's the name of this song?"

"Fallen Angel, by Coro. I'll make you a CD."

"Oh cool. I'd like that."

In the minutes before we pulled up to the Showcase Cinema in Revere, my mind was in utter chaos. I thought of how crazy I was for keeping the gun; Calvin's call reawakening my heart to sorrow; my dreams were strange; and Ray's presence blew my mind.

"What did Andre say about you taking me out?" I blurted.

After turning off the engine of his car, I thought he'd answer my question. Instead, Ray gently slipped his hand behind my neck and in the depths of my hair. With his touch the chaos in my head became calm. My mind slowed down and caught every detail of his move. He leaned in, turning his head, and pressed his lips to mine. Slowly we opened our mouths, swirling our tongues together. I felt the rise and fall of his breathing. I was lost in the sensation of it all. My hand flattened against his chest, slid upwards over his shoulder. I felt a pinch of sexual desire in between my legs. Then he made little butterfly kisses around my face towards my ear. To my pleasure, he whispered that he wanted me.

And then, there was silence; that calm, deadly silence that makes you feel worse than getting yelled at. We barely knew each other but he wanted me. That feeling alone made me feel a bit uncomfortable. Was he pretending to like me just to get me in bed or did he like me enough that he didn't want to wait? Would he still like me the morning after? Would the thrill exist after the chase was gone? Then I thought of how his kiss sent a charge through my body.

I pulled away. "Give me time to get to know you better." He didn't take it as a rejection. He found it more challenging.

"I respect that." He smiled at me. "Come on, before we miss the movie."

We walked across the parking lot to the cinema and I remembered he didn't answer my question. "What did Andre say when he saw you in the driveway?"

Ray lifted his shoulders high and with a deep voice mimicked Andre, "Keep your hands off my step-daughter or I'll break your neck."

"He didn't say that," I laughed.

"Damn near," he laughed back, making it impossible for me to believe him.

"No seriously, did he say anything?"

"All jokes aside, he said you're a little rough around the edges but that you are a good girl. And if my intentions weren't to take you seriously, I should drive off his property immediately."

This sounded more like Andre. He told me before, in one of his kinder moments, I showed great potential and with time I'd blossom into something greater.

"What was your response?"

"I told him we're just having fun. I'm getting to know you, you're getting to know me and time will tell where we end up. Then I said, with all due respect Andre, but if you don't approve of me seeing Sky then you need to speak with her. Then he said it's not that he doesn't approve of it, he's making sure you don't get hurt. I told him I'm not out to hurt anyone, we're just having a good time."

"You said all that to him?"

"I'm twenty six years old, sweetheart. I don't need another man telling me how to treat his step-daughter. I have sisters, a mother, and two girls of my own. There won't be any misunderstanding as long as we're both clear as to what we want."

The step-daughter comment made me cringe but I refrained from barking at him. I was more impressed that Ray stood up to Andre. It must have been a cop thing, where they sword fight with their dicks.

"I just don't want to catch feelings for you and then end up getting sandbagged."

"Oh yeah? Well I don't want to fall for that innocent act, and then I'm found stiff somewhere from poison!"

I punched him in the arm and laughed. "That's not funny."

After the movies, a wave of hunger cramped our stomachs. We drove to Revere Beach and bought two shrimp plates with fries

253

from Kelly's Roast Beef. We sat on the beach's stone wall and ate. We watched State Police drive by numerous times watching the area. It made me question his career and what type of officer he was. He seemed so laid back with a humorous personality, unlike Andre who was an asshole for a cop. The more I listened to him, the more intriguing he was.

"I'm an honest cop. I'm just as much a cop to the blacks as I am to the whites, Hispanics, Asians, rich, poor, ugly, and the uglier. I could care less. You break the law; then I'm taking you in. What bugs me the most is when people test me. Don't confront me when I'm giving you the chance to move it along. Everyone wants to challenge the policeman. We're chastised if we use force on someone, but it's perfectly fine for a criminal to do what he wants against me or other people, but in no way can I touch him. I don't see the logic in that."

He got up and threw away our trash. I raised my napkin to cover my smile so he wouldn't notice how giddy and child-like he made me feel. When he came back he took me by my hand. We started to walk, hand in hand, towards the edge of the breaking waves.

"I think I want to challenge you, Officer Povez," I teased.

"If you want to challenge me, you better be a real good bad ass to take me." He gave me a big smile.

"I don't scare easily, officer. I'm dumb that way."

I took off my shoes and let my bare feet dig into the sand of the beach.

We stopped to look at one another. Nothing needed to be said, we just engaged in a kiss. He wrapped his arms around my waist as I stood on my tippy toes with my arms around his neck to kiss him back. He was affectionate; caressing my arms and hair while our tongues made out. Our kisses seemed to be getting longer, when he bent down to pick me up.

254

"Aah!" He surprised me when he lifted me and carried me in his arms.

"I hope you know how to swim because you're going in," he threatened to toss me in the ocean.

"No, I hate salty water!"

"I thought you'd be more worried about your hair," he laughed.

"I don't care about my hair! I hate beach water!"

He ran to the shore and dumped me right into the ocean. With no remorse, he just tossed me in. I didn't think he was going to do it, but he did! He stood there laughing at me. I got up and splashed water on him. He turned around to run off but I jumped on his back, trying to take him down. Even the laughter didn't make him weak enough to lose his balance. It was a great night and wet fun.

We walked back to the car and he went in his trunk, still chuckling as I stood there soaking wet. He pulled out a towel and a blanket. After closing the trunk he handed me the towel. I threw the towel around me and we returned to the beach. He pulled out the blanket for us to sit on. He told me he had planned on taking his daughters to the lake the next day so he had already packed everything to save time.

"It's late though. Shouldn't you be heading home to get rest?" I didn't want to be guilty of him being too tired to hang with his daughters; but he usually worked late hours and always functioned well.

"I'll be fine, don't worry about it. Unless you want to leave now."

"No, let's stay awhile."

Sitting up on the blanket, I sat in front of Ray with his arms around me. The ocean view was incredibly serene, that I rested my head back on his chest. We spent the entire night talking, learning all about each other, and shamelessly flirting. Occasionally he planted butterfly kisses on the side of my face, my neck, and shoulder. It was a sweet experience. We stayed there until the sun came up and started shining mildly at us. The huge red ball that made the whole world around us glow was also our cue to call the date to an end.

POLITICS IS IN

Autumn brought forth an unrivaled blaze of colors throughout the city, making everything vibrant. This wild season was showing me how to reach for a brighter horizon, clear away the pain, and create a fresh life.

"Michael is running for Mayor again," Andre poured himself a cup of coffee and stole the toast off my plate. "You should consider volunteering for his campaign."

"Volunteer?" I frowned.

"Yes, volunteer." He took a bite out of the toast. "What's the worst that can happen? You'll learn a thing or two about politics."

"I don't see the benefit of working for free." I stared at my mother's plate, contemplating on taking her toast.

"The point is, you scratch the Mayor's back now and later you may need him to scratch yours."

"Do you volunteer?"

"No. I'm a sponsor." He rubbed his fingers, indicating he donated money.

"Why can't I just *sponsor*?" I mimicked his hand gesture.

"You can if you want, but I'm telling you to support the campaign with your time and put that brain of yours to good use."

"I'm not interested. I have other things going on." I reached for the toast off my mother's plate.

"No you don't, Sky," my mother slapped my hand and I dropped her toast. "You're wasting your time partying with Sasha. This is a good opportunity for you to get involved with politics."

"I'll make a deal with you, Sky." Andre set down his mug. "If you help with Michael's campaign committee, I won't charge you rent until December."

I didn't understand why Andre insisted for me to become this sort of political geek, but I threw up my hands in the air. "Fine! You got me."

The weeks following the election in November, Mayor Kirsch asked me to collect all donations at his fundraiser event and help his campaign manager look over the finances. I even attended the candidate's debate at City Hall where I picked up a few tips on how to argue a point without losing patience. Kirsch did an outstanding job debating. Many were upset that his opponent was being interrupted, saying Kirsch was rude for it. But he did it to get the truth out. When his opponent would claim he did something for the community, Kirsch would laugh and say no you didn't.

Working with the campaign committee during the day and going to work in the evenings, kept me so busy, I didn't have any time to myself. My co-workers constantly told me that I sounded tired. I sounded tired, because I was.

Meanwhile, back in the political scene of Headquarters, new supervisors were transferred to the Communication Center. Now we had two lieutenants and three new sergeants. Lieutenant Apple Crumb, Lieutenant Mocha, Sergeant Honey G, Sergeant Blueberry Muffin, and Sergeant Coffee Roll. Out of the five, Lieutenant Apple Crumb, Sergeant Coffee Roll, and Sergeant Honey G were assigned to my shift. And I was grateful that this new group of supervisors was excellent, with the exception of one, who didn't have the sense to blow hot soup.

Lieutenant Apple Crumb was a tall and slim Caucasian man. Those who knew him spoke highly of him. He was down to earth, funny, and slow to anger. But when he got upset, it was in our best interest to stay out of his way. I heard once that his ancestors belonged to the Klu Klux Klan, but I didn't believe that. He had so much soul and was genuinely good to us minority civilians. There wasn't a racist streak in his bone. Although in the back of my mind I

258

sometimes thought if he came from a line of KKK's, were they turning over in their graves.

One sergeant in particular couldn't have been any more perfect in my eyes—a Mark Wahlberg look-a-like. He wore his uniform with an air that said he knew he looked good in it. A man of few words, I thought, not that it mattered. It wasn't his vocal dexterity I was attracted to. He was an alpha male; confidant, handsome, and dominant. His name was Sergeant Honey G.

Sergeant Honey G was a well-respected man. He pulled no punches with anyone, but he was fair with how he treated us. One time, I lost my temper with another co-worker on his watch, forcing him to give me an oral warning with the threat to write me up if it ever happened again. As his reprimand faded into the background, all I thought was how sexy he was when he got mad. It really turned me on, but I didn't want to provoke his anger because the result wouldn't have ended with makeup sex. It would have been a suspension and another strike on my record file.

To some degree, the treatment we were receiving at work was appeasable. I gained a whole new level of respect for these supervisors. When they came on board, things changed. They cultivated the right attitude and were more engaged in what we did; which built a good working team.

All these changes, along with helping Mayor Kirsch's campaign became overwhelming. As it turned out; that had its flipside. My new love interest with Ray and friendship with Massiel sifted away like sand. I maintained a guise as a strong woman but inside I felt I had been trampled under a mob. My saddened heart had to accept the fact that Ray and I were in two different places in our lives. He worked overnights and did a lot of overtime in the day. All while trying to gain equal custody rights over his daughters. Massiel, on the other hand, was close to seven months pregnant and was a completely different person. Any time I was around her I felt a dense and heavy energy. We weren't vibing like before, yet I thought it was just the pregnancy.

NEVER KNOWING WHERE YOU'LL FALL

The sparkling colors of the autumn leaves were starting to fade and the colder period was setting in. The leaves descended sadly to the ground as the wind howled. A haunting sound came as I walked through the crispy leaves in my driveway. In no rush to go upstairs, I circled the house slowly. The lights on the first floor were on and the shades all drawn. Something deep inside me didn't feel right.

I couldn't explain what I was feeling but some things in my life were unpredictable. Sort of like the way weather forecasters are blindsided with storms, even with loads of data at their fingertips. Some days I was ecstatic; my entire being seemed to be one with luminance. Other days I was melancholy and didn't know why my life appeared to be one horrid pandemonium.

I came home to an empty house. I picked up my phone to call Ray, just to hear his voice, but I hung up before I finished dialing and tossed the phone on my bed. Instead I turned on my stereo to listen to the CD he made for me. I forwarded to song 8. It was the song that mostly reminded me of him; Fallen Angel by Coro.

After playing the song a few times, I turned off the stereo and went to my room. I searched through my grandmother's old books for a simple spell that would lure Ray back. As my eyes skimmed the pages of the book of love spells, I found a tobacco prayer to Saint Martha. This prayer would have me on his mind.

Because I didn't have a cigar to smoke with the prayer, I used a cigarette. I went to Sasha's room. She always kept a box of Newport on her dresser. I stole a cigarette and made my way to the attic. I lit an old red candle on my altar and sat Indian style. Pulling on the cigarette, I read the prayer.

"I offer this prayer to the charitable spirits of the Guardian Angel of Ray Povez, for the holy day on which he was born, to the four winds and their places in which they're found. Have him cling to me, love me, and do not let him forget me." I took another pull off the cigarette. "Spirit of force, give strength to Ray Povez, so he can love me and come to me wherever I am. Spirit of illusions, let the illusion of Ray Povez be over me. Spirit of despair, let the desperation of Ray Povez be over me. Charitable spirits, here I surrender the body, soul, and will of Ray Povez. Do not let him eat, sleep, drink, walk, or work without thoughts of me indelibly etched into his mind, that my name is Cecilia Pino." I finished the cigarette by completely focusing on him.

The following day, I bought a new Saint Martha candle and dressed it with Come To Me oil. I read the tobacco prayer every twelve hours for three days but kept the candle lit in the attic in hopes of him returning. The timing, I thought, was perfect. Sasha was out all weekend with a new guy she was seeing so I didn't have to explain the smell of smoke on me.

Days went by after my prayer to Saint Martha and yet no result. So to take my mind off it and allow things to fall into place, I decided to share brunch with Andre and my mother. It had been a while since I ate with them on a Sunday afternoon. When I walked downstairs, I found it odd that there wasn't any smell of cooking in the air.

I knocked on the door a few times but there was no answer. I assumed they decided to eat out instead. Just as I was making my way back upstairs, I heard a car enter the driveway. I turned back around to open the front door and see who it was. Two officers in an unmarked cruiser were stepping out.

I closed the door behind me and walked out to the porch to greet them. In front of me stood a tall, slim black gentleman with a shiny bald head. His partner was a tall, medium build, Hispanic man with salt and pepper hair. They asked me about Andre.

I pressed my hands against my face and rubbed my eyes. Something wasn't right. Where were Andre and my mother? Why were these FBI looking men inquiring about Andre?

The Hispanic officer must have asked me in three different ways where could they find Andre. Scratching my head, trying to understand why they were there, I questioned them as well.

"Can you tell me what this is about?" I thought something tragic happened to my mother and they came to notify Andre. "Oh my God, is my mother all right?"

"Nothing we can talk about in specifics. Are you Officer Medeiros' daughter?" the black officer took over the conversation when he saw that I was concerned about my mother.

"No. I'm his wife's daughter. Is he in trouble? Is my mother in trouble? Can't you tell me something?"

"We just have some questions for him."

I stared at them. It takes a lot to surprise me but not much to leave me speechless. When the officers left, I flew upstairs. Halfway up, I stopped. I turned around and flew down the stairs thinking I should check the garage. When I reached the bottom of the stairs, I thought let me get a hooded sweatshirt because it was cold outside. I turned around again to go back up the stairs to my apartment. I was so nervous that I couldn't think straight, running up and down those stairs. Then a headache came on. I threw on a gray sweater and grabbed the keys. I ran outside, opened the garage doors, and found both their cars parked there.

Fortunately, they never changed their locks to their apartment when I moved upstairs. Not that I ever used the keys to walk in; I didn't want to risk catching them having sex or walk in the middle of a fight. My mother was feisty when provoked. Andre caught a slap in the face once for accusing her of flirting with the cable guy.

But that morning, I turned the key in the door. I searched around the entire house and found all the lights on and their bedroom ransacked. Clothes were thrown all over the bed and floor. The closet was wide open with empty shoe boxes and hangers scattered around. Some drawers were open with few undergarments in them. My mother's purse was gone. Andre's safe was empty. These two pulled a disappearing act.

The kitchen was left clean. I checked the medicine cabinet and my mother's prescription bottles were gone. My mind was racing, intensifying my headache. Andre's office was locked, as usual. So I climbed up the kitchen counter looking for the office key inside the cabinet.

I unlocked his office door and found that his computer was gone. The only thing left was his desk and a few boxes. I looked through the boxes and found pornographic DVDs. Strange enough, each box contained a different type of film, but they were all brand new, as if they were for sale. The only thing these movies had in common was their production label: Silk Stockings. I took one of each and brought it upstairs.

All this confusion was making me sick to my stomach, so I called out sick from work that afternoon. I went to my room and placed the movies in my underwear drawer. The phone rang, startling me. I didn't recognize the name on the caller ID so I answered it in a low tone, "Hello."

"Hey Sky, it's Massiel."

"What's up?" I tried sounding like she had interrupted my sleep.

"Can we talk?"

"Right now is not a good time. I'll call you back later." That was a lie. I wasn't in the mood to hear her. She hadn't spoken to me in over four months and she caught me at the wrong time.

I lit a joint in my bedroom to shut off my mind. That attempt failed, so I pulled out one of the porn videos and inserted one in my DVD player. From my bed, I reached over to lock my door. Sasha wasn't home and I sure didn't want her to catch me watching a freak show.

The video began with a young woman in a teddy alone in her bed. Oh the irony! I was never into porn but Calvin made me watch them sometimes. After a few seconds another woman came in and joined the woman in some foreplay. I had never watched lesbian eroticism but this was a fantastically lustful view.

My body was starting to relax and my mind clear. I wondered how many people did what I was about to do. I slowly spread my legs apart. My fingers lightly brushed over my stomach making its way down my sweatpants. It slipped between my folds and I began to work my hand in circles round and round on my clit, pushing my hips against it. The rest of my body was enjoying the pleasure of my hand over my sweet spot. A sensational feeling started rising and growing stronger. Suddenly, I stopped. I thought I heard someone at the door. But then I realized I was just high.

I dipped my fingers back down to that area again. I gathered some of the moisture there and spread it along my nubbin, increasing the speed and force. It was Calvin's hand I was imagining touching me as my body tensed up for two seconds before erupting into a powerful climax. I gasped out loud sending me into tears. Why the fuck was I crying? The hand that was pleasuring me was mine— not his. I had only experienced orgasms with him. My climax brought me back to the time we were together. It's probably why I ended up crying.

I turned off the DVD player and ran to the bathroom. I switched on the shower as I undressed myself. The house phone started ringing again. I just ignored it and jumped in the shower.

Later that evening, I sat on my couch, still in my bathrobe, smoking what probably was my fifth joint. The living room smelled heavily of pot but it was almost impossible for me to be sober without knowing the circumstances behind Andre and my mother's disappearance. In the midst of my thoughts I became aware that my wish for Andre to disappear became a reality. I found myself in the position during my grandmother's ritual, of deciding Andre's fate, and it wasn't done in a small way. A simple divorce would have worked for me, but at the time I was angry and wished for it in haste.

I turned on the television to BET Rap City: The Basement. Watching rap videos was helping me escape this harsh reality. As soon as Hot Boyz by Missy Elliot featuring Nas and Eve came on, I curled up into my oversized leather couch. I was calm. I was numbed. I was zoned. I nodded off and fell asleep.

It was nearing ten o'clock when Sasha came rushing in the house. The place was in darkness, apart from the television that was still on. She came in squealing. Her voice was loud but her words weren't clear to me until I heard her say, "Turn on the news!" She grabbed the remote and tuned it to the local news channel, "You're not going to believe this shit!"

CURRENCY OF CORRUPTION

I tuned in to the news channel. "Breaking news…Former Senator Alan Thomson faces felony charges stemming from an unusually sophisticated prostitution ring that spanned across Massachusetts, New York, and Florida. A search warrant affidavit filed recently in Superior Court provided a glimpse into what authorities say was a high end prostitution service that financed Thompson's extravagant lifestyle. Court documents have also named thirty women in Massachusetts alone, who were required to bring in a minimum of $500 a night. Authorities believe the ring had been in operation since 1990. FBI special agents implicated two City Police Officers, Andre Medeiros and Richard Hesse in the illegal scheme as well. A spokesman for the City Police Department declined to comment but are launching an administrative review of the fellow officers…This is Karen Davis coming to you live with this coverage…We'll keep you up to date with new developments."

I was in total shock. Sasha sat down to console me, but it was in vain. Learning that Andre was involved in this brought my spirit to the pits. I wasn't equipped emotionally or physically for the hardship this was going to bring me.

When I thought of prostitution, I imagined ladies of the night standing at the Combat Zone in Chinatown, with their pimps driving around the block over and over again. My emotions were distorted. One thing I knew for sure was, officials were bringing down this prostitution ring like the titanic, but only Andre had the life jackets, and took them with him and my mother.

I started to wonder if Massiel's call earlier that day had anything to do with this. Since she was indifferent, why all of a sudden was she calling me? Did she know and wanted to give me the heads up? Did she want to apologize and be a friend? When I remembered my dream of the Star Trek ship with all the naked women inside and suddenly the dream book interpretation was clear to me. I was facing that puzzling situation that made no sense to me. What role did Andre play in all this? One thing I was sure about was that the FBI was going to dig deep into our background.

The dizzy ring tone from my cell phone rang at midnight. It was Ray. I hesitated to take his call. Oh the humiliation! He was a decent officer who had no business getting involved with someone of my caliber.

"Hello." My voice was low.

"Are you home?"

"Yeah...have you heard?"

"I'm working half a shift tonight. I'll come by around 4:00 so we can talk. Is that cool?" He knew exactly what was going on.

"Sure. I'll leave the door unlocked. Just let yourself in."

"No. I'll call you when I get there. I need you to come out."

"Okay. Bye."

Ray showed up at four twenty that morning, outside in the driveway waiting for me. I threw on a gray sweater and black sweat pants. I ran my fingers through my long black hair, twisting it up in a bun, and securing it with a clip. As soon as I stepped outside I shivered from the cold wind and the anticipation of seeing Ray.

He greeted me with a kiss on my cheek. "Are you all right?"

I barely looked at him. "No."

Ray drove out the driveway. I leaned back on the passenger seat without saying a word. A part of me suspected he had some sort of secret recording device; to try and set me up. He drove into the parking lot of the Agazziz Elementary School, on

268

Child Street. He did most of the talking as I responded with a nod or shrug.

"I'm letting you know, entry into your house is going to come quickly through a search warrant. Be ready for it. Andre's been AWOL since Thursday night and the department is calling a high-level meeting of commanders to figure out who warned him that a corruption probe was underway."

"What else do you know?" I mumbled as I stared at the school's playground from the passenger window.

"Thompson admitted he operated the escort service from one of his houses, in Walpole. That was the call center where they coordinated all their client calls. Officer Hesse claims he and Andre only shielded the Senator, but when the FBI looked into Andre's finances, they discovered from 1993 increasing amounts of money were deposited into his bank accounts. It's looking real ugly."

He explained to me how the search would go down, how to stay calm, and read the warrant carefully to know what they were entitled to go through. We watched the sun come up talking about this scandal. Once the conversation shifted, I noticed Ray, had changed. He had lost weight and had dark circles around his eyes, made him look drawn and tired. Turned out he lost the custody battle, he had been fighting for. He didn't want to touch the details of his situation and I didn't press him to know.

The sun was rising and we were still sitting in the lot. Ray gave me the impression he didn't want to leave. "You've been on my mind lately."

I started fidgeting with my nails. "What about?"

"I thought about our first date when I tossed you in the water." He reached over and grasped my hands. My stomach did cartwheels.

"Is that the only part you remember well?"

269

"No, but it made me laugh. Then I thought of how we watched the sun come up."

"We definitely had a good time...I think about you too."

We reminisced about that night as he drove me back to my house.

"When are we going out again? I owe you dinner."

"You do?"

"Yeah, I think you said your favorite ice cream was cookies and cream."

"No. My favorite ice cream is mint chocolate chip." I remembered our deal the first night we met during the new moon phase. If he got promoted to the Drug Unit, dinner was on him. "You made detective?"

He gave me the first smile of the night. "Yes, I did."

"When were you going to tell me?"

"Over dinner."

"Congratulations, Ray. I'm really happy for you," I said, with no emotion. With all that was going on, I didn't have the energy to show excitement even though I was truly proud of him. "Can we wait for all this to die down before we go out?"

"I agree. Let me get myself situated as well and I'll call you."

After he dropped me off, I walked up the stairs, eyes half closed, and crawled into bed for a little daylight hibernation. As I closed my eyes looking to rest, our conversation played in my head. The threat of the search warrant woke me back up. I took out the .380 and its ammunition from my closet but I was clueless what to do with it. I picked up my cell phone and dialed up the only person I trusted. Xavier.

"Hey X. Are you busy?" I could hear background noises, men working out in the gym.

"Never too busy for my homegirl. What's up?"

"Have you heard the news?"

"No. What's going on?"

"Before I give you the details, I need to know where to dispose a .380 before the Feds come in here and find it."

"What the fuck, Sky?"

"I can't explain now. Where can I hide this thing?

He paused. "Dump it in the sewer."

"I don't want to throw it away."

"Sky, dump it! Get rid of it. Because if that's the gun that I think it is, then you'd be stupid to hold on to it."

"All right, all right."

Xavier stayed on the phone with me. He instructed me to walk to the complex near the basketball court to a sewer, where I carefully scanned my surroundings before tossing the gun. On my way back up the hill, I jabbered away about the scandal.

NO TEARS TO SHED

The Feds and local police came in as I was leaving to go to work. One officer flashed his badge in my face and shoved the warrant at me as he moved forward into the house.

I called Lieutenant Apple Crumb and told him I was in the middle of this situation. He gave me permission to come in late. When I opened the door to my car, an officer scolded me to get away from it. According to the warrant, the entire house was subjected to searching, along with my Audi that Andre helped me finance because his name was on it.

Meanwhile, I sat on the swings and chatted with a friendlier cop who was flirting with me. I wondered if that was his way to get me to open up. It was a tacky approach but I preferred that over an arrogant officer.

The Chevy Tahoe was safe from the hunt, because it belonged to my mother. So when the search was over I sped off to work. Luckily there was no traffic because my nerves were on edge. At Roxbury Crossing I jumped on the brakes when a huge pothole emerged in the center of the road. That's when I heard something heavy shift in the back of the truck. Not paying much attention to it, I continued to drive.

At 11:30pm, Massiel came wobbling in to begin her midnight shift. She plopped her pregnant behind next to me, asking why I didn't return her call. She had a nerve to question me about not calling her back, when for months she stopped speaking to me.

"Are you ok?"

"I'm fine," I said with a stuck up voice.

"I know we haven't spoken in…"

"No." I interrupted, "*You* haven't spoken."

"I'm sorry. This pregnancy has been hard on me."

"So what was the urgency behind your call?" I raised my eyebrow in annoyance.

"I just thought you may need a friend."

"Thanks, but I'll be fine."

I left her sitting there with the words in her mouth, while I unplugged my headsets and walked away. As I was leaving the department, I snuck a newspaper out of the break room to read at home. I walked out of Headquarters with my head hanging low, avoiding eye contact with everyone. I jumped in the Tahoe and stopped at the complex to pick up a good size bag of weed. When I drove up to the house, I was relieved to see that the search was over and Sasha was home.

She was packing her belongings to move out. She didn't want to get involved in all that was going on. So her new love interest, Anthony, invited her to move in with him. Who could blame her? But it was inconsiderate to leave me hanging at the most difficult time. Here I thought we were like sisters but instead she's leaving me behind to sort this thing out alone. My head was full of sadness and confusion. Therefore I did what I always did for mental comfort—smoke.

While Sasha packed her things I pulled out the newspaper to read. The prostitution scandal had grown in scope: *Disgraced Former State Senator Alan Thompson was released today on a $75,000 bail following charges with his involvement in an organized escort service that procured prostitutes for top-class clients. Thompson became the subject of a vice investigation for six months after authorities received a tip from an anonymous source....Thompson's assets included two houses, three cars including two Mercedes and a Land Rover were seized...Court documents named a decorated 23 year veteran of the City Police* *force, Andre Medeiros, and another officer Richard Hesse, who face charges for allegedly helping run the business...Hesse will appear in court on January 9th for arraignment on pandering...Medeiros is now a fugitive of the law...Authorities also arrested 25 year old Robin Gantz on suspicion of threatening a witness, Sharon Miller, who helped police investigate the case. She was booked for bribery and intimidation of a witness...Gantz was placed under judicial control and was forbidden from contacting defendants or witnesses regarding the procedure...*

Sharon Miller. Andre's old mistress helped bring the operation down.

I waited for Sasha to hit the sack or hit the road so I could go pray in the attic. I thought she was staying another night when she locked herself in her room. I quietly went up to the attic to light some candles and pray to Saint Michael and the rest of the saints that were stationed on my altar.

My altar was small so if there was anything out of place, I would immediately notice. And of course, one of my statues was missing: Ochosi. He represented justice. This meant my mother took it with her. He was their protection for running from the law. Strangely, my mother replaced it with a Native American porcelain doll, holding a dream catcher, and wearing a multi-colored head dress with a cream and brown feather. It was almost humorous to see a porcelain doll in the place of Ochosi, but because things were already odd, I didn't laugh. I took the doll down and placed it on the floor.

I burned a bit of sage in an abalone shell and let the smoke lift. I carried the smudge all around the attic, allowing it to trace the edges of the wall. Then I got on my knees, with my rosary beads in my hand. I centered myself, cleared my mind of all negative thoughts, and prayed, "St. Michael, by your divine power, I seek refuge and protection, for Andre Medeiros and Lucia Velez-

Medeiros. Free them of evil intentions of others. I invoke you, St. Michael, with your justly goodness, to protect and bless them where ever they may be. As you do this for them, I humbly pray you protect and bless me also, for in you I have the utmost faith. Amen."

When I stood up from the floor, I knocked over the Native American porcelain doll that was beside me. As I reached to pick it up, I noticed a rubber stopper at the bottom of it. When I pulled the stopper out, I found three bundles of money rolled up with rubber bands. I drew them out and found a note tucked in there also. My mother left me a message. It took me several times to decipher her clumsy handwriting.

Sky,

If you are reading this note I assure you that I am saddened for the burden we have placed on you. Even though money will not compensate for the trouble this will cause you, we left you something to help you get by. You'll find it in the shed. Please forgive us. Until we meet again.
L.V.

I felt lost. I wanted to break down but I couldn't bring myself to tears. To make matters more confusing, what shed did she mean? We didn't have one.

I walked back downstairs to my bedroom. Everything was dark except for the kitchen light. When I went in my room, I caught a glimpse of Sasha walking to the bathroom from the corner of my eye. I didn't say anything. I waited for her to come out. If I showed her the note, she would help me figure out where the money was and maybe change her mind to stay.

I sat in the dark, on the edge of my bed. Sasha was taking a long time in the bathroom. Then I thought the shed was maybe a code for basement. I waited for Sasha some more. A car pulled up in

275

my driveway. I ran to the window and saw Sasha stepping out of a red jeep. What? Sasha wasn't in my bathroom. Who was? I ran around the house switching on all the lights like a maniac. Then I ran down the stairs and approached her in the hallway.

"When did you leave? And who's that in the jeep?"

"Anthony. I made him turn back around. I feel awful leaving you like this. Please don't be mad."

"Too late."

"I'm pregnant, Sky. I think it's best if I stay with Anthony."

What could I say after that? Nothing. My blood boiled inside. Walking out on me at such a difficult time was hurtful. Finding out she was pregnant didn't help much either. I locked myself in my bedroom and searched for a candle. There was something wandering in the house and that made me feel worse. I had always found candles and light the easiest method of ridding myself of those unwelcomed spirits. So I prayed myself to sleep.

TURNING AWAY

Days went by and nothing had changed. Doctor Wesley came to mind first thing in the morning as I laid in bed. It was time to schedule an appointment with him. His secretary told me he had an opening but I would have to rush to get there on time. That wasn't a problem.

Rambling to Dr. Wesley always helped on some level. For example, things I couldn't say on the job could be said in his office. I expressed to him how 911 call takers didn't get the proper respect. With the middle to high class people, you could really feel their putdown. They would try to ruin you. They would call the Chief's office or write out a formal complaint if they didn't like the tone of your voice.

"I feel like the piece of equipment I use to answer calls. Picture yourself listening to a bunch of callers screaming hysterically because they witnessed a jumper's brain splat on the sidewalk, a raped woman sobbing, or a young boy holding on to dear life because he was stabbed over sneakers. Then suddenly there's a moron crying murder over a parking space he felt he was entitled to. What do you want the police to do? Make the other person move his vehicle for you? Seriously, get over it and move on. But no, that's the asshole who for some reason believes he pays my salary!"

After my rant, I brought up the news about Andre's disappearance and the ordeal behind it. Doctor Wesley had been keeping up with the story. In the years I had been his patient, he never showed any type of emotion. As a therapist, he was trained to always remain neutral without getting excited over anything a patient said. But his eyes opened wide and his jaw dropped when I told him about the great escape. It actually made me laugh because his facial expressions conveyed a great deal of humor. He apologized repeatedly for his shocked reaction, but I took no offense to it. I appreciated the laugh.

By the end of our session he prescribed me a low-dosage of Valiums.

Over the course of a few months, the stress was weighing down on me. The scandal was still prominent over the news. The job and co-workers treated me like an outcast. I resented everyone that turned their backs on me. That resentment was attached to my emotional body, making me sick. Therefore I paid my physician a visit.

"So, what are you here for, Cecilia?"

A little embarrassed, I replied, "Um, I'm getting a lot of headaches, dizzy spells, and I, um...bleed every time I use the bathroom."

"In your urine?"

"No."

"In your bowel movement?"

"Yes, and it feels like it's ripping my insides when it comes out, leaving a bloody mess in the toilet. It's pretty scary."

"And that started when?"

"A month ago."

The doctor paused to look through my medical record. "Are you on a new, special diet?"

"No."

"Have you experienced anything stressful in the past month?"

"Yes."

She typed in the computer, then stood up. "Okay, let's have you undress from the waist down."

I laid on my side with my right hand covering my face from the discomfort of her finger examining my rectum. She told me I had an

278

anal fissure, a small tear. How on Earth can stress cause a crack in my skin? Every day I was learning how this drama was hurting me.

The doctor was concerned. "You have to find a way to make your mental well being a priority. If stress is what's creating this, then you have a problem."

When I got home, I took two Valiums to settle my nerves. Within minutes, Ray called me to invite me out for dinner that following Friday. I needed entertainment to provide an escape from work and the horrors of my mind.

It had been a while since I had spoken to Sasha and I wanted to mend things, so I invited her shopping to help me pick out something nice to wear. She left work early that Friday. It was the only thing I was looking forward to all week; a little retail therapy and my dinner date with Ray.

When Friday came, I drove to South Station to pick her up from work. A remix of I Turn To You by Melanie C was blaring from the speakers of the Tahoe when I pulled up.

"Oh my goodness, Sky." Sasha gets in the car. "Someone is excited for tonight."

"I've been waiting all week for this, girl." I moved my shoulders to the beat and turned down the sound of the music. "How's that belly?" I rubbed her stomach.

"Tired of carrying it. I can't wait to have her in my arms."

"It's a girl?"

"Yes and I want you to be the godmother."

I was honored that she chose me. After all I was going through and how secretly I was dreading to be alive, this gave me something to look forward to.

We walked around the Square One Mall in Saugus and I bought new clothes. The anticipation of seeing Ray later that night and being asked to be a godmother had me go crazy on a shopping spree. I bought a new cell phone, intimate wear, two pairs of baby sneakers, and five outfits for the new baby.

Sasha and I finished shopping and we headed to the parking lot. When I opened the back of the Tahoe to place the shopping bags, I noticed something tucked under a bed sheet. It was the heavy thing that made noise whenever I slammed on the breaks or made sharp turns. I gave Sasha the key to get in while I arranged the bags and take a peak. It was Andre's desktop computer. It was one of the things the Feds were looking for the day they searched the house. It contained vital information to the operation he was running. I also found a large orange envelope in the corner. It was the deed to the house and other documents left behind with everything that was under my mother's name. I tucked it back underneath the sheet and drove off.

"What's wrong? You seem out of it," Sasha asked.

"I've never been with anyone besides Calvin." The computer was what set me off but I couldn't tell her that.

"If you're not ready then don't do it. Don't let any man pressure you into having sex with him if that's not what you want."

"I want him. I'm just scared."

"You are *not* a virgin. What the hell can be so scary?"

"Him turning away."

"He's not Calvin. This guy is really into you. Ask him what he wants."

"He wants me; in his bed."

"Then you have your answer. Nothing wrong with that if that's the same thing you want."

The anticipation of seeing Ray was coming down like when I came off a weed high, humdrum. Sex was fun but if that's all he wanted then I thought I better be careful how I played along. I was pretty sensitive underneath all my gruffness.

When I arrived home, Ray called. "My sister and nephew showed up from Puerto Rico to surprise the family. They're all coming over my house tonight."

"Oh. I guess I'll take a rain check."

"I'm not canceling, Sky. I want you to join us. My partner is having a few people from the job come by too. It's going to be a small party, nothing big. My sister and I are going to make dinner. I also bought you cookies and cream ice cream." He chuckled.

"Mint chocolate chip, Ray!"

"Yeah, whatever. I told everyone to be here by 8 o'clock but you can swing by at anytime."

"What's your address?"

"Whitten Street, in Dorchester. Call me if you get lost."

"I know where it is. I'll see you tonight."

I left my house at exactly 8 o'clock. As I locked my front door I looked down at the correspondence piled up on the porch. I found a letter from Calvin and another letter my lawyer sent me to sign in order to receive my check from the accident claim with Coco. I inserted the mail in my purse and continued to Ray's house.

On my way, I called Coco to tell her we were going to receive the money soon. She didn't sound thrilled over the news so I suspected she wasn't going to pay me. If she didn't kick in my one thousand for adding her into the scheme, her face and my fist were going to meet.

At Ray's house, I spotted him outside on his phone. As I slowly approached him, he hung up and surprised me with a hug. He made me smile as he took me by the hand to bring me in the house.

I pulled back and stopped him. "Please don't mention that I work for 911. The last thing I want to talk about is work."

"Okay, so I'll tell them you're a mortician." He laughed and slapped my ass.

I didn't care what he said, just as long as he didn't reveal I was a police employee. Ray opened the door to a neatly ordered home: wooden floors, light colored walls, and the windows were opened to let the breeze in. The living room was connected to an open kitchen where everyone stood around and mingled. He introduced me to everyone before getting me a drink. There were many people there, mostly his family and a few people who worked with him.

He brought me back a milky drink.

"What's this?" I asked.

"Try it."

I took a sip.

"No seas tan mistica, carajo!" (Stop being so finicky, shit.)

"No me hables malo." (Don't swear at me.) I rolled my eyes at him.

I stood in a corner of the parlor watching the Celtics with a White Russian in my hand. Ray, towering over me at six feet, two inches, stood close to me during the night. Yet I was nervous whenever he flirted with me. I tried to ignore his candid assessment of my charm and physical appearance but I had a foolish smile on my face making it impossible for him to stop.

He bluntly asked me to sleep with him. Without answering him, I politely turned away from him, and retreated to the kitchen. I stood in front of the sink, gulped the last of my White Russian, and washed my empty glass out. He came from behind as his hand slid down my back and rested at my waist.

I turned my head to look up at him. "May I have another one?"

He made me another drink and when he handed it to me, he smoothly took my cellular phone out my other hand, placing it in his back pocket. He left to continue hosting the other guests. I scoped out his mannerism thinking about everything I wanted to do to him.

He ate a traditional Puerto Rican dessert called arroz con dulce; that his sister made, while he engaged in conversation with the others. As he savored the sweet rice pudding, I wondered how his cunnilingus skills were.

The atmosphere changed as I stood there in the kitchen, drowning my nerves in the alcohol. The conversation about the prostitute scandal came up. The ones who were in the kitchen discussing it were three officers and Ray's brother. I noticed how Ray's partner excused himself when the topic came up.

Officer No. 1 said, "The FBI were watching and filming from the house across from the Senator's call center."

"Someone from inside had to have warned Andre to leave right when the plan to move in was hatched. I wouldn't be surprised if it came straight from Anti-corruption. You know he and Brown were good buddies," said Officer No. 2.

Officer No. 1 continued. "I'm with you on that. He had to be the one to warn Andre to leave because the phone was tapped for months. No one saw that coming. How did he just disappear with his wife?"

"That's crazy," Ray's brother added, "A cop with a side career in pimping. I'm shocked it took them this long to find out. Supposedly he was running this operation since the early 90's."

"Everybody was surprised, as well as disgusted," said Officer No. 2.

"Not as surprised as I was when I saw Massiel's baby." Officer No. 3 raised his eye brow and swigged his beer.

No fucking way! Massiel's baby was Andre's son? The skeletons were falling out the closet one body at a time. I understood why she acted funky during her pregnancy and why the urgency to talk after the scandal. I wanted to run out and show up at Massiel's house right then and there.

283

"I heard the baby is Andre's spitting image," said Officer No.1, "but that's what happens when you deny a child."

"I wonder if she knew all along," asked Officer No. 3.

"About him being a sack of shit?" Scoffed Officer No. 1.

Ray made his way back to me with a smile. "We have unfinished business, you and I."

I held up my hand. "Hold up, let me hear the last of this conversation." My eyebrows pulled together in a tightening position indicating I was angry.

Ray was alarmed. "What's wrong? What are you guys talking about?"

"Nothing," said Officer No. 1, "We were discussing the shit that went down with Medieros and Hesse, we wasn't…"

Ray interrupted his gossiping friend, "I told you not to bring that up!"

"I'm sorry bro, I thought you didn't want us to discuss it with you…" Officer No. 1 apologized.

Ray cut him off again. "No. I meant don't bring it up at all."

I slammed my empty glass on the kitchen counter, "You can gossip about my step-father with me out of earshot now." I turned away.

I stormed out the house and jumped in the truck. With angry tears flowing I drove to Massiel's apartment. I couldn't believe I called Andre my step-father. The vodka made me say it. When I got to her place, Massiel's lights were off. It took me twenty minutes to compose myself and wait to see if any of her lights came on. But nothing happened.

The thought of Ray not calling me after I left his house angered me further. That's when I realized he had my cell phone in his back pocket. After thirty minutes of highway driving and curvy roads, I made it back to Ray's house. He was standing on his porch with his brother. I made my way to the bottom of the steps.

"I believe you have something that belongs to me." I had the palm of my hand facing up.

He stepped down and grabbed my hand. "Come back inside. You ran everyone out except my family."

I pulled away. "I can't go back in there."

"Don't let that get to you. Let's finish the night like it never happened."

I followed him back inside the house. He gently caressed my hand. "You want another drink?"

I liked his coy manner. "Are you trying to get me drunk, Officer Povez?"

"I'm trying to get you back into a good mood."

He replaced everyone's old empty glasses with new drinks and his brother a fresh cold beer. The family played dominos with Ray while his brother pulled me aside to apologize. He didn't know who I was or any of those officers. He only knew what he had heard over the news and was stunned at what happened earlier in the kitchen. He mocked the officers' expressions when I revealed who I was. I could tell he ran in the complete opposite lane than Ray did, and that's probably the reason I was getting along with him.

There was a more positive energy in the house thanks to all the liquor. I knew the alcohol would lower my inhibition and give me some sort of courage to sleep with Ray. I didn't even consider the fact that hooking up with Ray was probably going to leave me feeling shameful the next morning. But my sexual drought had passed the one year mark and time was beginning to steal the bloom from this flower. A fling seemed ideal for the time being.

After everyone left, Ray grabbed me by my waist and kissed me. The session started in the kitchen. He removed his sneakers and unfastened the belt of his jeans. I was immediately taken to the place I fantasized about during masturbation, only this time, I was being caressed by a real man. Ray's hand bridged the crest of my breast,

285

sending a wave of pleasure through my body. I started to ask myself what the hell was I doing, but I shut down the thought when he slid his hand down my pants. His fingers reached my clitoris, giving it a quick tease. He pulled his hand out and unbuttoned my slacks. After my pants were off, he worked his way to my top, unbuttoning my shirt. Ray placed his hands around my torso, lifting me up onto the counter top. My legs were spread open and he made his way down south kissing and licking me. I moaned. My body writhed and bucked; but no wave of climax.

We made our way to the living room. Once we were both on the couch, I lifted one of my legs higher so it was over his shoulder, pointing straight up in the air. Then he paused, mid-thrust, and withdrew. I swung my legs over to the side to a new position. He took hold of my hips and plunged back into my slit; thrusting like a wild man. I fell over halfway; my hands caught my fall holding my upper body up from the floor. We increased the pace and ferocity until he pounded one last time to climax. We collapsed on the floor in giggles and breathless panting. Our limp bodies slowly got up to slouch on the couch. Even in the dark, I could see Ray sitting there in the afterglow.

We were both completely spent, slumped there with our naked bodies. He pulled me by my arm towards him and I rested on him. I never expected to feel so comfortable in my own skin with another man. He played with my hair until I dozed.

"What do you expect will happen with us?" He spoke gently.

"It's not good to have expectations. I'm just going with the flow."

"Damn, there goes my expectation of you bringing us some ice cream from the freezer and doing me again."

I laughed. "I'm your guest. You should be serving me."

"Oh I served you. I put in all the work while you just moved your legs around."

"Oh you think so?"

"Should I rewind the tape?"

"What!"

I tried to get up fast but he reached forward, grabbing my arm and pulling me against him. I squirmed, trying to break free from his grasp. He was much stronger than me but I didn't stop trying.

"Let me go, you bastard!" I kept trying to release his grip.

"Stop! I was kidding, relax! Come here."

I cooled down. "Tell me again that you were joking."

"I was kidding. Seriously, come here."

I sat down next to him without taking my eyes off him. He stood up and walked to the refrigerator. I looked around the living room to see if in fact it was a mean joke and there was no hidden camera.

He came back with the ice cream and one spoon. I gave him a dirty look and he just laughed as he took a spoonful of the mint chocolate chip ice cream and fed it to me.

"I know you been wronged and you're real defensive. I don't blame you. But one thing you should know about me is I'm not that guy. I won't lie to you. I won't burn you. I won't talk about you." He fed me another spoonful of ice cream. "I'm a private person. Yes, I love to joke around and have a good time, but I keep my personal life personal." He tried the ice cream but wasn't too fond of it. "I think you're sweet, outspoken, a little ghetto, and you have the craziest laugh I have ever heard. If I feel that things aren't going well between us, I will tell you. So let this be the last time you get up like you're ready to fight me, because I'll slam you next time." Then he smiled, with the bite of the tongue that I loved.

THE SECRET IN MY SLEEP

The sun barely beat me home when I left Ray's house. Despite the visible hangover I left with, it felt amazing starting over with a sexy and fun-loving man. I shaded my eyes with my Gucci glasses and cranked up the radio to Kiss 108 FM when U2 came on, It's A Beautiful Day.

When I got home, I pulled out Calvin's letter to read it before taking my day time hibernation. He was now at MCI Concord State Prison doing his bid. I opened it with unsteady hands. In the letter, Calvin pointed out all that he was going through the past six months.

Nicole stopped bringing their son to see him, his family abandoned him, and his so-called friends were strangers. He was alone and desperate for a friend; just one. He had no canteen money, no visits, and no letters. It was disturbing to read that he told his cell mate to take the pillow from behind him and smother his face with it. The letter made me sad. But he knew how to manipulate me. I put the letter away and thought I'd give myself some time to think things through before visiting him. My heart was all in but I had to mentally prepare myself before stepping foot in another prison. They say love hurts and some people will leave footprints on your heart. But he left a stomp print on mine.

Later that evening Ray called me at home. His sister wanted to go out dancing and he suggested I take her to Copas Night Club in Saugus. He offered to watch his nephew so she could have a girls' night out. I was looking forward to it because I knew that would get me back to his place by the end of the night.

I called Angela, Sasha's friend, to join us because Angela loved to party. She was a replica of Sasha which is why they got along so well. The three of us headed out to Copas for a night of dancing, drinking, and laughter.

Copa had three rooms of varied music selection. The first room had the largest dance floor that played Salsa, Merengue, and Bachata music. The second room, decorated with palm trees and railings made out of bamboo, was the jungle room. The best of Hip Hop and Latin Freestyle were played in there. Then in the back of the club was a small room just for Reggae. It was the hottest club to be at on Saturdays.

Ray's sister, Evelyn, was really enjoying herself; toasting away with Angela all night. Neither one ever left the dance floor unless it was to guzzle the drinks I was watching for them. I sat on the speakers in the jungle room, while they danced the night away. The most I did besides babysit the drinks was bob my head up and down to the music, thinking of Calvin. I chose not to drink that night. It wasn't like me to stay sober but I didn't want to show Ray that side all the time.

Evelyn and Angela had left the club in a highly excited state. Evidently they had a little too much to drink. As we walked towards the rear of the parking lot to my car, a brawl broke out between two gentlemen. I stopped to watch as a crowd gathered around them. Angela pulled me away. She wanted to prevent me from catching another arresting charge.

We laughed all the way to the car. Soon after slowly pulling off, Angela saw one of the brawlers go to their car and grab a gun from under his driver seat. We tried to drive off but people were in our way, running all over the parking lot. I prayed we could make it out safe. Luckily we did.

I arrived at Ray's house to drop off his sister. Evelyn sat in the passenger's seat almost helpless, claiming that she was too lit to move. All I did was laugh. I then called Ray and asked him to come out and get her. He jokingly said that was the last time he was going to allow her to go out with me.

When he came out, in his basketball shorts and white tank top, I had already helped Evelyn out the car. She walked up the stairs on her own but wouldn't stop laughing at herself. I looked at him and shrugged.

"Looks like you guys had too much fun."

"We did. I just hope she'll remember it tomorrow."

"Are you going to remember?" he asked.

"Why wouldn't I? I didn't drink tonight."

"Let me see." He bent down and tasted my tongue.

"That's all I get?"

"I'll give you more if you stay."

I got in the car to shut off the engine and grab my purse. He stood there waiting for me. When we walked in, I could hear Evelyn vomiting in the first floor bathroom. I got a cup of water and brought it to her. She was on her knees bent over the toilet. I placed the cup on the sink and positioned myself behind her to pull her hair back and tap her back.

Ray stood there shaking his head. "Why are you hitting her that hard?"

"Can she have some privacy?" I handed her the cup, "Toma, bebete la agua." (Here, drink the water.)

She said no. I hit her harder. "Que te lo bebas o te lo mando ensima!" (Drink it or I'll pour it on you)

Ray doubted I would pour it on her. "I have to watch this."

"Water is always good when you get sick. It will help you no matter how you take it—inside or out."

Evelyn drank the water and I helped her stand. Ray carried her to the couch where he placed a pillow and blanket. When I turned to switch the light off in the bathroom, I noticed the basement light was on so I shut it off. I heard someone yell up, so I turned it back on. Ray's brother was in the cellar.

I told Ray I was going to say hello to his brother and I would meet him upstairs in his bedroom.

"What are you doing down here?" He tried to hide the joint he was smoking.

"I should be asking you that, but I see now that you're making out with Lady Jane. I just came down to say hello."

"Lady Jane? You mean Mary Jane."

"You say tomato, I say tomahto."

"Excuse me for smoking. I know this house if full of law enforcers."

I couldn't help but laugh. "Says who?"

"Your badges."

"I'm no cop, sweetie. Do me a favor, blow some of that smoke my way."

"You smoke?" His head tilted back and he raised an eyebrow.

"Of course I don't, silly. I'm a law abiding citizen." I chuckled. "I'll settle for a little contact smoke though."

Ray found women who smoked anything, unattractive. He made that clear when we watched Jennifer Lopez smoke that joint in the movie The Cell. I found it badass when I saw it, but I didn't say anything. I had to keep a low profile about my weed habit as long as I could. Now that he was in the Drug Unit, I really had to stay away from him while under the influence.

His brother shot the smoke in my face and I inhaled it with gusto. I said goodnight and made it up to the second floor. Ray's bedroom light was on. He was looking through his drawers for condoms.

"Can I take a shower to freshen up?"

"Let me get you a clean towel."

After I took a nice cool shower, I walked in Ray's room wearing nothing but the towel. He used his two fingers to slide it off. Then we kissed while I stood there in the nude. It was a sweet and sensual kiss that transported me to a peaceful place where the world couldn't find me. With wetted lips and a sliding tongue his hand extended to touch me. He began to play with my body like he was playing 88 keys. I didn't need much foreplay; I was yearning for him to be inside me.

The bedroom lights were still on but neither he nor I cared. I gently pushed him on the bed and undressed him. The first time we had sex he said he did all the work. This time I wanted to show him differently.

His cock immediately sprang out his boxers. I ran my nails down his abs while I bobbed my head on his cock. I placed it between my breasts and massaged it up and down while I licked the tip. He moaned before I released it. The sucking was turning me on that I had to stop and sit on it. Ray just surrendered to my control as I rode him. I leaned forward and the position triggered my building climax. It was like shaking a coke bottle and watching it explode when you open it.

Ray then flipped me over and got on top of me—missionary style. He grabbed my hands and held them down on the pillow, above my head as his thrusts were fast and hard.

"Talk dirty to me!" he demanded.

I thought of what to say but my mind went blank. I was trying to concentrate and enjoy every stroke he was giving me.

"Talk dirty to me!"

Ray, in an uncharacteristic act, slapped me on my face with such force, that my hips stopped moving. My body froze in disbelief. But he kept thrusting.

"Wait a minute. Did you just slap me?" It was the craziest thing ever done to me during sex. "I can't believe you slapped me!"

He placed his hands under the pillow and pinned me down with his body, almost suffocating me. He bit me on my neck and said, "Shut up." All I could do was laugh from the shock. My body stopped its rhythm but he kept going until he came. Our body fluids were all over the sheets. It was quite intense. The smack really threw me for a loop. We laughed uncontrollably when we were done. He was as shocked from striking me and told me he had never done that before. It was just the heat of the moment.

After the laughter ceased over that bold move, he asked about my night out with his sister. I told him how we had a good time and a good scare. When he asked what scared us, I recounted what happened after the club.

Ray asked, "You saw him pull out the gun?"

"No. Angela saw it. I was too busy trying to drive out of there."

"What were these fools fighting over?"

"Who knows? I hope it wasn't over a bitch. The cemetery is full of victims that dealt with people lead by emotions." I placed my hand over my chest and got theatrical. "I loved her and if I couldn't have her, no one was. How did that work out for you, buddy? She's dead, you're doing life, and now you have motherfuckers playing with your star fish!"

After Ray laughed at my butthole comment, he wrapped his arm around me. "We should hang out more; seriously. You're nice to talk to."

"That's it? Nice to talk to?"

"Well the sex is not that bad either."

I pushed his arm away. "Really?"

"Well I wouldn't kick you out of bed in the morning."

"It wouldn't surprise me if you did after that high-five to the face you gave me."

He squeezed me in his arms. "I had to lay down the law."

293

I placed his hand between my legs and closed my eyes. "Tell me what you look for in a girl."

Time with Ray was beginning to be more valuable than sex. After our romping sessions, I enjoyed our conversations.

"Women come up with weak game all the time because they think their looks and sex is all that matters. But what they don't understand is that doesn't impress me. Anyone can be a woman in the bedroom. My criteria's are: Is she caring? Is she sincere? Is she smart? Those are the things on top of my list. Yes, I want someone attractive, but looks can go. What about you?"

"I need someone that can handle me. I like real people to call me out on my bullshit. That is what I respect. So, if a man is afraid to confront and correct me, I have no time for him. A person who agrees with everything I do is enabling me to fuck up. I learned that from watching my father try to help my mother. But she was set in her ways and never listened to him."

"Ok then."

Hours later when I woke up, Ray wasn't beside me. I was never a cheerful riser but I woke up feeling like I could smile sky borne home. The time was 2:15 in the afternoon and I had to rush home to get ready for work.

"Do you know you jump in your sleep?" Ray asked when he entered the room, holding a cup of coffee.

I knew my body did this at times before going under, but I wasn't aware it happened during a deep sleep. "Now I do."

"So who's Calvin?" His tone shifted from concerned to investigative.

I didn't reply right away. My heart dropped. How did he find out about Calvin? He glared at me, waiting for me to respond. What do I say?

"You're not going to tell me who Calvin is? Then answer me this...am I the only one you're sleeping with?"

294

"What? Wait a minute...yes, you're the only one I've been seeing. Where is this coming from?"

"You."

"Me?"

"You called out his name this morning in your sleep. Then you said he was the only one; nothing would ever come between you two; and something about his secret being safe."

I couldn't believe it, but he had no reason to lie. We were doing fine. It was that stupid letter Calvin wrote me that somehow set into my subconscious state. I think of The Romantics when I think of that moment: I hear the secrets that you keep, when you're talking in your sleep. Only it wasn't about wanting Ray.

"You know what, I'm not even mad. It's not like you're my lady anyways."

His words couldn't have been any harsher. I had no time to explain who Calvin was. I had to get home to get ready for work and walking down memory lane wasn't going to matter to Ray after that statement. Before I left, I looked at him with teary eyes and said, "Last night was the most fun I've had in a long time, but I hope I never see you again."

295

KAT IN THE MOON

A week passed and I didn't hear from Ray. I stayed busy trying to catch up with more important things like therapy, bills, and searching for the money Andre left me. It was hard, though, with how things went down between Ray and me. I called out from work to stay home and relax. I went through my mother and Andre's mail that I let pile up. We didn't have the best relationship, but I missed them.

My utilities were separate from their apartment so I took care of my bills. Their light and gas had been shut off in the recent months. My eyes began to get weary until I opened the urgent letters from the bank threatening to foreclose the house. It was time for me to leave that haunted place and start fresh somewhere else. My card readings always showed that I would be moving out and I was beginning to see the signs. The bank told me the last mortgage payment they received was in March. That was impossible. They left in December. Someone was paying with a money order from Florida. That meant that someone in my family was mailing out the mortgage payment on behalf of my mother. It was hard to imagine that she was still in the States. She always said she wouldn't stay here when she retired. The severity of what was going on had to have made them leave the country. They were outlaws now, not retirees. I felt a little trip to Florida was in order; but I needed to take time off.

The following Thursday, July 12, was my turn to leave early from work. I ran into Katana in the elevator on my way out. She invited me to a college party outside of Cambridge. I had no interest in going but I didn't know how to turn down her invitation. She asked for my address and told me she would pick me up later that night.

While I waited for Katana to pick me up, I played back a message Massiel left on my voicemail. She was still on maternity leave and wanted to show me the baby. I believed she also wanted to confess that Andre was the father, to clear the air. I was fine with that. I would never trust her again but she deserved a chance to tell her side of the story. I returned her call and we made plans to meet the next day.

Later, Katana picked me up at about 10:00pm in a raggedy red Ford Escort. As I locked my door before stepping foot outside, I rehearsed in my head how I was going to pretend that I wasn't feeling well to bail out early. I opened the car door and greeted her.

During the ride, I noticed there was something odd about her. She was talkative. This was the opposite of what I was accustomed to seeing at work. She went on and on about some guy she met through an on-line dating service. It was the first time I had ever heard of such a thing. They weren't as common then as they are today, but she was comfortable with it.

"I regretted bringing him to my house. He seemed like the stalker type. I mean if he was going to do it then I couldn't stop him. You want to watch my house from across the street, be my guest, just walk a fine line and don't cross me. I didn't mean for him to sleep over. I woke up early, made breakfast. He came down and ate. I wanted the day to myself. After he ate he went back to my bed to sleep. We are not hanging out today! I had to wake him up and say its 11:00, I have to be somewhere. I was not going to spend my day off with him. The night wasn't *that* special."

Not only was I lost in her conversation, but the ride was long and I didn't know where we were. I was too distracted by her behavior. We arrived at a two-story house located outside the college. A short, but good looking guy greeted us. He wasn't steroid muscular but his body was nicely toned. The frat brother was Stanley, a 21 year old senior.

Stanley escorted us into the party room and introduced us to the president of the fraternity, Timothy. Katana was smitten by

297

Timothy's endearing charm. He was the one who invited her. How they met is beyond me, I never bothered asking.

This party was boring. About forty people sitting around drinking and mingling. It was more of a private setting. I went to a couple of college parties before and they were nothing like this. I partied with students who build pyramids with beer cans, played hard rock till the speakers blew, with a lot of weed smoking and girls going wild. That was a normal college party.

Stanley handed us a fruity concoction in a red cup called Trash Can Punch. It was a mixture of Everclear Vodka and fruit punch. I took it to be polite but I wasn't going to drink it. This drink was poured out of a trash can—literally—which is how it got its name. I was grossed out by the appearance of the house too. Even in the dim light I could see how dirty they kept the place. I just settled onto an old green couch with dingy cushions, staring at the cracked ceiling.

After a while, Katana went upstairs to use the bathroom. She came out acting more bizarre and had glassy eyes. A frat member changed the music to techno. He played an awesome mix by The Supremes, You Keep Me Hangin' On, with a heavy trance sound. Katana gyrated to the music. Everyone was staring at her; a few were murmuring and snickering. It was mind blowing how she handled herself outside of work. Who was this girl? A light bulb must have gone off in her head mid-song when she stopped. She found herself out of place and accordingly withdrew from the middle of the floor.

Stanley came over to me. Our legs touched when he sat down. A couple of frat members were in a corner whispering in each other's ears and looking towards where I was sitting. Stanley pulled out a joint and asked if I wanted to go in a private room and smoke. *Rule No. 1, never smoke with anyone who has a joint already rolled up. You don't want some scumbag lacing the weed with anything...*

were Xavier's words that came to mind. I politely declined; I had enough for me at home.

A few minutes later Katana pulled me into the kitchen. She was definitely the center of attention. She rambled continuously as if every word was just flowing. Was she high on something? Timothy offered us another drink. I left the first one behind but Katana sure didn't hesitate to have another one.

"Have a drink, loosen up," Katana said.

"No thanks, I'll pass."

"Okay Miss Goody Two Shoes."

The guys who were whispering in the corner earlier made their way to the kitchen. One by one they approached me, giving off a shady vibe. I couldn't explain why. They were all well mannered college guys.

Then I heard, at a little distance to my right, and partly in front, something, which I didn't understand but made me leery. One guy said to the other, "Consider her Rohyphnol worthy."

He turned to look at me up and down with a perverted stare and proceeded to walk towards me, "What's your name, pretty?" He leaned on his side with his elbow on the counter top.

"Sky."

"What do you like to do for fun?"

"I like to go to the shooting range with my dad. He's a sniper in the army."

I succeeded in getting rid of him faster than the rest of them.

Shortly after, I saw Timothy put his arm around Katana as he kissed her on the neck. She shied away and tried to slow things down. A few minutes later he made another attempt to kiss her. He was starting to get a little aggressive with her and I was ready to leave the party. I rushed to the bathroom to use it before leaving, but it reeked of urine, alcohol, and sweat so I rushed back out without bothering to wash my hands. I stood in the hallway looking down while I fixed my shirt and buckled my belt.

When I came back everyone was out of it. I barely saw any girls around but the few who were there had wobbly bodies. There was no sign of Katana. I made my way back up the stairs when I saw Timothy trying to pull Katana into the bedroom. By that time, she was stumbling and slurring her words. She could hardly remain standing.

"Hey, I was looking for you." I said. "I'm ready to leave."

Timothy interjected, "She's not leaving."

"Excuse me?" I asked.

"You're more than welcome to leave but Kat wants to stay here." He kept trying to pull her in the room.

I ignored him. I shook her shoulders to get her attention. "Where are your keys? I'll drive."

Timothy then stood in front of me in a threatening manner and told me she was too drunk to drive. Not wanting to appear rude, out of fear, I let him grasp my arm. Stanley walked out of a room and came over to us. While I spoke to Stanley amiably to get him to convince his buddy to let us go, Katana made her way into the bedroom. I rushed in behind her and locked the door behind me. I struggled to find the light in the room.

"Enough with the bullshit, Kat! We need to get out of here; and safely," I said, on the edge of panic.

I placed both hands on the wall and moved them around in a circular motion until I found the light switch. Katana covered her eyes as the light was too bright for her. Timothy banged on the door. Adrenaline gave me the strength to push a small table against it. I paced around the room thinking how I was going to get us out, but Katana passed out on the bed.

I pulled out my cellular phone and called Xavier. Even though he was in New York, I knew he would help me find a way out because I couldn't think straight.

"Hello," a girl answered softly. It was obvious I had wakened her up.

My voice trembled. "Could I speak to Xavier?"

The girl passed the phone to Xavier and he answered, "Who is it?"

"X! It's me, Sky!"

"What's wrong?"

I explained to him how I was trapped in a frat house with a co-worker and no way of getting past these guys. No way was I going to call 911 and draw more attention to myself with the department if they found out we worked for the City Police.

Xavier told me to hang on and he would call me back. The banging on the door got louder. I yelled out, "I just called the campus police and they're on their way."

The banging stopped and I tried to wake up Katana by pulling her up from the bed and smacking her in the face. "Kat...Katana, wake up please. I need to know where we are."

I grabbed my cellular phone and decided to call the police for help. The phone rang before I could dial 911. It was Xavier. He had Rodney on a three way conference with me.

"Where exactly are you?" Xavier asked.

"I don't know."

"Look for mail or something that may have an address on it," he instructed me.

I began to look around and inside the drawers of the night stand. "I found a wallet!"

I read the address on the school ID. Rodney told me to stay put. He was on his way. Xavier stayed on the phone consoling me as I cried. I looked at the time and saw that it was half-past one o'clock.

"Nuh come to me with that fuckery, yah bumbaclot!" (Don't come to me with that bullshit, motherfucker) Rodney was in the house and I could hear him coming closer. He sounded angry, "Me nah guh without Sky!" (I'm not leaving without Sky)

The thud in my chest was strong from hearing his voice. I pushed the table back and ran out. There stood Rodney, with his brother Sean, walking through the hall opening every door and looking inside.

"I'm over here Rodney!" I shouted.

I ran back in the bedroom to try and wake up Katana. Sean and I carried her out.

"How many drinks did it take ar to conk out?" Sean asked.

"Two, three, I'm not sure. She was acting strange all night; then after she drank, she passed out."

"They probably slipped a roofie in ar drink."

That's when it all came back to me; the conversation in the kitchen, the persistence of giving me a drink, and Timothy trying to force Katana in the bedroom.

We carried Katana to her car and Sean jumped in his tow truck and zoomed off. Rodney stayed behind so I could follow him out that place. Before we left, I asked about his girlfriend, Coco. He told me she was doing fine and that she had just bought a car. I told him I wanted my money but he told me I had to take that up with her. It looked like I had to confront Coco myself. I hugged Rodney tight and said, "Thank you. I owe you."

"It wah nutten! Take ar home." (It was nothing. Take her home.)

I jumped in the Escort and followed Rodney. When I arrived home Katana wouldn't wake up. I sat in my driveway questioning whether I should bring her to the emergency room or let her stay in my place for the night to sleep it off. The possibility of her being slipped a rape drug bothered me. She was breathing but appeared to be in a coma. I walked up to the house to open the front door first. I left it open and went back to pull Katana out the car and carry her up the stairs.

Once I was inside, weary and breathless, I dragged her into the bathroom. I sat her on the floor against the wall in an upright position. I took a towel and ran it under cold water. When I looked down, her lips were blue. I threw the wet rag to the side and dropped to my knees to face her. She was foaming from the mouth and convulsing. I opened her mouth, closed my eyes tight, and stuck two fingers down her throat to provoke her vomit. I screamed out of disgust when it gushed out all over me but I wasn't going to let her die. I took the wet rag, wiped the vomit off her, and called 911.

When the ambulance arrived, I gave them a false name of Catherine Greene. I felt I was compelled to lie. If anyone in the department heard about this, it would be another full blown scandal. My story was she arrived at my house drunk and asked to stay over. I was completely oblivious to what was going on with her or her whereabouts prior to her arrival. That's the story I stuck with.

I followed the ambulance to Brigham and Woman's Hospital. After spending the rest of the night beside her, the doctor informed me that Katana tested positive for the date rape drug, Rohyphnol. However, it was more disturbing to me to find out that she also tested positive for cocaine. The only confusion the doctor had was how she made it to my house in her condition. Evidently, the doctor didn't believe she drove herself to my house, but I wasn't going to recant my story.

It was now 6:36 am and I was exhausted. I decided to walk outside to catch the morning air. The sliding doors to the emergency room opened up as I approached it. I stepped outside and took a deep breath. The horizon was tinged with red and the sun appeared. I just stared at the sky and played that frightening night over and over in my head like a movie. My mind recalled the last time my

303

grandmother gave me a reading. I remembered how she screamed at her vision of someone trying to poison me. Before I took my eyes off the sky, I mumbled, "Gracias, Abuela." (Thank you, Grandma)

I walked back in the hospital and found Katana awake and pale. She looked at me with shameful eyes.

"I guess I have some explaining to do," she said with a weak voice.

"I signed you in as Catherine Greene and no, you don't have to explain anything to me." I spoke quietly just in case any staff came in. "You almost died, I didn't know what else to do, but I'm glad you're okay now."

"What happened to me last night?"

After I told her everything about the night, she dropped a bomb on me. "The department is watching you."

"What?" I thought she was still high or the after effect was tripping her out.

"The department is watching you. I overheard a conversation between my father and a sergeant. They were trying to bring someone in to Anti-Corruption to interview them about your step-father. I didn't tune in too much because I don't get in my father's business but ever since you found my wallet, you earned my respect. And after today—you've earned my trust."

"Wow. I don't know what to say. Thanks."

"No, it should be me thanking you. You saved me. I will forever be in debt with you."

I almost chuckled at the thought of how things are discovered, but I just smiled at her. I didn't want her to feel that she owed me anything. Snitching on her father was gratifying enough. Superheroes don't go around saving lives and asking for compensation. They do it because they have a supernatural power and it's their obligation to protect. Even though I wasn't a comic book hero, I felt that my instincts were powerful enough to stay alert and watch over her. At the end, I saved her.

COCKTAIL ANYONE?

After the ordeal with Katana, I made it home in time to get ready to meet Massiel. I stopped at Toys R Us in South Bay and picked up a few things for her baby. This was going to be an interesting conversation. I was meeting Andre's first born, who was conceived out of wedlock, by a former friend, and possibly the very person Anti-corruption wanted to interview. I felt the need to drink.

We met at Uno Chicago Bar and Grille on Huntington Ave. She was already there waiting for me with the baby in a car seat. The waitress brought us to our table before I got a chance to greet her and peek into the car seat. But when I sat down, I took a good look at the baby and handed Massiel my gift bag. There was no denying he was Andre's seed.

The waitress, who seemed like she hated her job, reminded me of Eeor from Winnie the Pooh. "Could I get you guys something to…"

"I'll have a strawberry Daquiri."

"You are in rare form. I don't think I've ever seen you like this; a drink in the middle of the day?"

"I didn't sleep well last night. I'm waiting to hear what you have to say." I spoke fast while staring down at the menu. But I wasn't hungry.

"You already know who the father of the baby is."

I turned the menu page. "I have a pretty good idea from looking at him."

"I wanted to apologize for everything."

"What's everything?" I picked my eyes up from the menu to look at her.

Massiel pointed at the baby. "Him."

"He's everything?"

"He's everything to me, Sky." She stared at him. "I'm really sorry that I befriended you just to keep tabs on Andre. I never expected you to be as cool as you are. Andre use to say you hated him so I thought there was probably something wrong with you because he was loved by everyone. But we have different eyes for him. You're his step-daughter."

"Mother's husband! I dislike the term step-daughter and I don't feel any different about him now than I did growing up. I'm not going to sit here and explain my reasons but this little precious thing right here has no fault in any of this." I rubbed my hands against my lap nervously, "Can I hold him?"

"Of course you can." She pulled the baby out the car seat and placed him in my arms.

He was the first baby I had ever held. Once he was in my arms, tears were streaming down my face. The poor thing must have sensed I was uneasy because he pouted his lips and began to cry. I handed him over back to Massiel.

"I think he knows that I hate his father." I chuckled as I wiped my face.

"He's just hungry. It's his feeding time." She pulled out a bottle for him.

"Did you know Andre was married when you slept with him?"

She opened her eyes wide at my question as if she were offended. I didn't care, though. The respect was lost when I found out about their affair. She was still trying to formulate her words after that. So while she thought of something to say, I continued.

"You know I'm a straight shooter, so if we're here to clear the air, let's put it all out there." The waitress stopped at our table and I said, "I'll have another cocktail, please."

As soon as the waitress left, Massiel put the baby back in the car seat and turned her attention back to me. "I don't have to give you every intimate detail of my affair with him."

"I didn't ask for an intimate detail. I asked about your knowledge of his marital status before you fucked him."

"Why does it have to be a fuck thing?"

"Because that's exactly what it was—a fuck! Or did you really think he was going to divorce my mother to be with you? Pff," I spurted. "Let me tell you something," I waved an accusatory finger, "You weren't his only mistress and you better thank your lucky stars my mother didn't catch you, because she would have wrung your neck."

"I didn't invite you here to fight."

"I didn't come here to fight either, but don't expect me to be fine with all this. You befriended me to get close to Andre—my mother's husband. It doesn't get any shadier than that."

"I'm trying to make things right here."

"Make things right with who? Me? Or are you under investigation too? Is this your way to patch things up, so you can know where Andre is? Save yourself the trouble. I'm done with you. Now if you'll excuse me, I have somewhere to be."

I threw my money on the table, guzzled my cocktail, and stormed out without giving her a chance to come back with an answer. When I got in the truck I regretted the way I came off. I even slammed my hands on the steering wheel, wishing I had stayed calm. I should have let her speak; that way I could have probably found out something I didn't know, but my approach was poorly delivered.

My drive back home was a bit reckless. I was anxious to plunge in my bed and sleep the rest of the day. Although my body was exhausted, I was too deep inside my head to sleep.

At about 4:00 o'clock I gave up trying to fall asleep. Instead I started cleaning while blasting my mother's Latin CD by La India; who is known as the princess of Salsa. I didn't know much about Salsa music, but it reminded me of Andre and my mother, since they were no longer around.

I found myself listening to La India's lyrics, and not just the tropical beat I used to when my mother played it. There was a song titled Dicen Que Soy (They Say That I Am), where she says people call her hechicera, which is someone who practices voodoo. In the song she describes how people accused her of cursing a man's life, dominating his mind, and is an evil snake in disguise.

In her lyrics she also sings, *they say that I am bad luck, they say that I am a poison apple, they say that I am more thorns and less of a rose.* Then she says how she doesn't care what people say and they can continue to speak about her because it makes her happy. I thought it was brave of her that she didn't care what people thought of her, especially because everything that she was being referred to in the song had to do with her involvement with Santeria. Interesting how she put it out there with her head up high and a beautiful voice to back it up.

Listening to La India was putting me in a bittersweet mood, which was quite different than how I had been feeling earlier. After I spic and spanned the house, I took a break. As I sat on the couch, listening to the CD, the last track came on. It was an upbeat house-music song. I found it strange that this kind of music was on my mother's CD. First, she didn't listen to this kind of music. Secondly, I've never even heard this play in the house.

I looked inside the CD case to see if the person who dubbed it wrote the name of this song. While I read down the list, a mystical chant came on. I thought I was tripping for a second. But as I listened closely, it became clearer to me. I was definitely familiar with incantatory singing because my grandmother listened to the fast Caribbean sounds that chanted to the spirits during her rituals.

It was strange to hear a chant on a house-music beat but it sounded cool. The title of the song was Love and Happiness (Yemaya y Ochun), also sung by La India. I didn't recognize the deities, Yemaya and Ochun, which were written next to the title, but I knew she was praising them. So I went through my grandmother's books to do my research as I replayed the song a few more times.

In Santeria, Yemaya is the goddess of the ocean. She offers protection to women and one of her areas of influence is fertility. Ochun is the goddess of love and her areas of influences are romance, seduction, and marriage.

Later that evening, in sheer exhaustion, I got under the covers and went under. And then a door in my mind opened. Voices from outside my ear rushed in on me. It was as if they were competing for attention, in brusque, choppy phrases and even the laughter of a baby came in: *Leave now...time for supper...the shed, look for the shed...listen to...no listen to me...one day he'll scratch yours...I didn't choose...peaches.*

My body froze, waiting for the voices to stop. And they did; until one voice whispered in my ear. "Hello."

I shot up from my bed and staggered to the medicine cabinet, covering my ears. I grabbed the bottle of valiums and drank some milk out of the container. I turned up the volume to the television and watched it until I fell asleep again.

Sometime in the middle of the night the smoke alarm went off. I propped myself up onto my elbows, blinking my eyes, and hoped I was dreaming. But the alarm was loud and clear. I put on my sneakers to check what was going on. When I opened the front door, a plume of black smoke surged past all of my sensory organs. I immediately shut the door and found my way towards the back door. It was clear of smoke so I rushed out.

Sirens wailed. I ran to the front of the house and saw flames coming from the first floor parlor. The suffocating air knocked me down against the side of the fence where it was free from smoke. I sat curled up on the ground. When was this nightmare going to end? Then, as the neighbors put their noses out of the windows while others came out upon the steps of their houses, the fire fighters and police responded.

Four firemen jumped out the fire truck and got set up. They braced themselves for the kick of when the valve on the hose opened. It started whipping around about fifty pounds of pressure, knocking the helmet off one of them. I sat there; dazed, watching how they attacked the fire.

The officer called for an ambulance. I couldn't move. I was catatonic. Meanwhile, the fire fighters did their investigation and determined that someone threw a Molotov cocktail through the window causing the blaze. Luckily I was able to escape.

The paramedics arrived shortly thereafter and transported me to the hospital for an evaluation of smoke inhalation. There I learned that I had a bladder infection and my potassium level was so low the doctor couldn't believe I was able to even stand. All this was caused from the depression I was in. This depression combined with my lack of nutrition continued to affect me physically. I was prescribed an anti-biotic and potassium citrate and later discharged from the hospital.

I walked to the Brigham Diner down the street from the hospital and bought a bacon, egg, and cheese croissant with an orange juice. I waved down a taxi cab and got in. He brought me home and I instructed him to wait until I went upstairs to get my money. The window that caught the Molotov cocktail was boarded up. I was starting to look at it like the house of Amityville Horror. After I paid the cab driver, I got in my truck, and drove to Reynalda's house.

"I'm sorry for showing up unexpectedly, but I had no one else to turn to." I was in tears.

"Come in, Sky, you don't have to apologize. What's going on? You look like you were caught in a tornado."

I laughed and sniffled at the same time. I sat down in her living room and told her what had happened that night with the voices that invaded my head and the home-made bomb. She gave me the phone and told me to speak with Xavier while she went to set up her reading room.

Xavier was worried. He invited me to go stay with him in Queens, New York. I told him I would go after the storm calmed to get him to stop worrying. But I had no intentions of going. Reynalda handed me a St. Michael candle and told me to follow her to the kitchen. Her clients were starting to come in for their card readings so she told me to wait for her until she finished working.

By late afternoon, Reynalda was done with her clients and fixed me something to eat. She also made me some tea and told me everything was going to be all right. She offered me a spare bedroom to stay in for the time being, but I didn't want to be a burden on anyone. She insisted. I refused.

"That house is not safe for you. I just consulted with my saints and my advice is to take only what's important out of that house and leave everything else behind. You are welcomed to stay here if you change your mind." She grabbed my empty dish and cup. "Xavier is coming to Boston soon. He is really worried about you. You should consider going back to New York with him. Get away for awhile and go see the big city. You'll love it out there."

She assured me things were going to get better and many changes were in the near future. One only hoped that everything would turn around for the better.

Back at the house, I found a swarm of reporters and police gathered outside. Apparently, another fire bomb was thrown while I was gone. It was early in the evening and the media followed me. Questions swirled about Andre's involvement in the prostitution ring, were the bombs a form of retaliation, and could they have an exclusive interview with me. I tried to push my way through. I even slapped a microphone out of my face because I was so angry.

The officers on scene disbanded the reporters, but someone then grabbed my arm. I hit the person who held me. That's when I heard his voice.

"Sky, it's me."

Ray! "What are you doing here?"

He walked me to the back of the house where we could speak in private. "It's all over the news. I came to see if you were all right. I heard you were in the hospital last night."

"I'm fine, thank you."

"Is there somewhere safe you can stay for the time being?"

"Yeah."

"Are you sure?"

"I said yes."

"Take down this number." He pulled out his cell phone. "My friend Benji is a realtor. He'll help you find a new place if you're interested."

I took down the number. Neither one of us brought up what had taken place the last time we were together. As soon as he left, I sat on my back steps with my head down, touching my knees and my hands holding my ankles, waiting for the rest of the squad and media crew to leave me alone.

After all was clear, I went to the attic and lit the St. Michael candle Reynalda gave me. I sat in the attic by a window and fiddled with my gold rosary necklace. The window was facing Mrs. Jankowski's lonely, small house that stood vacant for years. I stared at the waste and shambles that littered her property. Garbage was strewn about her yard, weeds grew wild all around the fence and none of it was ever cleaned up.

313

Before I turned away, I noticed the shed. I pressed my face against the window to get a better view. Mrs. Jankowski's shed was where the money was stashed! But I needed to wait for darkness to fall before going over there.

When the night came, I went through my flashlight bin. I held on in the dark stairway and walked out the back door towards the fence. As I climbed it to cross over, I heard a police radio and, "Hey!"

There was an officer in my yard pointing his flashlight at me and I did the same to him from the top of the fence. He caught me in the act.

"What are you doing up there?" he asked.

"I heard something, sir, so I came out to check." I jumped from the top of the fence back to the ground. "What are you doing on my property?"

"I've been ordered to watch the house. You can go back upstairs; you're safe here with me."

"Who assigned this fixed post?" I walked closer to him to get a better look at him.

"I'm not sure. I just do as I'm told."

Sure you do. "Well, if you need anything, feel free..." Damn it! I had to wait.

"Thanks."

SETBACK JOURNEY

Finding things unbearable, I decided to visit Calvin at Concord State Prison. If there was someone else who understood what it felt like to be all alone, it surely was him. I filled out the visitor's form with a shaky hand. The front desk officer ordered me to let my hair out and make sure I had nothing in my pockets besides money.

"I can bring money in?" I asked.

"Yes, but only for the vending machines, and it has to be in a clear plastic bag."

She kindly gave me a zip lock bag and pointed to the change machine. I walked over to it and made change. After I put all the quarters in the bag and all my belongings in my assigned locker, I was called.

I walked through the metal sliding doors which were loud and ancient. A heavy set woman instructed me to take off my sneakers and belt, go through the metal detector, and stand to the side. Then I had to go into a separate room where I was patted down. The woman went up and down my legs, all around my waist, and under my breast. I thought she was going to have me bend over and cough by the way she thoroughly searched me.

Another woman visitor walked with me through the other metal sliding doors and told me the search was mainly for first timers or anyone who looked suspicious. I was relieved to hear that because there was no way I would have continued visiting him if that was going to happen to me every time.

I followed the rest of the women into one huge visiting room. There were chairs lined up, each row had a pair facing another. I sat down all the way at the end of the room near a window, far from the correction officers who sat near the doorway. I watched all the inmates come in one by one.

Calvin finally came out and looked around to see who had paid him a visit. I didn't wave at him to see how long it would take him to find me. When he saw me, he smiled and made his way over.

"Can I get a hug?" He stood in front of me with open arms.

I rose up on my feet and hugged him. He held me tight and kissed me twice on my cheek. He looked really healthy and nicely tanned. Jail made him look better than he ever did. He sure enough didn't appear to be stressed, unlike me who went in there, ten pounds lighter, pale, puffy eyes, and messy hair.

"Talk to me." He leaned forward and put his hands together, waiting for me to speak.

"I don't know where to begin."

I leaned forward to avoid speaking loud. Obnoxious chattering throughout the entire visiting room made it hard to hear him. I told him everything I was going through and he told me about his troubles. By the end of the visit he asked me if I would return.

"I'm not sure. I have a realtor helping me search for an apartment and a few other things I need to handle, so don't expect me here any time soon."

"Come see me Friday."

"Calvin." I threw my hands up in the air. "Did you not just hear what I said?"

"Come see me Friday. I need a favor."

"What? Is this why you wanted to see me? You need me. Oh, I see now, you haven't changed."

"Sky, you're the only one I have right now."

"What's the favor?"

"Come see me Friday."

316

"Fine, you'll see me Friday."

We stood up, hugged, and I left the prison. On my way home, Benji the Realtor called me. He had an apartment for me to look at. I scheduled an appointment to meet him and we hung up.

When I arrived at my house, a woman in a dress suit waited on the porch. I asked her if I could help her with anything. She was from the bank and was putting the padlock on the doors, foreclosing the house. I begged her to let me run upstairs and allow me to pack my things, but she declined. I insisted until my nagging became annoying. She gave me exactly 24 hours to pack my things. She would return the next day and put the padlock on and that was final.

I went upstairs and took a long shower. I packed my birth certificate, jewelry, the doll coin bank my mother left me, my CD collection, and my clothes. The only thing I had to think about hard of taking was that black wooden box I made in high school. It only brought bad memories for me. I went downstairs to the basement and unlocked two windows in case I had to return for anything.

After putting my belongings in my ride, I sat on the porch thinking about where I was going to stay. My options were to sleep in the truck, a dirty motel, or someone's house. I didn't want to burden any one with my troubles. Besides, I lived in total freedom, coming and going as I pleased. That was something I didn't want to compromise just to have a roof over my head.

Another thought was getting to that shed to retrieve the money Andre left me. I wondered how much was in there. I'm sure he left me a good amount.

I went back upstairs one last time and looked around to make sure I wasn't missing anything. Up in the attic, I blew out the candle. I brought down my altar and placed my spiritual icons in a box. Finally, I made sure to unlock all the doors throughout the house. Before I left the apartment, I returned to my bedroom and decided to take my hideous blackmail box. I rushed out the door. This house, where I was brought up, had breathed its last. That night I said goodbye. Its existence had been no more.

At exactly 10:30 that night, the officer assigned to watch the house took off early. I left the truck's engine idling so no one would hear me climbing the fence to Mrs. Jankowski's yard. I jumped over it, landing on my two feet. Like a missile I made it through her backyard and ransacked her shed.

"Out of all places to hide money, this son of a bitch really chose this dump," I growled. "Ah—there you go!"

I picked up the green camouflage duffle bag, and judging by the weight of it, it appeared to have more than what I had imagined. I shivered with excitement, trying to make it out of there without running into any shed creatures. I swung the bag over the fence and then I jumped over it.

The mission was accomplished and I anticipated the moment to count how much was in the bag. I drove around thinking where I could station myself without getting caught sleeping in the truck. The only place I could come up with was my job. So I drove to the city.

The parking lot across the street from Headquarters was extensive. There was a section that few people knew about, behind a high fence covered with trees and tall shrubs. I discovered it one day when my mind drifted off while looking for a parking space. I thought it was my safest bet: I could sleep there and shower at the gym at night when no one was around.

I stayed up the first night converting the back of the truck into a sleeping nest and counting the bundles of money that were tied up in rubber bands. It was more than I could count; and more than I could bank, but I couldn't get an accurate number because I kept losing track. One thing was for sure, Andre's pay out was seriously large.

Days went by. I lived out of the truck, showered at the gym, and ate from the cafeteria. I could afford a hotel room but I didn't own a credit card. I couldn't have a credit card because my credit was ruined when my Audi was seized. Searching for a new apartment wasn't as easy as I thought it would be. Most property owners were doing credit checks and those that didn't were renting out slums.

The discomfort of my secret hideout affected my sleep. I grew thinner, lethargic, and found it increasingly difficult to concentrate. I was a communications person but I didn't want to communicate with anyone. I dreaded getting up in that truck every day. All I did was cry in it.

In the last days of summer, I decided to pay Benji the realtor a visit and have a serious talk. I pulled out his business card to get the address. It read: King Realty, on Beacon Street, in Brookline, across from the Golden Temple Restaurant. I knew exactly where that was.

I made a stop at the Copley Mall where I bought a nice dress at Neiman Marcus, a pair of stylish sandals, and a black designer tote bag, made out of calfskin, to store some of my money. Having no safe place to leave the cash, I bought this trendy bag to carry most of it around. I was reluctant to part with it until I found a place to live. After I got dolled up in the mall's public bathroom, I drove to King Realty.

"I'm here to see Benjamin King," I told the receptionist.

"He's with a client right now. Do you have an appointment?"

"Yes. Can you tell him Cecilia Pino is here to see him?"

"Of course," she looked at me up and down, "have a seat."

She dialed his number and spoke softly over the phone. Ten minutes later, Benji walked out his office with an older gentleman. Benji was 5'9", 200 pounds, with medium brown hair and light green eyes. He had a beer belly that would turn the corner before he did. Although his physical attributes were in a low category, his persona was larger than life. The client was talking his ear out. Benji gave me a sideway glance and winked, then turned his attention back to his client. The conversation didn't seem important from where I was sitting. So I stood up, adjusted my tote over my shoulder, and waited for Benji to finish up with this man.

"Good morning Cecilia, or should I say good afternoon?" He turned his wrist to check the time.

"It's afternoon." I giggled.

"You look very nice today."

"Thank you."

"What can I do for you?"

"Well I was going to have lunch across the street and I thought I'd invite you to join me so we can talk." I raised my eyebrow hinting that I needed to speak in private.

He turned to his receptionist and said, "Dana, could you cancel my one o'clock?"

The receptionist picked up the phone to cancel his appointment. Benji then politely held the door open for me to walk out. As we crossed the street he answered his ringing cell phone. For a moment I entertained the idea of explaining my situation to him but it was going to be a lengthy story we didn't have time for. Suddenly he threw his right arm out to stop me from getting hit by a car. I was embarrassed that I wasn't paying attention when crossing the street.

We walked in to the restaurant and ordered lunch. His cell phone rang continuously the first fifteen minutes we were there. I

320

waited, trying to figure out how I was going to ask him to bypass the credit check, if I ever got the chance to speak to him with all the incoming calls interrupting us.

"I'm sorry. It's a busy time with all the college students moving in."

"I bet. It's back to school season." I took a sip of my soda. "So Benji, I um, I really need an apartment." I pulled out a thousand dollars folded in half, and slid it across the table to him. "Can you find me a nice place where good credit isn't a requirement?"

Benji grabbed the money and flipped through it. "I'll see what I can do."

The waiter brought us our food. As we ate, his cell phone rang again. Only this time I was attentive to his conversation. A friend of his wanted to sell her townhouse and asked for him to help her find a buyer. I wasn't interested in buying property even though I had enough money to purchase a townhouse and more.

"My friend Andrea has a beautiful place in Roslindale; three bedrooms, two and half bathrooms, fireplace, laundry room, I mean it's a beauty, too bad you're not able to buy because you would love this place; but anyways, let me see if I can find someone who is willing to rent without a credit check."

"What if I told you I could afford to buy this townhouse with straight cash?"

"I would say that's a questionable purchase. Then I would tell you the IRS would look heavily into that."

I regretted speaking in haste. Benji was good friends with Ray and all I could picture was him running back telling Ray, an honest cop, to be leery of me.

"I'll tell you what...if you can afford this place, hypothetically speaking, and you're interested in buying it, I suggest you get someone to put it under their name. Or, speak to the bank and work something out to fix your credit."

Benji explained to me how important it was to have good credit and how to go about getting it. I sat there quietly eating and listening. He gave me useful advice but I was desperate. How could I worry about rebuilding credit when I was sleeping in the back of a Chevy Tahoe?

Time was ticking and I wanted to make it to Concord to visit Calvin. How could I tell him everything without worrying him?

When I got to the prison, I was sick. My stomach was nauseas and a bad headache came over me. I sat in the visiting room with my head leaning on my hand against the chair. Calvin hurried over to me, kissed me on the cheek and asked was I all right.

"I swear every time I see you, you're skinnier. What's going on?"

Tears ran down my face. "I just got sick all of a sudden."

"Are you pregnant?"

"No!" I was offended by his question but usually when a woman says she's not feeling well, pregnancy is the first question out of a person's mouth.

Calvin attempted to make me feel better by telling me how pretty I was dressed and how happy it made him feel to see me. That only made me cry more. One of the other visitors handed me toilet paper to wipe my face. I was behaving extra sensitive because of everything I was going through.

Calvin finally dropped the bomb on me that he wanted me to smuggle blow inside the prison. When my stomach tightened up and my headache intensified, I realized that all these secrets and emotions I was keeping to myself were hurting me.

I stood and glared at him. "Have you lost your fucking mind?"

322

"Sit down, Sky."

"I left you canteen money. That should be good enough."

He didn't want to hear that. He had a hustling spirit that even those prison bars weren't powerful enough to separate. I thought it was insane, though, that he would even think I'd consider such a thing. But it wasn't only about money. It was about respect and power. He didn't say it, but that's what I thought.

I broke enough rules and laws in my lifetime—I didn't want to press my luck. I refused to help him but I was curious to know what got into him to think that we would get away with such a thing.

"I called Rodney one day and told him to come up and visit. He said he couldn't because he was on probation but Sean could. I told him no, because I don't trust his brother. He knew right away it was about business so he sent his girlfriend, Coco."

"Coco?" I interrupted.

"Yeah, but check this out. She comes up to visit and right from the jump I get a bad feeling about her. But I'm thinking I have no other choice but to use her. I'm explaining to her that my cell mate cleans the visiting area including the bathroom. All she had to do was bring the product inside a maxi pad. Chew gum during the visit. Then five minutes before leaving, go to the ladies room, and stick the bag behind the toilet with the gum. My cell mate picks up the supply after visiting hours. That's it."

"That's it?" I asked sarcastically.

"That's it." My sarcasm went over his head. "But the trifling bitch never brought the product. She sat here chewing the gum like a cow, didn't make much conversation, and looked uncomfortable. Then she went to the bathroom and claimed she left it there. It was total bullshit. I called Rodney and told him she came up empty but he didn't believe me. I was pissed off, Sky! I've been doing business with Rodney since I was fourteen. He meets this chick yesterday and now I'm the liar."

Calvin grew heated as he told the story, giving me no chance to tell him what I was going through. Our time was up and I had to leave. We hugged each other. Only this time Calvin held on tight and longer than last time.

"I love you," he whispered in my ear before kissing me on my cheek.

I didn't say I love you back. A simple goodbye was sufficient. I stomped off and left Concord feeling extremely sick. I even took off those new shoes to drive barefoot.

When I arrived to Headquarters, I grabbed a change of clothes and took a shower in the gym. But I felt terrible; I decided to take a cab to Brigham and Woman's Hospital. After going through my medical file, the doctor learned I had a manic depressive disorder. He began asking me questions regarding my mental state and how I was feeling at the present time. I admitted that I was depressed and was experiencing suicidal thoughts.

Next thing I knew I was committed to Arbour Hospital, a private psychiatric facility in Jamaica Plain. It was a nightmare I couldn't believe I was in. They found traces of marijuana in my urine and refused to let me go because they thought I would harm myself. I tried explaining to them that the difference between insanity and normalcy is I could think of driving my car into a crowd of people verses doing it. Just because you think of something crazy doesn't make you crazy, it's the act of your thought that puts you in that category. That theory went nowhere.

From the hospital bed, I could hear people screaming and crying in other rooms; begging to leave. A pregnant Nigerian woman pleaded with her husband to pick her up. One elderly lady would scream for hours that she wanted milk. Another man posed as a nurse, going into everyone's room asking if they needed anything. When he entered mine, three staff nurses apprehended him and he fought with them. Fear iced through me. I believed I was never going to make it out. I was allowed a fifteen minute break outside but I was surrounded by brick walls. It took every bit of strength I had to stay calm.

My first night there I had to be sedated. Even though I wasn't much of a pill popper, a good night sleep was my first step in letting go of the stress of being there. I fantasized about being famous and how the whole world loved me. Then other weird thoughts played into my subconscious at night causing wild, silly dreams.

My dream took me to the Communication Center where a union representative asked me if I wanted to sit in a meeting. I thought I had nothing better else to do on my break so I agreed. I informed Sgt. Honey G that I would be at the union meeting. He spoke about coming back from my break on time but I was too busy thinking how attractive he was. Even in my dreams this Boy Scout made me lust.

The dream jumped to the meeting which was being held outside in the parking lot across from Headquarters. They planned on protesting an increase of pay for the 911 call takers. When the meeting was over, everyone was standing around talking among themselves. That's when I noticed my belongings were on the ground. I started picking up my things and thinking my secret has come out. Everyone was going to find out that I slept in that same parking lot. But no one else seemed to be paying attention to me.

The more I picked my things up, the more items were surfacing. Suddenly I saw water near my feet. I was next to a shore. None of this seemed strange because it was a dream but the water caught me by surprise and swallowed me. I let out a scream. My body was being shoved around by angry waters. My body went from side to side, upside down, and back up from the tide. I reached over to the sand to pull myself out but the water dragged me back in.

When I found myself breathing under water, I realized I was dreaming. I yelled out at the dream, "Wake up, NOW!" The dream then shifted to an unknown arena where the rock group ACDC was playing Thunderstruck. I was on stage with them; rocking out. The crowd was cheering and I fell in love with the sound of their applause. It appeared like I was a rock star that rose to stardom overnight. It felt real. It felt right. That's when I woke up—still in that psychiatric facility.

After spending a couple days in that mental ward, I was ready to go home with the promise of seeking treatment. During my breakfast hour, a doctor came in to check on me. An older woman with greasy gray hair that was parted in the middle, she wore enormous, outdated glasses. Her eyes jiggled from side to side as she spoke to me but never looked at me. I pushed the emergency button and a staff member came over the intercom.

"Hello."

"Um, I um, need someone here right away."

"What do you need, Ms. Pino?"

"Can you just send someone to my room, please?"

The doctor had a confused expression on her face. "Is everything all right?"

"Who are you?" I asked, just as confused as she was.

"I'm Dr. Lebec."

The intercom was still on. "Dr. Lebec are you all set in there?" the voice asked.

The doctor smiled. "Yes, I think there seems to be a misunderstanding."

"I'm sorry doctor. I had a patient pose as a male nurse my first day here and I wasn't sure if you...well, you know...were posing as well."

"That's quite all right. I will get you your discharge papers ready for this afternoon."

Great. I didn't have to call out of work again because I still had time to make my shift. After that experience I vowed to never share, my upper body felt a sudden burst of energy from the wind the second I stepped out those hospital doors. I couldn't fathom what Calvin was going through in prison. I wasn't built to be confined with no freedom. It made me think I would never admit to suicide again. If I ever felt the need to end my life, it would get done or it would get pushed out my head.

There was tension in my walk as I entered the Comm Center. It was the tensity of hoping I would be working somewhere other than 911. By chance, the supervisor in charge assigned me to the Support Room. I worked in the Stolen Car Unit, but it wasn't the quiet evening I had hoped for. One of our long time employees, Helen, broke the receiver against the desk after she was denied a day off by the office. Everyone tried calming her down and agreeing to let her out early the day she was requesting. But whatever climbed up her ass, went sideways.

17:02, glared the large clock at the head of my cubicle. Helen was found in the break room crying. Sergeant Coffee Roll, who had heard about what was done to the phone, sought out more details. He questioned her, provoking an intense reaction out of her. Then he instructed her to write out a report when suddenly there was a small snap in her psyche. Whatever support column that helped organize her behavior went tumbling down. I knew her pretty well, so the structure was already weak. A small kick was enough to make it collapse.

Captain Lyons stepped in to diffuse the argument but it only made Helen angrier. She was shouting and flailing her arms. The sergeant used a wrist lock on her to gain control. She shouted, "I'm going to cut your dick off!"

327

I took malicious pleasure in knowing this madness was going to take some of the attention off me.

Days later, Rasheeda told me that our crazed coworker was forced to go on medical leave. This gave me the idea to request a medical leave as well. Helen and I weren't that much different, except that I wasn't going to use her tactic in getting time off.

As I went over the manual that explained the different types of leave of absences, I decided to put in for the personal leave of absence.

I presented to Human Resources my request of six months—unpaid. Time off was exactly what I needed to retreat and recharge. I was trying to return to normalcy; if it were ever possible. After several days of waiting for a response, my submission was denied.

I crumbled the letter and closed my eyes; only to find pain with disappointment. My mind was so far gone from the dark emotions that gripped me, that I was oblivious to what had taken place in my homeland: America had fallen victim to a horrific attack on September 11th. I watched it over and over on television, everyone was talking about it, and yet it didn't hit me until I heard one of my sergeants' say, "This city better tighten up because it's bound to happen here next."

I decided to visit someone with power and authority. I needed to speak with Mayor Kirsch. The mayor had a good reputation and plenty of clout. If the police department wasn't going to grant me my request, maybe they would listen to Kirsch. His name held a lot of weight and I was certain if he spoke on my behalf the department would hear him out.

I took a deep breath and straightened my back before walking into his office. "Hi Mayor Kirsch," I greeted him, "Could I speak with you?" Sadness seeped in my voice.

328

Mayor Kirsch welcomed me in to his office and we spoke for two hours. He emailed the Chief asking him to grant me my leave of absence. Within days I received a call from Mayor Kirsch. It was approved. Thanking him for his kindness, I hung up feeling weightless.

THE SMILE THAT LIGHTS THE HEART

I called Jade to meet with her. She was the only one that I could think of to help fix my credit and start a loan application for that townhouse. She asked me to bring her my pay stubs and bank statements. She doubted I would get approved because Andre ruined my credit, but she was willing to show me how to repair the damage.

That evening I stopped by her house with all my documents. She still lived with her mother on Hyde Park Ave. That didn't come to a surprise. She was the favorite twin. And after years of her mother not approving of my friendship with the twins, she learned to accept it. She realized I wasn't a bad person—mischievous—but not bad.

"Jade, you're the Bank Manager, make it happen," I asked with enthusiasm. "I'll give you five hundred dollars, straight cash, if you finagle that loan for me," I bribed her. I really wanted the townhouse.

"First we have to find out if Audi is willing to take a settlement payment before anything else."

"That's fine with me. Where's Sasha?"

"She's home, still pregnant and miserable." Jade rolled her eyes.

"What are the plans for her baby shower? I haven't heard anything from you guys."

"We're trying to find a hall for the party."

"I just got some time off work so I'll get the hall. That's my goddaughter we're welcoming!"

The next couple of weeks I helped Sasha's mother set up the baby shower. But when I wasn't busy party planning, I was visiting Calvin. He started to notice the difference in my attitude. I was more relaxed and smiled more. We spent our visits reminiscing and opening up.

During one of my visits, he confessed that he did business with Andre. This was how Calvin came up in the drug game. Clients of the prostitution ring that Senator Thompson ran brought him serious money. He agreed to keep the drugs outside the house and keep his mouth shut, which explained why Andre looked the other way when I allowed Calvin to live with me.

Everything started to make a lot more sense to me. The reason Andre lost his temper when he found the drugs in the attic wasn't because he was concerned about me. He was worried about his own neck. And the interview with Internal Affairs when Calvin was arrested in my car after shooting Nicole's brother had Andre on edge because he was tied to Calvin just as much as I was.

Calvin and I went back to the days when things were less intense between us. We spoke of the times when we had snow ball fights during blizzards, being egged on Halloween by the rest of the gang, and the infamous fight with his cousin Charlene that landed us both in the emergency room.

Somewhere in between laughs, he managed to ask me one more time to sneak cocaine inside the prison. I stopped laughing. He wouldn't let it go. He was hammering the subject and against all common sense, I gave in.

After agreeing to bring in some Columbian marching powder, I paid the supplier a visit. Rodney. I walked in the complex and met him outside his mother's building to pick up the product. He gave me a hug by wrapping one arm around me and we discreetly switched money and product with our right hand. Rodney laughed and called me crazy. I laughed and asked about Coco. I hadn't dismissed the fact that she bamboozled me out of a thousand dollars. He always had an excuse why she wasn't around, but I knew eventually I'd run into her.

The day I brought Calvin what he ordered was nerve racking. I sat in the lobby shaking my right leg and drinking ginger ale for my upset stomach. I stared at the entrance door with my back towards the front desk to avoid eye contact with any of the correction officers.

A hand crept up on me and tapped me on the shoulder, causing me to jump and spill some of my ginger ale on my lap. The woman who brought me back to Earth was another frequent visitor who informed me I had been called. I made it through the guards and sat in the visiting room waiting for Calvin. He was excited to see me. The thrill of him knowing his product was between my legs drove him to kiss me on the lips. The kiss caught me by surprise. I hit him on his arm and wiped my lips with the back of my hand.

We sat down and I spoke about Sasha's baby shower to distract myself from feeling paranoid. He didn't care about a baby shower or how nervous I was. He instructed me to go to the vending machine and buy gum. When I returned to my seat he told me how much he loved me and I reminded him that it was the first and last time I was going to make such a bold move. He lowered his head and pouted his lips. I was serious about not pulling it off ever again but he insisted that the plan was flawless.

Exactly eight minutes before our visiting time ended, I walked to the restroom and attempted to stick the gum on the bag behind the toilet. My hands were shaking and the gum was too wet. I put the gum in between the palm of my hands and rolled it back and forth to dry it up. I stuck it firmly to the bag and porcelain and waited to make sure it stayed there. I flushed the toilet twice.

Calvin stared at me when I returned to my seat. His eyes were gleaming from the thought of knowing his plan was half way executed. The hard part was over. It was now up to his cell mate to retrieve it.

Saturday morning, the day of the baby shower, brought with it some sunshine. Even though summer was officially over, the warm weather remained. I stopped at Dunkin Donuts for a coffee to wake me up. My body was tired from the lack of sleep the night before. I rode the orange line train to Downtown and spent the day shopping for Sasha's baby and myself.

By 7:00 o'clock that evening, I snuck in to Headquarters to shower. After I was done showering I threw on my sweats and walked down the corridor to the other side of the building. I saw a back door and approached it. I placed my hand on the metal bar across the door to push it open but I was hesitant. What if an alarm went off? Did I want to bring attention to myself? But did I really want to walk all the way back to the front? I pulled my cap down over my forehead and proceeded out the door. No alarm went off but my heart took two minutes to settle back down.

I crossed the street back to my mobile home in the isolated parking space I stationed the truck. I pulled out my outfit from my Macy's bag and got dressed inside like I usually did. Jade called my cell phone and I answered. Sasha wasn't picking up her phone because she was fighting with Anthony and she was taking out her frustration on everyone. It looked as if Sasha wasn't going to make it to her own baby shower.

If Jade couldn't get Anthony or anyone to get Sasha out, I was going to spoil the surprise and drag her out the house myself. I hung up with Jade who decided to figure it out so I wouldn't have to spoil it. The night wasn't starting off on a good note, I thought, but I felt everything would work itself out eventually.

I called a taxi to pick me up and drive me to Our Lady Of The Cedars Of Lebanon behind Jamaica Pond. There was no way I was going to expose my truck and my entire luggage. The taxi driver took an hour to arrive. And when he did, it smelled musty inside. I usually didn't talk to cab drivers, but that night I initiated a conversation to ignore the stint.

At last I arrived at the function hall. The place was nicely decorated in pink and white. Jade ran up to me and told me Anthony had to tell Sasha about the baby shower and they were on their way. I was a little bummed out she had to find out about it but it was the only way to get her out the house and I'm glad it wasn't me who spoiled the surprise.

I found an empty table where I chose to sit alone. As I'm going through my purse searching for my money, someone stood over me waiting to get my attention. I looked up and jumped from my seat. It was Xavier who came down from New York to attend the baby shower. We hugged each other tightly. It was the best surprise I had received and it surely was going to be a pleasant one for Sasha.

He joined me at the table along with his brother Miguel. I offered to buy them the first round of drinks. Xavier walked with me to the bar to help me carry the drinks back to the table. He wore a smile that lightened up my heart and I had a smile that was inerasable. From the bar I could sense Jade giving us the evil eye but I was too overjoyed by his presence to even care.

We sat at the table drinking, waiting for Sasha to arrive. Meanwhile, Angela showed up and sat with us cool folks.

"Where's Sasha?" Xavier took a swig of his beer.

"She's on her way. Chill out."

"She needs to hurry up. My stomach is empty."

"Like your head?" I let out a chuckle.

When Sasha walked in with Anthony, I immediately noticed her flawless skin and blushing cheeks. The pregnant glow was real. She began to cry when she saw us all gathered together celebrating this special moment in her life. But Xavier brought out the biggest smile in her.

SNAPPED PATIENCE

The baby shower ended at midnight. Xavier left a little early but I stayed behind finishing my last drink with Angela and catching up with Sasha while others cleaned up.

I asked Angela if she would kindly drop me off at the complex where I was going to meet with Xavier. The neighborhood was sure to have a good crowd gathered around him, drinking and smoking. Although Xavier quit smoking marijuana, that didn't stop the rest of us from enjoying the herb.

Angela dropped me off in the parking lot where I could see a small crowd outside Xavier's building. The person who stood out to me the most was Coco. Anger played havoc in my mind causing a wave of nerves to build up inside my stomach.

As I walked towards the building, I heard footsteps behind me. I turned to find Charlene, Calvin's infamous cousin, walking in the same direction as me with crack-head Bob, the neighborhood news anchor. He knew everyone's business and loved to gossip. Crack-head Bob always claimed you never heard it from him. But you did.

Even though I was never fond of Charlene for initiating our fight when we were younger, I remained cordial with her out of respect for Calvin. I stopped her in her tracks.

"Charlene, I need something to tie my hair."

"Why? Your hair looks nice out." She lifted a strand of my hair and let it go.

"Go get me one, I need it." My tone was a bit forceful.

"Okay, damn."

Charlene turned around and ran back to her building. She knew I was about to throw down with someone and her being a trouble maker herself, wanted to get a front row view. Crack-head Bob just stood there in the parking lot with me, waiting. He tried starting a conversation.

"Have you heard from Calvin?"

"No." I responded coldly, with my arms crossed and shaking my right heel.

"You guys don't speak?"

"No." I refused to make eye contact with him. I moved my head around wishing Charlene would hurry up.

"Why are you so nervous?"

I didn't respond so he would catch the hint that I didn't want to speak to him. That's when Charlene ran back to us, handed me a hair ruffle, and I put it up in a bun. The three of us walked to where everyone was gathered.

Knowing that Xavier was there made me feel safe enough to fight. He wouldn't let anything happen to me, so I tossed my purse on the bench. I knew this beef with Coco was going to get ugly. I stood in front of her while she sat on the bench and stared daggers at her. The White Russians I sipped on during the night served to embolden me.

"You're a piece of shit!" I waved my finger in her face.

"Whatever, get out my face, Sky," she tried to dismiss me by waving her hand back at me.

"Make me, bitch."

"Get out my face, Sky."

"What are you going to do? Nothing!"

I let my clenched fist swing. I caught her square in the face. She got up from the bench, swinging her fists at me but I managed to pull her down by her hair back on the bench. I was throwing blows with my right fist, while she was throwing blows back from underneath me.

The guys jumped in to separate us. Once we were untangled, Xavier grabbed me to leave, but I elbowed him out of anger. Suddenly, Coco ran up behind me and brought me down to the ground by my hair. I landed on one knee. Xavier pulled her off as I rose up on my feet and lunged at her with rage.

Someone yelled for me to let her go. But I wouldn't. I held on to her hair while punching her in the face. The more she caught a hit, the better I felt. There was so much commotion that I could hear the guys arguing with one another. Rodney was furious that Xavier was holding Coco, giving me a better advantage in the fight. Xavier didn't back down to Rodney, but I feared they were next to brawl. Xavier dragged me away.

Xavier walked me to the steps near the basketball court. We sat there like we did when we were younger. I bit my lips nervously as I tried to look at my sore fingers in the dark and wipe the dirty streak from my dress pants. A taste of blood lingered in my mouth from a busted lip.

"What was all that about?" Xavier said, checking my face for marks.

"I did an insurance scam on my car and I put her on for a thousand..." before I could finish my story, Xavier snatched me by my hand and sprinted up Jamaica Street.

Out of breath and not knowing why we were running, I let go of Xavier's hand. We stopped half way up the hill and Xavier looked around. He walked into a bunch of bushes, so the street lights wouldn't catch him.

"What the fuck are you doing?" My breath was fast and deep.

"I have to take a leak." He unzipped his jeans and urinated in the bushes.

"No fool, what are we running from?"

"Jakes."

"For real?"

"I saw a cruiser pulling up to the parking lot." Xavier zipped his pants back up. "You brought heat, girl."

We continued up Jamaica Street to my old house. Its existence was completely solitary, bringing sadness to me. There was no breath of wind and the trees watched us silently. I didn't want to be there so I turned to Xavier to tell him to walk me to Forest Hills Station to catch a cab. His face was pale as death, eyes wide open, as though something of horror had come before him.

"What's wrong, X?"

"Let's get out of here." He took a few steps backwards in slow motion.

"What's wrong?" I didn't dare to look back. "You're scaring me."

"Look at your old window."

"No, just tell me what you see." Struck by the unfeigned horror expressed in his face, I made two steps forward with an anxious yet puzzled expression.

"Someone is up there."

"Stop playing X, that's not funny."

A soft breeze rustled my hair giving me chills that felt like a million ants running up my skin. My nerves tingled as I rubbed my head. Xavier turned around and walked off unsteadily. I ran behind him, taking hold of his shirt.

"What was it?" My voice was panicky.

"I saw a face in your window." He rubbed his forehead.

As we continued down the hill, I asked, "Are you sure? You freaked me out back there."

"I didn't mean to scare you but that shit was crazy."

"Can we go back to find my purse?"

"Nah. Wait for me down the ramp while I get it. I don't need you going back there."

"Don't leave me by myself." I held on to his forearm as we headed down the hill.

"Where are you staying, that you're out this late—fighting and running from cops? When are you going to stop borrowing trouble?"

"For one—I'm homeless." I retorted. "And secondly, I believe you ran from the cops. I just followed suit."

"Homeless?" Xavier was concerned.

"Yes, homeless. Now can you please get my purse? I'll be here on the steps."

"You can stay with my pops. He won't mind."

"No, that's fine. I need to get going," I sat on the steps.

Xavier became upset. "Going where? You just said you were homeless."

"Yes. I don't have a home, but I do have somewhere to lay my head."

"Sky, stop with the bullshit."

"Go get my purse, please." I buried my face in my hands.

"I see you haven't changed." Xavier walked off mumbling, "difficult as always."

When he returned a few minutes later with my purse, he held on to it until I answered him truthfully. I was too embarrassed to say I was sleeping in the truck because I knew he wouldn't have given me my purse and would have forced me to stay with his father. I told him I was staying with a girlfriend. He knew I wasn't telling him the truth but he let it go.

"How much time you got off work?"

"Six glorious months." I pulled out my cell phone to call a cab.

"Come to New York with me."

"I would love to go to New York, but I can't get up and leave. I mean, I can, but I really can't right now. I have a few things to

340

take care of. Besides what am I going to come back to if I leave? The same shit I'm in now?"

"Sky, I've known you for a long time, and it seems at every turn, there's a problem. Then you put up defenses with me when you feel uncomfortable talking about them. I know you're not telling me the whole truth. And holding back some truth is kind of like a lie because you're trying to deceive me."

"Okay genius, I'll leave to New York with you." I mumbled with my head down. "But I really do have to take care of a few things out here before I leave."

LONGING FOR A HOME

The following morning, I woke up agitated, a remnant of all the tension from the night before. Then the sun was beaming through the back window of the truck. I tried to cover my eyes from the lights but it was no use, I was awake. My head and body were sore from the fight with Coco, making me uncomfortable in that tight space.

I got up to smoke a joint in an effort to numb all the physical and mental pain that was overpowering me that Sunday morning. I sat on the driver side thinking of all the things I had to get done before leaving to New York. Calvin was first on my list. I needed to get rid of the rest of the coke I had left. Dr. Wesley was also on my to-do list. I needed a prescription refill. Even though I didn't take the medication as prescribed, they did seem to help when needed. And I had a hunch I was going to stay in New York for a while.

Not having a place of my own worried me the most. I had a ridiculous amount of cash, yet I was homeless with bad credit, no safe place to store my money, and no place to call my own. I started to think Benji was going to have to get an eyeful of this money and see that I was serious about an apartment. It was scary to think I would have to come clean, but I was desperate.

My cell phone rang, interrupting my thoughts. I flipped it open and saw Ray's name on the caller ID. I hesitated to pick up but I was curious to know how in the world he got my new number. I had changed it after he caught me whispering sweet nothings in my sleep.

"Hello."

"Did I wake you?"

There was an awkward silence. "I've been up for a while."

"Do you know who this is?"

342

"Yeah. How did you get my number?" I replied monotonously.

"I have my ways...I was checking on you to see how you've been. Benji told me you were having a hard time finding a place."

Closing my eyes, I put the seat back. "I am, but I'm leaving to New York soon so I'll worry about that when I come back."

"When are you leaving?"

"In a few days."

"When are you coming back?"

Slowly, my legs stretched out to rest on the dashboard. I tried not to moan from the pain. "I'm not sure, depends how much I like it out there."

"Can I see you before you leave?"

"You were pretty upset last time we were together."

"Can we talk about that when I see you?"

"Why?"

Ray got another call and told me to hold. While I waited, I entertained the thought of visiting him. I missed the warmth of another body next to me. It didn't seem like a bad idea to spend the night with him before leaving town.

He came back on the line. "Sky."

"Yeah."

"I was thinking if you were up to getting together later on."

"Sure. What do you want to do?"

"You." He laughed.

"Funny."

"Am I going to see you?"

"Yeah, just don't expect to see me naked."

"We'll see."

I drove around listening to Destiny's Child, No, No, No, and thinking about my trip to New York. In the midst of my thoughts I called Benji the realtor. He agreed to meet me at his office. I brought

343

in my tote bag with a good amount of cash to show and beg him to rush on my search.

As I pulled my truck outside of King Realty, I felt myself getting sweaty and my mouth drying up. It was a sign of nervousness. I pulled myself together as I stepped from the truck and entered the office. Benji was standing there waiting for me. He took off his glasses to alight his eyes on my poor appearance. I wore a pair of wrinkled gray sweatpants, a Red Sox t-shirt, and my hair was disheveled.

"Cecilia, right on time as usual."

"Call me Sky, Benji."

"What happened to your face? You look pretty banged up."

"Not as banged up as the other girl."

"Let's talk in my office."

I placed my tote bag on his desk and opened it wide. "Check out the faces, Benji."

"Jesus, woman! Why are you carrying all that money?"

"I was denied the loan even after paying Audi what I owed them. I need a place. I don't care where, how much, what condition it is, I just need a place."

Benji scratched his head. "My friend Andrea, who I was telling you about, is a Colonel in the army. After 9/11 she decided to hold off on selling her townhouse. She's going to rent it instead. Her father will be taking over once she gets deployed. I'm having an open house to show it in two weeks."

"I won't be here."

"Where will you be?"

"I'm leaving for New York in a few days."

"All right, I'll tell you what. Let's write out a letter, date it a couple of days after open house thanking me for showing you the place, and that you would really like to be considered as a tenant because the commute would be a lot easier. Fill this application out now but date it the day after open house. Leave the security deposit and last month's rent with me now. I'll have my secretary take out the money orders to submit with this application. What do you think?"

"Works for me." I sat down.

Benji typed the letter while I filled out the application. We looked over the paper work to make sure there weren't any errors. I signed both the application and letter, and then asked Benji how much he wanted for the trouble. But he wouldn't accept any money from me. The only thing he wanted in return was for me to be a responsible tenant and not make him look bad. We both stood up, shook hands, and he walked me to the door.

"Have a safe trip to New York and don't get into any more fights, Cecilia. You're too pretty for that."

"Sky, Benji. Call me Sky." I waved my fingers goodbye as he stood at the door behind me.

My body needed a good hot shower and a comfortable bed to rest so I called Ray. He gave me his address to the house he and his brother had recently bought, a nice two family home on Gallivan Boulevard in Dorchester. Before heading out, I threw a blanket over my storage in the truck to hide my entire luggage and computer. Even though the windows were tinted, cops are spooky on details and I didn't want to risk being caught homeless.

En route to Ray's house, I made a stop at a Chinese restaurant in Roslindale and bought a large order of food. When I arrived to the house, I noticed a few cars were parked in front of his two-car garage and on the sidewalk along his house. I managed to find space a little farther up from the rest of the vehicles. I got out, set the car alarm on, and walked in to the house. Ray's brother, Nathaniel, greeted me at the door with a kiss on the cheek.

"What's up, Sky. Where have you been, girl?"

"You don't want to know." I chuckled.

"I do!" He motioned for me to come in.

He led me to the living room where a few guys were playing dominoes and some were watching the game. Ray never got up from his seat to greet me. He concentrated on the game but lifted his head up and we kissed on the cheek.

Nathaniel introduced me to everyone. It wasn't just men in the house. A couple of girls were hanging out too. I politely excused myself from everyone and walked in to the kitchen. Nathaniel helped me set up the Chinese food on the counter. While we served ourselves a plate, he asked me about the scratches below my right eye and the small cut on my lip. I didn't want to tell him there. I didn't want anyone to eaves drop on our conversation. He told me to put down the plate so he could give me a tour of Ray's place. I walked around and noted how much nicer this place was than the one he moved from. Nathaniel then went back for his plate.

"Heineken?" he asked as he took one out the fridge.

"Yes please." I sat at the kitchen nook.

"I'm going upstairs to eat this. Come up when you're done, so you can see my side of the house. It's a lot nicer than Ray's."

"Are you smoking?" I whispered.

"No. I don't have any."

"Give me a few minutes and I'll come up."

Nathaniel instructed me to use the back door in the kitchen which would lead me to his apartment. When I finished eating I made my way back to Ray in the living room. I leaned in to his ear, resting my left hand on his back and spoke.

"There's Chinese food in the kitchen. I'm going to take a hot shower and get some rest. Is that okay?"

Without taking his eyes off the dominoes he covered with both hands, he simply nodded. I entered his bedroom and pulled out a joint, a half an ounce of weed, a lighter, a bottle of Visine, a head scarf, a hairbrush, and gum out of my tote bag. I stood in front of the mirror, wrapped my hair around my head and covered it with the scarf, poured Visine in my eyes, and stashed the weed in my pocket. Then I snuck upstairs to Nathaniel's apartment.

I tapped on the door and Nathaniel called out for me to enter. When I turned the door knob, he came to welcome me in.

"Come in, Aunt Jemima."

"Very funny. Can I borrow a sweatshirt from you?"

"Sure, let me see if I can find one to match that scarf." He laughed.

I lit the joint. When Nathaniel walked in with a sweater in hand, his jaw dropped.

"You walked in with that?" He handed me the sweater.

"I'm sorry. We can't smoke here?"

"No, it's not that, I thought you didn't smoke."

"In the eyes of the law, I don't." I took a slow drag of the joint and passed it to him.

"Sky, you are a scholar and a lady." Nathaniel took the joint. "Come on, I'll show you around."

He showed me the house while we smoked. He wasn't lying; his side of the house was nicer. After we finished smoking Nathaniel gave me another Heineken. We sat in the parlor and spoke about Ray. I confessed how intimidated I was by Ray, making me close up.

"Don't be intimidated by him. If anything, you should feel proud that you're different from other girls he's been with. As his brother, I can tell you some things about him. Ray is very intuitive. I'm sure he knows more about you than you think he does. It's probably why he likes you. You have a mysterious side like he does. I would have never taken you for a weed smoker. Daring—yes. A smoker—no. Ray can see right through people, so you may not want to hide too much from him. The difference between he and I is that he doesn't mince his words. He is highly opinionated so he doesn't waste his time on sensitive women. If you have traits that he doesn't like in a woman then you either hide it very well or he sees past it. Other than that, he's crazy about you. But just be careful because a woman who smokes is a major turn off for him."

"I know, I know. He definitely can't help but dispense his thoughts at times. Thanks for sharing that with me. It helps me understand him a whole lot better." I pulled the sweater over my head. "I need to get going. Here's your sweater back and you can have the rest of this Jacky White. There's half an ounce left. Enjoy it."

He was pleasantly surprised to have been given that amount of cannabis. He walked me to the door and we said our goodbyes. Halfway down the stairs, I removed my head scarf and let my hair down. I smelled it to make sure it didn't have the stink of smoke. Then I popped a gum in my mouth and snuck back in through the kitchen door. The party was still going strong in the living room, yet no one noticed my return.

The paranoia of being high brought me back to the days when I use to sneak in my back door on Jamaica Street. Luckily Ray's bedroom had a private bathroom, so I didn't have to bump into anyone. I looked around and admired the beauty of it all. His bathroom had a castle feel to it. The floor was tiled with gray, green, and dark rustic orange stones to accentuate the smooth gray walls. He had a deep soaking bathtub which was perfect for soothing and relaxing the body. And the linen closet was fully loaded with plush towels, soap, wash cloths, and other toiletries.

After this stressful long period all I wanted more than anything was a place to call home. I longed for a bath tub I could soak in, instead of quick showers in the woman's locker room. I longed for a bed with a mattress, not the back seat of a truck. I longed for home cooked meals, rather than take-out food. This night at Ray's house was exactly what I needed.

I went through a set of drawers in the vanity and found the Epson salt for my sore body. I ran the hot water in the tub as I began

348

gargling mouthwash at the sink. After I rinsed my mouth out, I poured the Epson salt inside the full tub and lit an apple cinnamon aromatherapy candle. I turned off the lights, allowing the small flame to send out a glow throughout the bathroom. I slipped in the relaxing hot water and closed my eyes.

Within a half an hour, I began to perceive a low sound; almost a whisper. I opened my eyes as a dark figure cut through the half darkness. It was all too familiar to me. There was a sudden rush for me to get up; splashing water on the floor. I grabbed a towel and reached to turn on the light. That's when I came face to face with the dark figure. I let out a scream and my body shivered. It was Ray!

He sought my presence by coming in quietly, thinking I was in bed sleeping. But the sudden shock, strung my nerves to tension, that I dropped my towel on the floor and I sank back in the bath tub. Ray couldn't help but form a mocking laugh. I rested my elbows on the sides of the tub and buried my face in my hands.

Ray continued laughing. He knelt down, grabbed my head, and planted a kiss on it. I couldn't help but laugh with him.

"You scared the hell out of me."

"You should have seen your face."

I stayed quiet for a minute. Although it was a bit funny to have screamed the way I did, a part of me knew that it wasn't all comical when I've been troubled by unnatural manifestations in my lifetime. Ray grabbed the wash cloth and began washing my back. He couldn't join me because he still had company. He felt he owed it to me to put me back in a relaxed state before returning to his guests. I pulled him by his t-shirt and kissed him fully on his mouth.

Fifteen minutes later, I got out the bathroom. I wrapped the towel around me and walked in the bedroom. I put on a t-shirt and panties to get into bed. Once I was under the covers, I turned on my Discman and listened to music.

I must have really been tired because the pillow was soaked with my drool. But I don't think I was out long because my Discman was still playing Mary J. Blige. So I turned the pillow over and fell back asleep, listening to My Life, on repeat.

Sometime later, My Life still played in my headphones, slowly waking me up. My eyes fluttered for a second, but I was still half asleep. The wall clock showed that it was ten minutes shy of two in the morning when Ray walked in the room. I closed my eyes again, removed the headphones, and just waited for him to get in bed.

That night I slept lightly, part of me always mindful not to give something away in my mutterings again. So while Ray snored the night away, I watched him sleep. The whole time I'm talking to myself. Why? Why? We just had sex and I still don't feel fulfilled. But it was my greediness of wanting to be with him one more time. I know that sex is just an act, but when it was over, I was left stuck in the vacuum of my loneliness.

HARNESS THE MULE

With only a few days left before my trip to New York, I paid Calvin a visit. I was prepared to tell him that I wasn't going to be his mule anymore. It was nerve-racking to sit there in the visiting room with mirrors facing me, prison guards standing on watch, and cocaine between my legs.

"I can't do this, Calvin."

"You can't fail me now, Sky."

"Oh yes the hell I can. Watch me."

"I have people depending on this delivery."

"I don't care."

"Chill! Go to the vending machine and take your time."

I got up and bought a bag of chips, a soda, and gum. Calvin was furious that I was going to make him look bad with the rest of the cell mates waiting for this delivery.

"This could have some serious consequences on me. Ask Charlene to do it."

"She has a big mouth and cracks under pressure."

"How do you think I feel with all the pressure you're putting on me?"

"We're doing fine."

"No, *you're* doing fine. I'm a mess!"

"Do this for me one last time."

"You mean right now?"

"I need another delivery after this one, Sky. After that you don't have to do it anymore. I promise. I'll settle with the canteen money."

"No! This is my last run. Look for another jackass to harness."

CITY OF DREAMS

I arrived at the bus terminal in Queens, eager to meet Xavier. I ran up to him with my arms open to hug him. He picked me up in the air.

"I'm so happy you came."

We stopped a taxi and jumped in. I couldn't stop smiling. Visiting Xavier was good for my soul. I stared out the cab window admiring the city.

"So this is New York, big city of dreams!"

He wrapped his arm around my shoulder. "This is where it's at, Sky."

When the cab dropped us off at Xavier's house, he paid the driver and carried my bags.

As I followed him inside, I sized him up. "Did you gain weight?"

"Yeah. I have a big fight coming up."

"I'm really proud of you."

"What's up with you? We didn't get a chance to speak in Boston because you went in like Mike Tyson on Rodney's girl. How are you holding up with all that shit that went down with Andre? Have you heard from him or your mother?"

"No, I haven't heard from them, but I'm all right. I hold my own."

"Sky." He stood in front of me swinging the backpack off his shoulder. "You're talking to me. No need to hold back."

I ignored him and scoped out his bachelor pad. "So this is what a single man's apartment looks like." I poked my head in every room.

"I get it. You don't want to talk about it right now. That's cool. Yes, this is my humble home and like the good old saying goes, mi casa es su casa. You can sleep in my bed."

I looked blankly at him. For a moment, I saw him in the same light I did when I first met him—attractive. He lifted his hands and said, "I didn't mean...you know what I'm saying. You can have my bed. I'll sleep on the couch."

Then I realized he was my best friend and nothing more. "You don't have to sleep on the couch as long as you stay on your side of the bed." I folded my arms.

He crossed his heart with his finger. "I won't do anything you won't let me."

I slapped his arm. "Show me around."

We took a stroll around Queens Village. Some girls stopped and purposely flirted with Xavier. A few times, I would glide my hand down his back or playfully wrap my arm underneath his, purposely giving it back to them. He loved the attention and I loved messing with these girls.

He brought me to a small hole in the wall Salvadoran restaurant. He ordered pupusas, which I learned were a thick hand-made corn flour tortilla stuffed with pork and cheese. We also ate panes rellenos, which means stuffed bread. It was a warm submarine sandwich served with marinated chicken, lettuce and tomato. I sat at the table observing how he interacted with the waitress. The look in her eyes when she saw us together told me she was one of his potential victims.

She tried to disguise her jealousy behind her smile but I knew better. Xavier was a ladies' man; a natural charmer. When she walked away to put in our order, I leaned forward and whispered, "Your dick is going to fall off!"

"Whoa, Sky!" He covered his crotch, "What's with all that?"

"Is there any girl out here for you worth settling down with?"

"Yeah, there was one. But she chose to be with my buddy Calvin because he had money, while I was just a poor scrub living in the projects."

I turned my face, breaking eye contact with him. He definitely hit a nerve. Although Calvin won me over because he was older, the money was a bonus.

"That's not fair, X."

"Hey listen, I have something Calvin will never get back, which is your trust and friendship. You can't beat that."

Dare I reveal that Calvin was back in the picture? "You're right. You can't beat that."

"Well, then again, I want to beat it, but you won't let me."

"Very funny."

After we ate that delicious meal, we walked back to his place. Xavier pointed out how much I looked like an outsider because I was always looking up, while the locals always looked straight ahead. I found the scene enchanting and breathtaking. I had a feeling I wasn't returning to Boston any time soon.

"How long can I stay?"

"You could move down here."

"What?"

"Why not? You can start working down here. You already have a place to stay. Start over somewhere new. What do you think?"

"I came with the mindset of getting away for a while, not permanently."

"You don't have anything holding you back in Boston. Or do you?"

"I may."

"Then at least stay long enough to consider it."

"If—and let's just say if, I decide to stay—I have to go back, get my truck and say goodbye to everyone."

"That's what I'm talking about, Sky. You're already considering it."

In the long silence that followed, I thought Xavier had a good point of me starting over. On the other hand, I loved Boston, and I was falling for Ray pretty hard. What should I do?

A BIRTHDAY HELD IN STORE

Xavier woke up early to hit the gym. He was training for a fight. I was awake but stayed in bed—eyes closed. It wasn't even seven in the morning; Xavier blasted the stereo in the living room and sang Ini Kamoze's reggae, "Here comes the hot stepper, murderer…" Clearly, he was in a good mood. I opened one eye and watched him standing in front of the mirror putting on deodorant and grooving to Hotstepper. I turned around and pulled the covers over my head. That's when the house phone rang.

Xavier sat beside me on the bed to answer it. "Hello…what's up? She's sleeping right now…sure, I'll let her know. When did you have her?"

I pulled the covers off. "Is that Sasha? Did she have the baby?"

Xavier ignored me. "You couldn't wait to have her on my birthday?"

I closed my eyes in an effort to remember Xavier's birthday. It was two days away. I sat up on the bed and nudged him. He passed the phone to me. "Hey Sasha!"

"Your goddaughter was born this morning."

"How are you feeling?"

"In a lot of pain but it was all worth it. She's beautiful."

"I bet she is."

"When are you coming back?"

"I'm not sure." I took a moment to stretch. "What's the baby's name?"

"Antoinette Marie Costello."

"Anthony must be a proud daddy."

"I've never seen him so happy, Sky. I'm a little jealous."

"You're funny. I can't wait to meet her."

"The nurse just walked in. I have to go."

"Get some rest and congratulations to the both of you."

Xavier left without saying a word. I took the liberty to smoke a joint and clean the apartment while listening to the sounds of Aerosmith. By the time I was done, I laid back down to take a nap.

Later on, I took a stroll around the neighborhood. I was lost in thought of what moves I would make to start a new life in New York. Job searching was the easy part. Saying goodbye to Boston was going to be tough.

On my way back to Xavier's house, I noticed him getting dropped off by a young lady in a green Honda Accord. Every woman who dealt with Xavier had a terrible disliking towards me, so I pretended not to have seen him. I continued to walk up the steps and open the front door with the spare keys he gave me.

In a mellow mood, I was preoccupied looking over my bank statements. Xavier barged in, slamming the door behind him.

"Are you okay?"

Xavier didn't answer me right away. He pulled out a cold beer out the fridge and sat down at the table. The expression in his face said the female in that green car must have spoiled his mood.

I couldn't resist the urge to get up and thrust out my hand by way of a greeting. "Hi, my name is Sky; and you are?"

Xavier put his beer down, to amuse me, and lightly shook my hand. "I'm fine, Sky. It's been a long day."

"So who's the new flavor of the week?"

"Her name is Crystal."

"And?"

"And that's all you need to know."

I walked back to the sofa, laughing. I put away my bank statements. Pushing back his chair and rising to his feet, Xavier turned on the stereo. Aerosmith came on blaring.

"What the fuck is this?" He turned it down before shutting it off.

I sang while leaving the room. "Dream on, dream on, dream on..."

Xavier put on Latin music. I came back out to the living room to find him Salsa dancing. I turned down the volume to get his attention. He didn't like that I touched the stereo. "What are you doing?"

"I brought you something."

"A SWAT t-shirt?" He said sarcastically.

"No silly." I handed him a brown paper bag.

"What the..." His eyes grew wide as he pulled out the content of the bag.

"Happy Birthday!"

"How much is here?"

"Ten grand."

"Ten large? Are you serious?"

"Yeah."

"I don't know what to say." He flipped through the bills.

"Say nothing. Ask nothing. Just take it." I smiled.

"Oh I'm definitely taking it. Thank you!" He hugged me without saying anything else about it.

The entire mood in that living room shifted. We were now drinking and listening to a complation of classic Salsa songs from hit makers like Hector Lavoe and El Gran Combo. I sat there enjoying Xavier move to the tropical sound. Something about him singing and dancing provoked a spontaneous pull when reached out to teach me how to dance. We spent the entire night

358

drinking and dancing. I couldn't wait to go out and party for his birthday.

I went out shopping the following day in Manhattan for a designer dress because Xavier told me to get dolled up. I even found an upscale salon where I got my hair done. As I waited for the stylist to finish with her last client, I gave Ray a call. "Happy Birthday to my favorite guy in the world."

"Thank you."

"How's everything?"

"Everything is good. I'm going to spend my birthday with my daughters."

"Oh that's great! I'm happy to hear that. How's my truck?"

"I had to borrow it last night. I hope you don't mind."

"Of course not."

"When are you coming back? I miss you."

"I'm not sure yet. I really like it out here so I may stay a while." There was an awkward silence. It was as if he didn't like what I had said. "I miss you too. I think of you all the time."

"Do you touch yourself when you think of me?"

I laughed. "Stop being nasty."

"You like it."

"Whatever."

"You sound like you're having a good time. Where are you?"

The salon was playing Back To Life by Soul II Soul. "I'm in a salon about to get my hair done. My cousin's birthday was Wednesday so we're going out tonight to celebrate." Ray thought I was visiting relatives in New York. If I had told him Xavier was a friend he would have guessed that this male friend had some underlying sexual desire for me—which was true.

"Well have fun and behave yourself. I'll talk to you soon."

"Adios mi amor."

359

I jumped in a cab which was costing me a fortune from Manhattan to Queens Village. The cost didn't bother me as much as the driving skills this man lacked. I was about to shout at him to slow down, when Sasha called me on my cell phone.

"Hello."

"Hi."

"What's up!"

"Anthony stopped at the post office to check your mailbox and I must say, Sky, you have quite the mail."

"Oh. What do I have?"

"You have a letter from Calvin."

I played like I was surprised. "Calvin? For real?"

"Yeah. You also have a magazine." She read the title over the phone and flipped through the pages. "Down & Out: In Depth Look At The Sweet Science. Is this a boxing magazine? That's all I see in here."

"Yeah, Xavier made me subscribe to it. There was an article on him last month."

"Is there something going on between you two?"

"Between who? Xavier and me?"

"Yeah."

"Here *you* go! We've always been tight."

"So you two have never..."

I cut her off, "No! Could you have Anthony send me the mail, please? I know you can't because you just got out the hospital, which reminds me, how's baby Antoinette doing?"

"She's good. She's sleeping right now. When are you coming back?"

"Honestly Sasha, I'm thinking of moving here."

"What?"

"Yeah, Xavier's uncle is a corrections officer at Riker's Island. He's going to try to get me in. If I get the job, I'm staying."

"Wow. I don't know what to say. Maybe you should think about it thoroughly. You just got there. What if you don't like it?"

"It's all I've been thinking about, Sasha." I regretted telling her this. Her doubts were going to invade my head and cause confusion.

"What am I going to do without my best friend?"

"I'll visit you. I'm only a few hours away."

"Well, I'm just saying, think about it carefully."

"I will. Listen, my cab just pulled up in front of the house. I'll talk to you soon and send me pictures of the baby."

"All right, Sky. Bye."

I climbed out of the cab, brushed off my jeans and walked to the house. A group of guys near the steps were hanging out. I could feel them watching me but I didn't make eye contact with any of them.

Suddenly I heard one of them speak. "Who's that going into your house, X?"

"That's my future wife."

I turned to the group and spotted Xavier wearing a sexy grin. "I'm your what, again?"

"You heard me the first time." He playfully pushed me inside the house.

As soon as we stepped in, I saw a prayer candle on the kitchen counter top. Xavier had placed a few twenty dollar bills on a plate beside it. It appeared to total a hundred dollars. I walked over to get a closer look. The candle jar had a picture of a man named Don Juan del Dinero (Don Juan of Money), with a prayer that read: I invoke the influence of the holy name of Don Juan del Dinero, so that you may offer protection and help, so that you may free me from poverty and need, that you provide me with abundance and happiness, that the star of good luck shine on me and may fortune and success accompany me in all that I set out to

361

do, I place myself under your patronage. Don Juan del Dinero, do not leave me in forgetfulness and always be by my side. Amen. Neither one of us said anything about it. After I silently read the prayer, I walked in the bedroom and watched Xavier take off his sneakers and his shirt. He had definitely put on good weight from boxing. I wondered what it would be like to sleep with him. I closed my eyes and shook the thought out my head. Then I went into my stash of money and matched another hundred on the plate along with Xavier's offering.

"So where are we going tonight?"

"Somewhere over the rainbow to find me pot of gold."

"Ha! Seriously dude, where are we going that I have to get this dressed up?"

"We're going to hit up Copacabana Nightclub in Manhattan; then back to Queens for a little Chinese delight."

The time arrived for us to head out. I had dressed myself in a short black fitted dress with a pair of black heels. Xavier was in black slacks and a coral blue dress shirt with no neck tie. I have to admit, I was giddy about that night.

Xavier put on his watch and pulled out the brown paper bag of the money I gave him. I saw him take out large amounts and place them in each pant pocket. A pearl white Lexus GS400 picked us up. The driver was a Japanese kid named Ren. He was good friends with Xavier since grade school. Ren had a hair cut to a length of half an inch with a spiky style that had a few unruly patches of cowlicks. He was slim build and stood about 5'7". He looked self assured and a bit defiant of authority. I liked that.

During the ride to Copacabana, the sound system to the Lexus was loud, making it difficult for me to listen to their conversation. Even though I was stoned, I could tell these two were up to something. I noticed Ren look down at Xavier's lap. Then Xavier pointed to the back seat with his head. Ren glanced at me and raised his head up at Xavier. I presumed Xavier was showing off the money.

When we arrived, there was no waiting in line. Xavier had become the person to know if you wanted to walk into a nightclub VIP style. A few of his cousins and friends joined us to celebrate the occasion. I was with a new boxing celebrity because everyone, including the bartenders, posed with him to take pictures.

Countless champagne flutes were passed around in our VIP section; I lost track after the third drink. At times I had one flute in each hand but Xavier would take them away from me and pull me out to the dance floor.

Before the night ended, we heard a live performance by Elvis Crespo who sang his hit song, Suavemente Besame (Kiss Me Softly). The crowd went crazy over this Merengue singer. Spurred by that song, I shook my hips side to side behind the banister, enjoying the show.

Xavier stood beside me. "You know what would make this birthday extra special?"

I shrugged. "What?"

His bedroom eyes were staring at me. "If I could have you."

I didn't answer him. He always had a way of slipping a come on into our conversations. Only this time, I didn't brush him off like I usually did. Instead I wrapped my hands around his neck and kissed him because I was elated. Someone popped open a bottle of champagne, splashing it all over us and breaking the kiss. We enjoyed every minute of it.

After Copacabana, we took off to Queens. I watched the streetlights from the back seat beaming like a streak going from pole to pole as we crossed the city. Ren parked in front of a Chinese convenience store. He went in the store while Xavier and I waited outside. I found my instinct to have been good; these two were up to something.

The November air invited a pleasant shiver to my body. I leaned on the car and rubbed one foot at a time because my shoes gave me blisters. Xavier pressed himself against me to warm me up. He leaned in for a kiss. This time the toe curling kiss was longer and passionate, causing a tingling sensation that ran through out my body and leaving a feeling of tapping feet in my heart.

"Get a room!" Ren yelled as he came back out.

"What's the word?" Xavier asked.

Ren flashed a red card and smiled as he jumped back in the Lexus. "We're in."

"Yes!" Xavier exclaimed. "Let's go."

"Can someone please let me in on this excitement?" I asked.

Ren turned around to reverse the car. "Do you play poker?"

"No."

"Well then, you'll learn tonight."

We stopped at a fancy Chinese Restaurant in Flushing. By then I wanted to take off my shoes and walk barefoot. Xavier asked me if I was hungry. I wasn't. But I still didn't see what poker had to do with Chinese food. The waitress welcomed us. Ren showed the red card and she escorted us to the back. Xavier instructed me to follow his lead and stay quiet.

We were led to a concealed door under a staircase in the rear of The Bamboo Palace Restaurant. It was impossible to make out any details of the illegal poker hall except that it was hidden underneath a row of interlocked storefronts and an upscale Chinese restaurant. Upon entering I squeezed Xavier's hand.

"Relax, Sky," he whispered.

The room fell quiet when we sat at the table with six other men. The dealer was a short, middle aged man named Huong. It was his poker palace and we were guests in it. Huong slid Xavier and Ren their chips after they paid a buy-in of $500 each. Ren sat there like a gangster smoking a cigar; looking intently at the cards he was dealt.

By some stroke of luck, Xavier was winning every hand. His stacks were growing while everyone else's chips were disappearing at a steady pace. Huong winked at me and asked if I wanted anything to drink.

Relieved at the chance of speaking, I threw in all my requests at the same time. "Yes, please. Could I have some water? I'm so damn thirsty. Oh, and could I take off my shoes?"

Huong smiled. "Do as you please."

"Is there a restroom down here?"

He pointed at the door behind me. I couldn't get up fast enough to run in, barefoot and all. When I returned to the table, there was a bottle of water waiting for me. I guzzled it down as I watched Ren throw away the stump of his cigar. He figured out he was the sucker in the game and quit. Xavier thanked the table and the three of us left.

X

Those hours of drunken happiness that Xavier and I spent together for his birthday put a lift in my step. When we arrived to his house, I jumped in the shower to wash off the sweat, champagne, and smell of cigar. I came out wearing only a towel. Xavier zoomed by me without making eye contact. He locked himself in the bathroom and took a shower too.

When he came out, he was in a tank and pajama bottoms. I, on the other hand, was under the covers naked, waiting for him to take me. Instead, he took a pillow and tossed a comforter on the carpeted floor. There was a rapid shift from bliss to head scratching. "You're not going to sleep with me?"

"I can't."

I sat up on the bed with the sheet covering my chest. "I'm confused. Did I do something wrong?"

"No, Sky. If you weren't high off X, you wouldn't think of..."

I interrupted, "Hold up! What did you say—high of ecstasy?"

"What did you think was in the champagne? I told you not to drink it and order something mixed instead, but Sky, as always, does what Sky wants!"

"I thought you said drink the champagne; don't order anything mixed."

"Why would I tell you that?"

"I don't know. I just did what I believed you said. Why didn't you stop me?"

"Every time I took away a glass, you had another one in your hand. I figured you were into that. Plus, I would never forgive myself if I took advantage of you. I'm not that kind of guy."

"Man, this is a good high. Now that I know the champagne had smiley faces in it, come lay next to me."

"No!"

I fell backwards on the bed and placed the pillow over my face for a second. After removing it, I stared at the ceiling. "Is this your payback from all the times I said no to you?"

"Men have been told no for centuries. We're immune to it. All those times you said no I thought, whatever, I'll come back later; she'll change your mind."

"I just changed my mind."

"This time doesn't count. It's the ecstasy talking."

I gave up. Overwhelmed by my senses and the subtle wetness developing between my legs, I decided to use my rich imagination and play with myself. But Xavier interrupted me. "With women you have to be smart, you have to be honest, and you have to be real. I learned that growing up. That's with the smart ones like you. With the dumb ones I get them a box of McNuggets and I'm in."

"That's funny—McNuggets."

"Yeah, like your girl Jade—pretty but empty. You can't have a long conversation with her. You get irked easily. Sometimes she would talk and I would say: damn when is she going to shut up, I just want to fuck."

My thoughts exactly. "Xavier!" I shot back up and looked down at him.

He had his hands behind his head. "Why are you looking at me like what I'm saying isn't true?"

"You need to be tamed."

367

"It's my mouth. I speak what I want, but because you can't handle what I say, I have to be tamed? A lion is a king of his jungle, who's taming him?" He laughed loudly.

"What the fuck are you laughing at?"

"I'm laughing at that hair bun of yours; it makes me think of Dr. Seuss."

I took my pillow and swung it at him. He caught it and pulled me down with it. I fell off the bed, holding on to my sheet, and landed on top of him. We both laughed at my elbow hitting the carpet.

"Ouch!" I rubbed it as I tried to untangle myself.

"Don't break down on me now. I'm going to have to take care of your ass when you get older. I need you to be a little mobile."

"You're still going to be there when I'm old and fucked up?"

"Sky, even when you're old, I will still love and take care of you. I'll make sure you go to all your appointments and tell the doctor: yeah, she's crazy! Could you up her dosage or something, I can't even sleep through the night, I'm afraid she's going to put a dead chicken under my pillow."

After all the laughing we did until dawn, my body gave up to sleep. My dreaming brain took me to a schoolyard where I was sitting on a cot, wrapped in a dirty blanket like a homeless woman. The day was warm and sunny. Boys were playing basketball across from me. A few girls were jumping double Dutch rope. To my right was a young couple holding hands; in love. And to my left were a few underage drinkers; passing a pint of dark rum.

The dream fleeted from outside the yard to inside the school. I found myself standing in a guidance counselor's office with two valley girls. The counselor was a heavy set Caucasian man with a full beard and mustache, glasses with black frames, and a buttoned up white shirt. He sat behind a teacher's desk with his legs crossed and a notepad on his knee.

One of the valley girls was pacing back and forth, speaking. She was dressed in a Catholic school uniform; short skirt, blouse, knee highs and dress shoes. The other one was sitting quietly near the doorway where I was standing, but I didn't pay much attention to her. My focus was on the one pacing.

"Tell me about Calvin," said the counselor.

"He was totally cool. Like, I loved him to the max. But he is so yesterday."

"And Ray?" He was naming the men in *my* life.

"Oh my God, Ray!" She placed her hands on her breasts and squeezed them. "He is, ya know, arresting."

"What about Xavier?"

She stopped pacing and slowly turned to me. Her voice had deepened into a hard demonic voice. "I ate him."

I ran out the office into the corridor screaming. "X! Where are you? X!"

The hallway was full of students with horrifying mutant faces coming towards me. I continued to scream for Xavier. When I saw them coming closer, I closed my eyes and forced myself to wake up.

When I woke up, I was still on the floor, naked under the sheet, and disturbed at my dream. Xavier wasn't beside me so I got up and tossed myself on the bed. Within a few minutes, he came in the room. I watched him approach me and attempted to peek under the covers. I kicked his hand away.

He laughed. "Oh, it's like that now?"

"Whatever. Are you going out again?" My voice was groggy.

"Yeah, I'm staying out so don't wait up for me."

THE UNKNOWN

Three weeks passed and I was still in New York. I received all the good news that strangely enough brought me down. Benji the realtor told me I was chosen for the townhouse I wanted in Roslindale. Rasheeda, my co-worker, gave me an earful about our union signing a new contract which would get us an upgrade and a retro pay of two years. And Rikers Island wanted a second interview.

Should I stay in Queens or go back to Boston? Things at home were looking up while things in the Big Apple were looking new. Xavier was pushing for me to stay with him. He harassed his uncle for me to get that corrections officer's position.

By mid December, I had Benji mail me the lease to sign. If I decided to break it, I agreed to pay the landlord for the remainder of the year. Still uncertain which direction I was going to take, my second interview at Rikers Island went well according to the director of Human Resources. I didn't give it my best but I didn't try to sabotage my chances either. I was curious about getting into the next training class. I was trying to leave it up to fate, sort to speak.

Winter was rolling in and I plunged into depression. I went into my shell and didn't leave the house for a week. I felt threatened by change and unsure about my decision to stay. I remembered Carmen the Santera telling me in my reading that things weren't going well for Xavier in New York. It seemed as if things were, but like she said, he wouldn't tell me if they weren't. I was battling with loss of appetite from the poor abstract thinking that swallowed me into a black hole. It wasn't solely on the choice I had to make; I felt empty and lonely at the same time. I had no one to bounce my feelings to. And I couldn't smoke to clear my head because of Riker's drug testing policy. I should have decided something, anything, but my thoughts were scattered.

Xavier was out most of the time. He said he was busy training for his big fight but I knew my toxic energy was weighing him down. That just added guilt to what I was already dealing with. Finally, I made my decision. There's a Spanish saying: el muerto despues de tres dias apesta (A corpse starts to smell after three days). Meaning I had overstayed my welcome. I decided to pack my things and head back North. A beautiful new townhouse was waiting for me to move in.

Xavier stopped me. As much as he didn't want to see me depressed, he didn't want me to leave that way either. He came up with a plan to drive me to Boston to visit Sasha and pick up the keys to my new place as long as I returned to spend Christmas with him. He had something special to give me.

We left at seven in the morning. The weather was cold and sleet but I found my trip to be a pleasant one. We reminisced about our childhood, listened to our favorite Hip Hop songs, and promised that we would always be the best of friends.

When we arrived at Sasha's house, we learned that she was engaged to Anthony. All were enthused with the engagement, but I was more excited to meet my goddaughter. I held baby Antoinette in my arms, to feed her, caress her, and baby talk to her. While I was catching up with Sasha, Xavier left to pay his father and brother a visit. Sasha told me she heard from her mother that Jade was infuriated that the night of her baby shower, Xavier gave me all his attention. Jade called his father's house a few times but there was no answer. So in her state of jealousy, she decided to drive by the complex and saw Xavier sitting outside with me late that night. She accused us of having sex because my hair was messy.

I explained to Sasha that I had gotten into a fist fight that night with a girl named Coco. Xavier was in the midst of all the

371

commotion and was waiting with me for my cab to arrive. Sasha barely believed me. I could tell she had her doubts, especially because she questioned everything about my living situation with him. It's a good thing I kept the ecstasy story a secret.

Later, I met with Benji to pick up my keys. I was excited to set foot in my new place. The townhouse was composed of highly polished, honey colored wooden floors from the entrance to the second floor. The second floor to the third had wall to wall Burr rug carpets. The place was enormous. It was any renter's dream to have such a beautiful place. I couldn't wait to get back to furnish it.

Before we headed back to New York, I called Ray. I asked if I could stop by before he left for work to see him and take something out my truck. He said he would wait for me. I was so eager to see him that I kept squirming in the passenger seat. The moment I arrived, Ray opened his front door. Xavier tried rushing me but I ignored him. I stepped out the car to meet Ray and he hugged me tight. I felt missed. We made small talk about my stay in New York and my upcoming plans. It was definite I would be returning to Boston. His presence alone confirmed that I belonged there.

Fifteen minutes into our conversation, we walked to the garage. I needed to take out another bundle of cash and discreetly stuff it in my backpack. Somewhere on Dorchester Ave, which intersected with Gallivan Boulevard, there was a metallic bang—two cars collided. Ray didn't flinch like I did. So when I ran out the garage to see if Xavier was still parked in front of the house; he wasn't. That's when I sensed something happened to him.

Ray and I ran down to Dorchester Ave. The brakes of a moving truck had failed and rear ended Xavier. After cursing underneath his breath, Ray called for help. Both drivers appeared to be hurt but Xavier refused medical attention. His uncle was expecting us to return that night with his car. And even though it was mangled from behind, it was still drivable.

We left Boston and I drove back to New York. I couldn't stop apologizing to Xavier. If I never stopped at Ray's house, that accident wouldn't have happened. He wasn't upset, though. He said he wanted to buy some snacks for us at Store 24 when the accident occurred. Xavier was always cool and collected about most things. It was a quality that he possessed that I admired. His uncle, thankfully, wasn't concerned about his damaged car, either. Instead, he made Xavier spend Christmas Eve in the emergency room to get checked out.

The morning of the 25th, Xavier surprised me with a Christmas card that held an airline ticket to Florida. He suggested I go visit my family to help me get out of my depression. Perfect. Along with the card he gave me a white bath robe with my name, Cecilia, engraved on it. I was touched by the holiday spirit.

My last night in New York, before leaving to Florida, Xavier slept in the bed beside me. During the middle of the night, I felt lonely. I shifted closer to him by pressing my breast against his back and wrapping my arms around him. His hand caressed my arm. I imagined how it would feel for him to undress me and take me in with every inch of what he had. He turned around and started kissing me. I became nervous but it was one of those moments where I was too scared to stop. His tongue danced in my mouth. I got a good feel of it, as I teased him with mine. He got on top of me and was grinding. My hips moved to his rhythm as I grinded back. He kissed me on my neck and took off my t-shirt. After unsnapping my bra, he cupped my breasts together and sucked on them. But I felt something was wrong—we were dry humping for too long. He stopped to turn on his back and pull me up on him. I was on top grinding him. That's when I noticed he couldn't get an erection. I turned on my back, embarrassed.

He was uncomfortable. "I've wanted you for so long and now that I have you, I don't know what to do."

The worst part was that I had to stay there with him. If I were in Boston, I would have run out the apartment and not look back. But I couldn't. You could feel the tension between us, in between those sheets. It was awful.

"Go down on me," he asked.

"Nah ah." It was safe for me not to try anything.

Then he put his hand down my pajama pants. "Sit on my face." I removed his hand and nodded no. I felt awkward. Why continue?

The following morning, we barely looked at each other. I stayed in the shower longer than usual. When I came out, hot and wet and clean, Xavier had McDonald's breakfast on the table for me. I picked at the pancakes. I just wanted to hurry out.

"I called a cab. I have to be at the gym early today." He clearly wanted me out of there or at least that's how it felt.

I took my bags as soon as I heard the cab driver honk the horn, but Xavier stopped me. "Wait for me. I'm sharing the cab with you."

The tension was slowly dying. He grabbed the bags from my hand and shoulder. "Go ahead, I'll meet you downstairs."

The cab ride, for the most part, was quiet. When we got close to the airport he said, "Make sure you call me once you get to your aunt's house."

I hugged him. "Thanks for everything."

"Have a safe flight, sweetheart."

I waved goodbye as the driver pulled off. When I entered La Guardia Airport, I remembered I had a bag of weed in my backpack. I found the restroom and sat in the stall debating whether to throw the stash away. I held it in my hands and knew I was going to need it in Florida. Eighty dollars worth of Purple Haze. I tried stashing it in my bra. No. It could fall out. Think. Think. Calvin. I had a few maxi pads in my duffle bag. I would smuggle it like I had the cocaine.

While I waited in line, security instructed us to check our pockets for any loose change or keys. I knew I didn't have anything metal in my pockets but I stuck my hand in to double check. That's when I discovered I had half a joint in my pocket. Damn, stupid me. I pretended to scratch my ankle and dropped the joint behind the table leg where we placed our bags. I then walked through the detector praying security wasn't watching me the whole time. I felt like such a bad ass when I sat on the airplane.

The rain was pouring hard in Miami when I arrived. I pulled a cab over and jumped in. The closer I got to my aunt Isabella's house, the more nervous I became. I asked the driver to drop me off a block away. The rain had ceased by then. I walked through the neighborhood thinking of what to say to my aunt for showing up unannounced. I made my way to her house from the back. The door was open but the screen was locked.

I pressed my face against the screen and called out. "Isabella!"

My cousin came to the door. She didn't recognize me. "Can I help you?"

"Raquel?"

"Yeah, who are you?"

"It's me, Sky, your cousin."

She rushed to open the door and hugged me. We were kids the last time we saw each other but she was excited to see me.

"Where's your mom?"

"She's at the store. Come in and sit down."

We spoke about her brothers, who were no longer in the house, and how much she had grown up. I invited her to visit me when she finished high school.

"I'm here because I think Isabella may know where my mother is. She left Boston with her husband and I haven't heard from them."

Isabella walked in with groceries. She was surprised to see me—but not pleased. I suspected she knew something. While I helped her put away the groceries, we spoke about my mother's disappearance. She denied knowing anything and Raquel sat at the table quiet.

"Do you have somewhere to stay?" Isabella asked.

"No. I was going to call my father's sister, I mean my aunt Dolores, to see if she had room for me."

"Nonsense! We have plenty of room here for you. Raquel and you can spend time together."

Isabella never left her house. She probably thought I would snoop around, which I would have. After two days of no leads, I asked Raquel to drive me to a travel agency to buy my airline ticket back to New York. Isabella invited herself. I found that strange. She was definitely staying on my trail. Raquel begged me to stay for a while longer. She was bonding with me. So I decided to extend my time there.

In the meantime, I was hoping my mother called the house or Isabella would slip out the secret. But I was tired of Isabella's presence; her continuous spying on me.

"Can we visit Enrique?" I asked Raquel.

"Sure."

We drove to Enrique's house. He was thrilled to see me. His wife and he welcomed us inside their home and cooked us dinner. Enrique asked me what was behind the surprise visit. I explained how I had time off work and just wanted to visit family. I reminded him how much I enjoyed him bringing me to church as a child. He had always been a loyal servant of God and I held that with much respect.

After dinner Enrique asked me to follow him to the back yard.

"For the past week, God has been waking me up in the middle of the night to pray. I've asked him to reveal to me what

376

exactly am I praying for. Even though I didn't know what or who I was praying for, I obeyed. Last night I had a dream with your mother. I saw her sitting on a porch. I asked her why she looked sad, but she wouldn't answer me. When I woke up, I prayed for her. My spirit became uneasy. I felt there was a spiritual battle within me. Every time I knelt down to pray for her, the phone rang or someone was at our door. Then, my wife fell down the stairs while mopping. There were so many interruptions that I knew the Devil didn't want me to pray. I said, Lord I need your strength to overcome the evil that's interfering with this. You are my rock and fortress Lord, I will not be shaken. God always will see through his plans, because he brought you to me."

I bowed my head to cry. He grabbed my hands and began to pray for me. "Father, I thank you for this opportunity that you've allowed me to spend with Sky. Thank you, for bringing her here. Thank you for your love and mercy. Even though I falter, You are still with me. Permit me to praise you and exalt your name before I begin to ask anything of you. Let me enter into your presence, oh Holy God. I give you my praise and adoration, because you are a faithful God. Thank you, Lord, for being visible in such an obscure place. Ephesians six, twelve says, for our struggle is not against flesh and blood, but against the powers of this dark world and against the spiritual forces of evil in the heavenly realms. In the name of Jesus, I pray that you grant Sky with your blood and protection without limits, throughout her journey. Amen."

The prayer was strong and comforting. I wiped my tears from my eyes and Enrique hugged me. Raquel came out and told me Isabella was ready to leave. I didn't get a chance to tell Enrique what I was going through but I'm sure he already knew. I believe I was brought to him for that prayer.

The night before leaving Miami, Isabella was in the kitchen making dinner. Raquel and I were watching the movie Matrix. We were lounging on the couch when the phone rang. Our cousin Felo called. When he heard I was there, he invited us over.

Raquel got in the shower and I went to the kitchen to eat. The house was eerily quiet when I heard a loud thump behind me. Isabella was on the floor convulsing. I jumped out of my seat but she stopped shaking and pushed me away.

"Keep your hands off me, Cecilia!" Isabella had a high pitch, nasally voice.

I stepped back, stunned at how the spirit who invaded her body knew my name. As she pulled herself up, holding on to the counter, she dragged her leg to get closer to me.

"I have come to communicate to you, not to ever come back here again."

"Why not?" My voice trembled.

"It's not safe. The answers you seek are outside this house. No one here knows where your mother is."

"Who are you? And what's wrong with your leg?"

"I was good friends with your mother before I passed. I know you're looking for her. You want to know where she is. When you find her, keep it to yourself. And if you ever have the chance to get that beautiful girl, Raquel, out this house; do it."

The spirit left Isabella's body and she dropped to the floor. I helped her up. After the convulsion, Isabella had no recollection of what took place. She told me she suffered from dizzy spells that knocked her down from time to time.

Raquel came walking down the stairs. "Are you ready, Sky?"

"Yeah, let's go."

Raquel didn't seem concerned at all about her mother falling victim to these epileptic episodes. She dived right into moving to Boston with me.

"I don't want to live in Miami anymore. Take me with you."

"Well, once I'm settled, I'll send for you."

"Seriously?"

"I don't see why not. You're going to have to be patient because I have things going on that I need squared away."

"I won't stand in your way, I promise. Please, just get me out of my mother's house!"

"How would she feel about you moving with me?"

"I don't care what she thinks. I'm turning eighteen in a few months."

I laughed at her rebellious attitude, so similar to mine. "Since we're visiting Felo, let's see what's in our cards."

The car turned into the driveway in front of the main entrance, where the headlights picked up a woman standing on the porch smoking a cigarette. It was Sonia, Felo's mother. As always, her eyes were somewhat dead; zombie-like.

"Look how much you've grown, Sky." She kissed me on my cheek, "Raquel, how are you?"

Raquel walked behind me. "I'm sad that Sky is leaving tomorrow."

Sonia opened the door for us. "Why don't you cut the umbilical cord and leave with her?"

"I'm planning on it. Where's Felo?"

As soon as we walked in, we smelled pine and cedar incense smoke. Felo came out and hugged us. It was nice to see him after seven years. He hadn't changed a bit except that he cut his afro. Sonia and I sat down but Raquel and Felo remained standing. He gave us the impression that he was ready to start reading our cards. Raquel went in first.

Meanwhile, Sonia and I spoke, alone, in the kitchen. "You should really consider having her move up North with you." Sonia spoke in a dull monotone, "That way you're not alone."

"I'll see what I can do."

"Whatever you do, be clever about it, because it will be difficult pulling that girl away from her mother's tit. Isabella can be overbearing."

"I noticed."

"Speaking of mothers, have you heard from yours?"

I put my head down and bit my nails. "Not yet. Hopefully I can leave here with some answers. I miss her." We weren't close but she was still my mother.

Raquel came out humming merrily. It was a sign she was satisfied with her divination. Now it was my turn to enter the room. I was anxious, but this was my usual emotion before a reading.

"It's been a long time, Sky. How have you been?"

"Out of my mind."

"I picked up that energy when you came in. I know things aren't the way they use to be with your mother gone, but my advice is for you to move on and feel blessed that you're free from that situation."

"Am I ever going to see her again?"

"Yes."

"How do you know?"

"That's the reason behind your visit. My saints are telling me you will. And...I spent a weekend with some influential people from the Yoruba Association of Santeros recently to learn more rituals and how to maintain the essence of my own gifts. I came out with a new sense of power."

"Really? Give me what you got."

"Let's see what else my saints tell me. You know the routine."

"Felo, before I break the cards, can I confide something in you?"

"Of course."

"I had a strange encounter at Isabella's house. She fell down on the kitchen floor like she was having a seizure. Then a spirit possessed her and told me I wasn't safe. When I asked her who she was, she wouldn't say. She stood up holding on to the counter as she dragged her right leg to get closer to me and said I was going to find my mother before her body fell back to the floor. Isabella had lost consciousness and didn't remember anything. Can you explain that to me?"

"Isabella secretly harbors hatred. That's the doorway which makes it easy for her to become possessed. This spirit manifested itself in the same manner it died; by dropping to the floor. I know who she is. She was a Santera in her day. Her foot was amputated due to diabetes. That's why Isabella's body couldn't hold up."

"Why did she say I'm not safe?"

"You know the FBI raided Isabella's house, looking for your mother and Andre?"

"I didn't know that."

"When we lived upstairs from you, Andre took good care of us. Even when we came back, he made sure we were fine. When the scandal came out, your mother sent us money to pay the mortgage for a few months so you wouldn't be out in the street. The FBI tracked it back to Isabella's house. She was offered a pricey reward for Andre."

"So you know where they are?"

He nodded yes. "First I have to make sure it's safe for you to go. Now, break'em."

Felo was still placing all the cards on the table when he started to tell me that he needed to expel a pestering spirit off me. "You're vulnerable on the emotional front. You are easily manipulated into making choices that will only benefit others. I see that you're confused about making some type of move. Where are you living now?"

"I'm staying in New York with a friend but there are things in Boston that I'm interested in."

381

"Things or someone? I see your interest right here. He's tall, with light eyes."

I smiled. "It's funny, I had a dream last night that I was living in New York. It was weird. I had a nice apartment and Boston was like a memory. It didn't exist anymore."

"What did you get out of that dream? You have the answer...think carefully."

"It means I desire to escape and find out how big the world really is. It's not a sign for me to stay there. I belong in Boston."

"You got it. But a woman is taking up this man's time. It's not serious between them, but if you don't return in time, he will end up with her. This gentleman is looking for more of the domesticated type. Yes, you appeal to him but he's not going to wait around for you too long. What's his name?"

"Ray."

"Ray wants to talk to you. It could be a conversation about moving forward and having children or it all ends with a simple goodbye...your call. Now who's the guy in New York that you're staying with? What's his story? I see numerous women surrounding him. I see confusion. I see a lot of conflict."

"That's my friend Xavier who's always had a thing for me but sometimes I don't feel the same way. At times I want him but something stops me."

"Now I see what all the confusion is about. He's not for you, Sky. Is he sick?"

"No, why?"

"I see him speaking with doctors. He's plagued by bad spells on top of bad spells. Whoever is harming him is stepping out of her boundaries. She's demoralizing what we practice. Advise him to get a cleansing."

"Alright...I will."

"As for you, brighter days are ahead. Go back to college. Stay on track and pursue knowledge. You have a smart head for money. I see success and attainment. When you reach the top, Sky, don't forget about me." He winked.

"I'm cool with that."

Much more was said but those things will remain private. Felo performed a small purification ritual on me. He slapped me numerous times over my head and back with a pile of wet herbal leaves and warned me not to open my eyes. Then, he spat rum in my face. I flinched. Eew! He prayed in a language I didn't comprehend while smoking a cigar. It brought me back to the day when my grandmother carried out her first ritual on me. Only this time it wasn't as intense—just gross.

Next, he made me pick off the leaves from my body with my left hand and place them in a white handkerchief that he tied up. The leaves were to cleanse me and remove the evil omen that was bothering me. Finally, he donned black and white sacred beads around my neck and handed me the white handkerchief to throw in the ocean at midnight.

"Here's your mother's last known address. Be safe." He handed me a piece of paper.

I slowly reached for it with a trembling hand.

Life had placed many challenges at my feet, and this one was no different than any other. Now there I was, on the other side of something, thinking this journey just turned into a labyrinth. I had no map and no sense of direction. But I couldn't ignore my heart that spoke so loud and tamped down all fear: *go...there's nothing in your path that's beyond the realm of possibility.*

HERE ENDS BOOK ONE OF
BROKEN VOODOO DOLL, ONE SKY ONE SOUL

THE STORY CONTINUES IN BOOK TWO,
A RAYLESS MIND

Follow me on Twitter: @OneSkyOneSoul

Made in the USA
Charleston, SC
11 July 2014